ANCIENT STONES OF DORSET

PETER KNIGHT

Local history from the same publisher
A Century of Cinema in Dorset
Thomas Hardy in Wimborne 1881-1883
Ferndown – A Look Back
Hampreston's Pictorial Past
Famous Women in Dorset

1st edition published December 1996

ISBN 1 898073 12 0

Power Publications
1 Clayford Avenue
Ferndown
Dorset

Publishers note
Whilst every care has been taken to ensure the accuracy of
all the information contained in this book neither the
author or the publisher can accept responsibility for any
mistakes that may occur.

Cover Illustrations and photographs: Peter Knight.
Cover and book design by: Graham Whiteman.
Printed by: The Baskerville Press, Salisbury, Wiltshire.

CONTENTS

acknowledgements

To pay due tribute to everyone who has helped during this project would be a very lengthy process indeed. But some special 'thank you's' are necessary:

I thank Gordon Harris for placing his original research material on leys at my disposal; Mike Casserley (Forestry Enterprise), Pam Reeks and other members of the Verwood Historical Society for their efforts with the Verwood stone; Wessex Dowsers members Bob Sephton, Paul Craddock and Roger Sleet for advice on dowsing and site information; John Morby for the loan of several old manuscripts and books; Derek Sowton who did some field-plodding when requested; the staff of various libraries across the county; David Haith whose article in 'The Advertiser' bought about a huge response from readers.

The following people submitted information that has been incorporated in this book, either by letter, phone or verbally in the field: Jeremy Harte, Sandra Harding, Michael Hodges, Rev. John Coombs, J.E. Burrell, Valerie Ciukaj, John Freeman, Robert Courage, Leslie Maskerey, Margaret Firth, Jenny and Eric Roberts, P. Bowyer, Gordon Cottell, 'Anne of Corfe Castle', Pat Law-Ibison, Sheila Cutts, Diane Coade, G. Smith, Dave Freeman, Jeff Bull, Barry Cuff, James Rattue, 'Mr Foley, Corfe Mullen' and John Day.

I thank George Terence Meaden for his kind permission to reproduce two photographs from 'The Goddess Of The Stones'.

Thank you to Graham Cheater for the sketch on page 36; thanks to my wife, Gemma, who did the artwork for the drawings in the Folklore chapter as well as correcting innumerable typing and grammatical errors; appreciation goes out to Paul Devereux whose work is an inspiration and who gave permission to use material from 'The Ley Hunter' as well as an entry in the Contacts column, which proved useful.

I wholeheartedly thank Mike Power, the publisher, who had faith in this book when others had not.

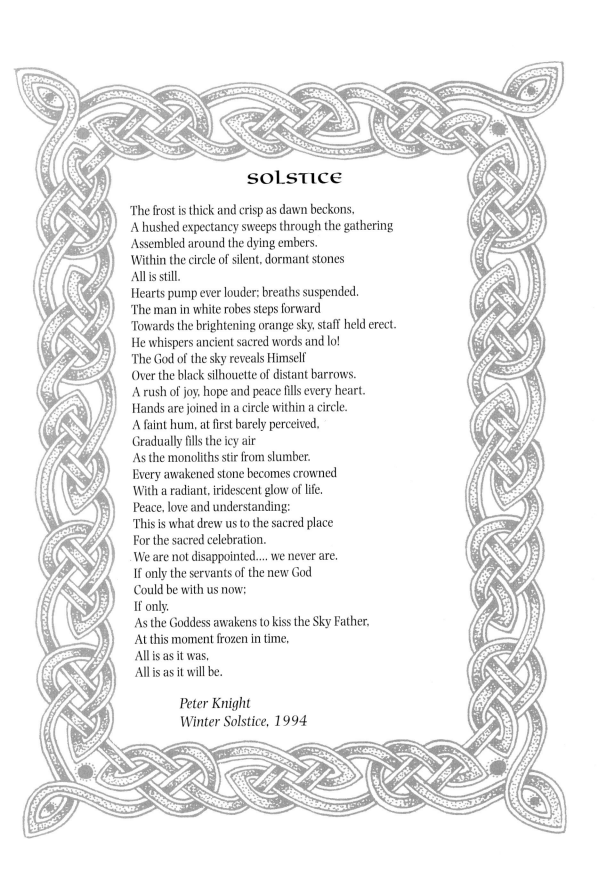

SOLSTICE

The frost is thick and crisp as dawn beckons,
A hushed expectancy sweeps through the gathering
Assembled around the dying embers.
Within the circle of silent, dormant stones
All is still.
Hearts pump ever louder; breaths suspended.
The man in white robes steps forward
Towards the brightening orange sky, staff held erect.
He whispers ancient sacred words and lo!
The God of the sky reveals Himself
Over the black silhouette of distant barrows.
A rush of joy, hope and peace fills every heart.
Hands are joined in a circle within a circle.
A faint hum, at first barely perceived,
Gradually fills the icy air
As the monoliths stir from slumber.
Every awakened stone becomes crowned
With a radiant, iridescent glow of life.
Peace, love and understanding:
This is what drew us to the sacred place
For the sacred celebration.
We are not disappointed.... we never are.
If only the servants of the new God
Could be with us now;
If only.
As the Goddess awakens to kiss the Sky Father,
At this moment frozen in time,
All is as it was,
All is as it will be.

Peter Knight
Winter Solstice, 1994

To the reader

a PREFACE

"ANCIENT SITES ARE PLACES OF LEARNING."

Paul Devereux (The Ley Hunter)

This book is the culmination of a very personal quest, going back several years. The manner in which I now relate to Planet Earth is radically different from when I started. Indeed, my study began as a part-time curiosity into early Man's use of stone and the erection of the megaliths and circles that festoon our magical land. This was all soon to change.

This innocent genesis was to blossom into an awareness of spirit that was to change my whole consciousness and, as a consequence, my whole life.

It gradually became evident to me that leys, circles, megaliths and barrows demonstrate a technology and a SPIRITUALITY in 'prehistoric Man' that is very much different from what I had been led to believe.

Over the past few decades the arena of 'earth mysteries' and 'geomancy' has developed and grown (after some pretty weird undisciplined false starts!) into a virtual science. Earth mysteries has come of age, so to speak. Pioneering work by Janet and Colin Bord, John Michell, Tom Graves, Paul Devereux, Guy Underwood and others led to incredible discoveries and a whole clutch of innovative books. I pay tribute to those pioneers who took the brunt of the academic backlash.

I felt that parallels and comparative results could be achieved on the ancient stone sites of Dorset if I was prepared to give it the commitment I knew it would require to do the task justice and to do it thoroughly and systematically. Circumstances in my life gave me that opportunity. I believe it was destined to be so: nothing is by chance.

Endless hours were spent sifting through countless dusty books and manuscripts, searching piles of Proceedings and Yearbooks and visiting and writing to many people I felt could help my Quest. But the most satisfying and uplifting times were the days (and nights) I spent out 'in the field', for this is the only true way to learn about the landscape and the enigmatic secrets held within it.

Gradually I developed an intuitive eye and 'feel' for aspects in the land I had previously not been aware of. Re-visits to many sites revealed to me subtle details, such as alignments and skyline features, that had eluded me on prior trips. Those aspects had been there all the time, but I was only now in the right mental and spiritual state to receive the knowledge.

I would welcome any comments from users of this book. I have striven to produce a usable book for readers to take out to sites, rather than the coffee-table format. I have provided the information I like to see in field handbooks. I do not pretend to have included every stone site and ley in Dorset. Many more await discovery by anyone who is dedicated and AWARE enough to take them past that point where the logical brain still rules. Earth mysteries is not about logic, it is about awareness, feelings and life itself.

May you walk in peace on a beautiful, and forever giving, Earth Mother.

Love and light,
Peter Knight,
Spring Equinox, 1996.

PART ONE

'I AM AN INFANT: WHO BUT I PEEPS FROM THE
UNHEWN DOLMEN ARCH'.

(from 'Song of Amergin': Celtic)

Chapter One

INTRODUCTION

"STONEHENGE MAY BE
STUDIED BY REASON, BUT IT
WAS CREATED BY FAITH."

Jeremy Harte

Few people who visit ancient stone sites such as Stonehenge or Avebury could deny the mysterious pull and lure that these places possess. Every year thousands of latter day pilgrims flock to these sacred places (and they are indeed sacred in every sense of the word) to look at the stones and ponder. Who built them? Why are they here? For what purpose were they erected? Can sacred stone sites teach anything of use to us today? Many perhaps also feel they are connecting to their 'roots'.

A growing number of individuals and groups are being drawn to these places because they sense and feel something more, something deep and even sacred which stirs their inner emotions.

I believe that we are picking up on common ancestral connections, linking us to the builders and users of these sites. We somehow remember, subconsciously, that which has gone before. There is a phenomena called 'site memory', a process by which events of a strongly emotional manner can leave permanently imprinted energy records at stone sites. It is as if moments in time are frozen and encapsulated at a locality, to be released when conditions are right.

I initially set out to study the handful of well known stone circles and standing stones in Dorset, such as the Nine Stones, the Grey Mare and Her Colts, the Harpstone, etc. But my researches in the field, in numerous libraries and from word-of-mouth input,

released what proved to be an avalanche of stones, ley alignments, crosses, former sites (and their kin) such as took me by surprise!

Added to this was an expanding inventory of folklore, legends, unexplained phenomena and dowsing results. All this has changed forever the way I look at and indeed relate to Planet Earth and, in fact, the whole Universe. The wonder of it all was soaked up like a sponge into my being with a fervour of enthusiasm that persists to this day.

An awareness gradually grew within me of two primary reasons why this book HAD to be written. Firstly, Dorset needed to be pulled out of the relative obscurity I felt it had languished in regarding ancient stone sites and earth mysteries. I feel that Dorset research as a whole has been a bit slow in

Plate 1: Sarsen stone at Lulworth. Typical of many stones lying around across Dorset. Were many once utilised by prehistoric Man?

putting pen-to-paper, despite much excellent work being undertaken by local groups and individuals. I hope this book helps redress the balance between Dorset and surrounding counties.

Secondly, I feel strongly, and a little sadly, that this book may be vital to help many of the described sites stay in existence. Builders, genuine lovers of the Earth, local authorities, farmers and conservationists all need to be aware of what is actually worth preserving in our landscape, something not always immediately obvious. A lump of rock waiting to be unceremoniously tossed into a waiting truck may be a prehistoric track marker. The 'troublesome' rock a farmer removes from his field may have stood guard at the entrance of some ancient barrow. Clearly this must stop. The mistakes of the past are for all to see.

However, I believe that we all collectively share the responsibility for the demise of so much of our heritage, as well as a share of answerability for the future preservation and survival of such places. Let us not shrink from this challenge, the future of our planet may ultimately prove to depend on it, as we will uncover later. Earth energies and ancient

sites may well be one of the ways to heal our ailing planet and, as a result, to healing Mankind itself.

Chapter Two takes the reader on a journey through the various aspects of Dorset's ancient stone sites, starting with the archaeology, pre-history and indeed later history concerning the sites. We will take a look at the types of sites and the periods of time when they were erected and continued to be used. We look at how religious and political upheavals intervened in the history of sites, often drastically so.

Chapter Three attempts to delve into the often mysterious realms of the folklore, legends and unexplained phenomena of Dorset stone sites. I am of the opinion that a deep hidden core of truth is to be found in most of folklore's old tales. This knowledge must often be gleaned out of the material by careful deciphering and interpretation, rather than taking stories as word-for-word gospel. The books of Janet and Colin Bord deal with this field excellently.

Chapter Four then deals with what many would describe as the more 'alternative' end of the ancient sites study spectrum. Earth Mysteries is a term for an area of study that can hardly be summed up better than by Paul Devereux inside the cover of each issue of 'The Ley Hunter':

> "Earth Mysteries (EM) is a holistic or
> 'general systems'
> approach to ancient sites and their
> landscapes. It
> involves the study of the curiously
> interwoven areas of
> archaeology, folklore, geomancy (sacred
> geography such
> as leys), ancient astronomy, geo-
> physics, primary sensing,
> unusual phenomena, consciousness
> studies, etc. EM
> researches ancient peoples and their
> nearly-lost knowledge
> in order to uncover principles, insights
> and data from the
> remote past that might lay foundations
> for a wiser, more
> whole future."

Plate 2: The stone at Shorts Lane, Blandford. Who would guess at first glance that it is an important ley markstone? (See page 42 and Fig.128). The need for preservation of such stones is vital.

Here I take the reader on a crash course in feeling, of seeing with new eyes, and of attuning and connecting with our remote ancestors and indeed the very energies they sought to experience.

We will explore and encounter many fascinating places and touch upon often thought-provoking material. We will stand at Dorset's largest former standing stone (only recently discovered) in a quiet Verwood forest. We shall walk through a field near Dorchester where a mighty henge with standing stones was erected thousands of years ago. We will speculate as to why tumuli are to be seen on the skylines in particular directions as viewed from stones. We will dowse sites together and sense the pulse of Mother Earth. Together we will follow alignments of sites across the countryside for tens of miles, their paths marked out by churches, crosses and lonely wayside stones.

We will also look into the realms of the unusual, of the unexplained. The term 'supernatural' is often banded about to describe a very varied array of phenomena. We shall shed some light on several 'coinci-dences' we will encounter. Everything means something and our distant ancestors, the erectors of the megaliths and barrows, had sound reasons for undertaking such tasks.

I urge the reader to partake in the Earth Mysteries side of this book with as open a mind as is possible. Most of the ideas suggested here can be checked out (and in some cases phenomena EXPERIENCED) directly by the reader. Take no-one's word for anything. Intuition, a sense of adventure and a love for this beautiful planet is all that is required. Go for it!

Many achaeoligists still scoff and ridicule Earth Mysteries as a "science". They decry leylines and such. To this I say one thing – you've placed your bets, but the wheel is still turning!

> "EVERY CULTURE IS
> UMBILICALLY LINKED WITH
> THE COUNTRYSIDE."
>
> *John Michell*

Chapter Two

THE BACKGROUND ARCHAEOLOGY

"THE LANDSCAPE - THE EARTH AND HER SITES - ARE OUR FINEST TEACHERS, IF WE CAN BUT ALLOW THEM TO BE SO."

Philip Heselton

orset lies in the heart of ancient Wessex, a region incredibly rich in ancient sites dating back thousands of years. Evidence of the presence of early Man goes back some 8000 years in Dorset, to approximately 6000 BC. Flints, bones and occupational remnants, notably at Portland and Blashenwell, tell the story.

The people of the Neolithic Period, or New Stone Age, began to appear in Dorset around 4000 BC, some 6000 years ago. They were not nomads as before, but built causewayed camps and grew crops and domesticated animals. Trade and commerce was thriving and communities became more structured, both politically and religiously. Long Barrows, cursuses and stone monoliths were erected for ceremonial and spiritual observances.

By 3000 BC much of the chalk hills had been deforested, denuded by Man and his foraging stock of pigs, sheep and cattle. Clearance of the land was continuing for crops. At around 2500 BC (4500 years ago) the so-called Beaker People settled here from across the North Sea and bought with them the skills and sense of spirituality that was to lead to the culmination of megalithic build-

Fig. 1: Time correlation chart of ancient sites

4500 BC	4000 BC	3500 BC	3000 BC	2500 BC	2000 BC	1500 BC	1000 BC	500 BC	1BC AD 1	AD 500	AD 1000	AD 1500

NEOLITHIC AGE | BRONZE AGE | IRON AGE | DARK AGES

Long barrows

Roman stones

Round barrows

Stone crosses

Mount Pleasant

Henges

Stonehenge

Stone circles

Standing stones and ley markers

ing, with structures such as Stonehenge, Avebury and the stone circles of Dorset displaying the results of their efforts.

The boundaries between the various Ages in Fig.1 should be taken as somewhat arbitrary, as one Age very much runs into another without clear-cut division. So, too, with the periods of construction and usage of the various types of ancient stone sites shown. There is somewhat of a problem with standing stones, which have always been notoriously difficult to date due to sparsity of associated datable finds; this is compounded when one adds to them the marker stones of leys and other alignments. I have placed marker stones and standing stones on the same line in Fig.1 because although many standing stones were probably not ley markers, many undoubtedly were.

There is also the aspect of 'Site Evolution', a term denoting sites that have literally evolved, often over very long periods of time. For instance, in Dorset we have some fine examples that demonstrate the problem of dating usage of sites. Dorset's stone crosses, whilst clearly shaped and erected as such in the post-Roman Christian period of history, are often modified and reshaped standing stones and ley markers (such as at Minterne Parva and at Tarrant Crawford). The beautiful and very sacred site at Knowlton originally consisted of a prehistoric henge (probably with standing stones also) but was later 'Christianised' in the 12th Century with the construction of the church, the ruins of which can be seen today. Dowsing confirms this is a very ancient and Holy locality.

So things are not always what they seem, a theme that emerges repeatedly throughout this book.

We will now take a brief excursion into the various different types of ancient stone sites

(1) LONG BARROWS AND CHAMBERED TOMBS

These include the oldest sites dealt with here, most being constructed between 4000-2500 BC. The term 'barrow' refers to a mound of earth or stones usually (but not always) erected over the remains of human cremation or burials. There is an immense variety of types, but the commonest are long barrows (which are elongated and usually wider and higher at one end) and round barrows (which are very profuse in Dorset and the 'tumuli' of Ordnance Survey maps).

The long barrow we are concerned with here is the Chambered type, those which had stones incorporated in their construction to form a chamber at the burial end. Large stones (usually local sarsens) were placed on end to form the vertical walls and an often huge capstone (weighing many tons) was placed over the top to form the roof of the chamber. Internal anti-chambers also occur and some had hidden compartments.

What is often seen at a chambered long barrow is that the earthen cover that comprises the major bulk of the mound has been partly or wholly eroded away, either by the British climate or else over-zealous farmers, leaving just the stones standing or lying around. In Dorset the Hellstone, the Two Gates Stones and the Cromlech at Winterbourne Steepleton serve to illustrate this. The various free-standing 'quoits' of Cornwall and Devon also represent this type of site, any original earthen structure having gone. Original recent work, however, suggests that many may not have had an original covering at all and nearly always stood much as we see them today. Why did the wind erode some and not others? There appear to be few semi-denuded ones! Food for thought.

Perhaps many are so visually and architecturally inspiring that they were intended to be appreciated and USED as they stood. This was the opinion of master dowser Guy Underwood. He considered (in 'The Pattern of the Past') that dolmens were of special importance in terms of earth energies.

Some sites, such as at Wayland's Smithy on the Wiltshire/Oxfordshire border, show how chambered tombs were often built by remodelling existing earthen long barrow mounds. This would suggest a later megalithic culture that perhaps spread over from Brittany where such structures abound. This is early evidence indeed of the aforementioned site evolution.

Sometimes we are fortunate to have a chambered long barrow with both the huge entrance stones and the long earthen mound. Dorset's best example is the Grey Mare and Her Colts, near Portesham. Here the mound extends some 75ft from the large sarsens that form the chamber. Some long barrow mounds extend for 150-300ft, Wayland's Smithy, West Kennet and East Kennet being superb examples.

A curious feature of a chambered long barrow is that the chamber, the actual 'business end' of it, usually occupies but a small percentage of the total length. Some ritual aspect is suggested here. Paul Devereux quite brilliantly demonstrated at West Kennet that the barrow had been extended several yards to the west so as to produce a visual alignment from this extended end to Silbury Hill and onwards north to Windmill Hill.

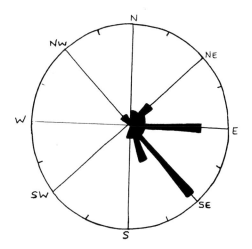

In Dorset it was noted how the mound of the Grey Mare and Her Colts points towards the Summer Solstice sunset point, with associated features on the visible skyline (Fig.17). To expand this, I carried out a study of the orientation of 47 Dorset long barrows. Of the chambered type, numbering 5, all had entrances orientated between east and southeast. All 47 long barrows are shown in Fig.2, and an instant bias can be seen in direction. 18 barrows point toward the Winter Solstice sunrise, some 14 towards the spring and autumn Equinox sunrises, and even some of the other directions denote other astronomi-

Fig. 2: The orientation of Dorset long barrows (their larger ends being used for compass direction). The circle circumference represents 20 barrows.

Plate 3: The Grey Mare and Her Colts, Dorset's finest chambered long barrow. The original earthen mound can be seen to the left of the sarsen stones, which form the chamber

cal events. It may be obvious also that here we have DOUBLE orientations. For a Winter Solstice sunrise orientation at the large (often chambered) end will give a SUMMER solstice SUNSET at the pointed end!

This is shown well at the Grey Mare and her Colts. Equally, Equinox sunrises in one direction will give you Equinox SUNSETS in the other. Studies of the complex astronomical alignments at Stonehenge and many other sites show us that Man of the Neolithic had a deep and practical knowledge of astronomy and geometry, and examples of this wisdom will be seen at various sites later.

Some chambered long barrows display crescental forecourts, noticeably at Grey Mare and Her Colts and Corsombe (although the latter has yet to be confirmed as a true barrow), again suggesting ceremonial activities. Many long barrows were re-opened to include more burials and we can only guess and wonder at the ceremony and atmosphere at such proceedings all those thousands of years ago.

To sum up, it is re-emphasised here that the LOCATION of long barrows appeared to be of crucial importance to their builders. Many lie on ley lines, others are sited to enable astronomical observations, whilst many more are situated in close proximity to other, obviously associated, ancient sites such as other barrows, standing stones, cursuses and the like. A theory to be repeated often in this book is that the LOCALITY is often of equal significance to the actual remains found at a site. This suggests early in our studies of a close and subtle relationship between early Man and the landscape.

(2) HENGES

"......ERECTED IN THE EARLIEST YEARS FOR OBSERVING THE MOTIONS OF THE HEAVENLY BODIES."

Dr. John Smith (1770)

A henge is a roughly circular area, surrounded by a ditch, which in turn has a bank of earth on the outside. The key thing to note here is that the bank of earth is on the OUTSIDE of the ditch, thus making henges ceremonial structures, not defensive. There are around 100 henges in Britain and Ireland and they are peculiar to these Isles and date from around mid-Neolithic to mid-Bronze Age. The word 'henge' in fact derives from the Old English 'stanhenge', meaning 'hanging stones', the ancient name for

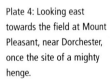

Plate 4: Looking east towards the field at Mount Pleasant, near Dorchester, once the site of a mighty henge.

Stonehenge, the most famous henge. What makes Stonehenge a 'henge' by definition is not the spectacular megaliths but the bank and ditch that encloses them.

More enigmatic and breathtaking to me personally than Stonehenge is the great henge at Avebury. This was perhaps prehistoric Man's most ambitious, and certainly one of the most sacred, structures. It has been estimated that up to 180 standing stones may have originally stood inside the ditch, with an added 400 in the two avenues adjoining it. Even by today's standards and methods of engineering, this was a staggering achievement.

Dorset has four henges that display evidence that megaliths were incorporated within their structures. The first, Maumbury at Dorchester, is reported to have had a huge megalith standing near its entrance, although this was probably not part of the original henge construction. Knowlton has a henge surrounding the ruined church and dowsing by experienced dowsers suggests standing stones once stood within the henge. The site of the Mount Pleasant henge, on the outskirts of Dorchester, is now an arable field, but excavations revealed evidence that a stone cove and an outlying monolith were later added to the original design. Two henges (for there are remains of 2 circular earthworks) near Litton Cheney had stones still lying around until recent times.

(3) STANDING STONES AND LEY MARK STONES

"......REPOSITORIES STILL OF ANCIENT POWER ......THE LIVING STONES."

Icthell Colquhoun (1957)

egaliths, those still erect and the more common prone variety, exhibit a vast variety of shapes, sizes and material of matrix. To a certain degree the shape and material of a stone will depend on the local rock type available; but we shall also see that many stones were beyond doubt fashioned into specific shapes as well as often transported into an area.

Clearly, our distant ancestors were often after a particular stone, often rich in quartz, as well as requiring symbolic and even FUNCTIONAL shapes to the resultant megaliths.

The term 'megalith' comes from the Greek words 'megas' and 'lithos' meaning 'great' and 'stone'. Another term used to describe standing stones is 'menhir', from the Celtic 'maen' and 'hir', literally 'stone' and 'long'. Another name we encounter often during this review of Dorset sites is sarsen stone. The word 'sarsen' derives probably from the Anglo-Saxon 'sar' and 'stan' meaning 'troublesome' and 'a stone', referring to the problems that many farmers had with these huge stones littering their fields. They are weathered-out remains of an extremely hard and durable deposit of sandstone which once covered much of the upland chalk areas of southern England.

The sarsen stones were particularly favoured by megalith builders as they were both very hard and durable. Sarsen stones come already weathered into big blocks, ready for transportation and erection. The fact that they frequently lie around in fields naturally (such as the Valley Of Stones near Little Bredy) does hinder somewhat the search for the ones that HAVE been moved and utilised for specific purposes thousands of years ago. A knowledge of the local geology, noting nearby associated sites, and an 'eye of awareness' for a stone of significance are all aids to decoding what Devereux terms the 'open secrets'. Master dowser Guy Underwood thought many sarsens were reworked for geomantic purposes.

Some stones certainly mark burial sites. Many others form avenues and outlying longsights for astronomical observations from stone circles. Many of the stones are mere remnants of once grandeur structures, which time and Man hath put asunder. For instance, the stones of the Two Gates Stones and the 'cromlech' at Winterbourne Steepleton are all that remain of once proud barrows, whilst the scatter of seemingly odd

Plate 5: Mark stone at Little Bredy. It stands at the meeting of two old roads and is not a sarsen stone, which abound in the vicinity, but is of limestone. Both of these features make it a ley marker candidate.

I note with some astonishment (but with little actual surprise) that in 'The Ancient Monuments of Dorset' (1972, Dorset Natural History and Archaeological Soc.) there are only 5 stone circles, 3 standing stones and 3 entries of stones associated with chambered long barrows listed in the 'Standing Stones' section. Equally enigmatic is the section on 'Crosses and Inscribed Stones' which contains a mere 17 entries as ancient monuments. I believe this situation needs to radically change if ALL our remaining heritage of stone sites is to be saved. By the time typing on his book had even began, I had uncovered over 150 STILL EXISTING stone sites in Dorset. These do not only include 'hard' archaeology, such as stones clearly put in a particular place up to the 16th Century, but also boundary stones of some antiquity and stones with folklore and legends associated with them, some of which are natural formations.

Gasps of breath I hear from many! But why should not natural stones with folklore be included? Were they not also associated with our ancestors and were they not held in reverence and esteem by the local populace? After all, many of these legends are in fact vestiges of descriptions of phenomena seen at sites, perhaps as a result of emanations of earth energies!

The hard fact to swallow for many, perhaps, is that many megalithic sites are where they are BECAUSE OF THE EARTH ENERGIES AT THOSE SACRED PLACES. I am not attacking the academic society as such, for they are people like the rest of us and have their own fixed ideas and beliefs like everyone else. But times change and people's minds change and we all need to be, I believe, more receptive to

sarsens at Littlemayne are the sad vestiges of at least one stone circle. There is even a seat-shaped stone at Corscombe.

Stones used as ley markers are often difficult to differentiate from odd stones used to protect the corners of buildings and others left lying around after roadworks, etc. However, these ley markers help define alignments of ancient sites, joining sites together in STRAIGHT LINES, often over tens of miles.

The whole question of leys is a very controversial one, with the majority of archaeologists generally still in denial (I wonder what would be the case if an archaeologist with lots of letters after his name had been first to uncover the ley network, instead of Alfred Watkins, an amateur photographer from rural Hertfordshire!). Many academics still dismiss the fact that leys have been statistically proven!

The latest theories will be discussed in the appropriate section later, and all that needs to be added at this point is that leys and their markers are not part of some long-forgotten and defunct system, but are very much part and parcel of geomancy, very much part of TODAY, and very much to do with an ultimate understanding that may help heal this planet.

new ideas. Some new theories will prove to be unfounded, others will be constantly updated. But this is how it should be, for a discipline that thinks it knows everything is doomed to die. For we are only at the tip of a beautiful earth mysteries iceberg and all that has gone before may have been preparation for what we are yet to uncover.

Dorset's standing stones need our help to survive. I believe that they have much more to offer US than we yet truly appreciate.

(4) STONE CIRCLES

Stone circles are amongst the most atmospheric and awe-inspiring places of our ancient prehistoric heritage. Few people who visit them can fail to be struck by that feeling of mystery; that strange sense of something almost indescribable, an 'experience' unlike anything today's technological society can give us.

A catalogue produced in 1976 listed 963 stone circles in Britain, and even this is probably not the true total. It is likely that this is but a proportion of the total original number, so many having been lost forever.

These circles were constructed over a period of some 2,500 years, between 3500-1000 BC, a vast period of time. Judging from the number of circles that were erected, we can deduce they were of vital importance to Neolithic and Bronze Age Man.

Arguments have raged for many years as to their purpose. Many of the stones in circles are so aligned as to allow often complicated astronomical observations. Another usage could have been as agricultural calendars, particular key sunrises denoting certain seasons. Also, in the field of earth energies, it has been demonstrated that circles of stones can store up and, indeed, amplify energies and that these may have been released or utilised by ancient rituals.

I think that all of these factors play a role in making circles such magical and revered places. They were made when people still held a reverence for the earth and 'spiritual technology', to use John Michell's telling phrase, was still being practised. Over many years

retired Scottish Professor of Engineering, Alexander Thom, studied hundreds of stone circles and came up with the discovery of the megalithic yard (M.Y.). He found that many circles were laid out using this common measurement, approx. 2.72ft/82cm. Many were not laid out as true circles at all, but used complicated geometry to produce ellipses, egg-shaped and flattened circles (see Bibliography).

Alfred Watkins noted that ley lines could strike a circle anywhere, but quite often passed through the edge of it, a fact subsequently borne out by modern researchers such as Devereux and Graves.

Dorset is privileged with 5 'official' stone circles, the Nine Stones, Littlemayne, Rempstone, Hampton Hill and Kingston Russell. However, others lurk menacingly at officialdom's door. Two possible circles have been recognised in the Valley of Stones south of Little Bredy. These were in fact mentioned on archaeology field trips near the start of this Century.

The two henges already mentioned at Knowlton and Litton Cheney, I believe, should now also be added to Dorset's stone circle list. And finally, we have a relatively new stone circle built in the 1970's near Rempstone. It is well worth a visit as it has several features in it that help us capture the magic of that which is rarest in Dorset, a complete circle of STANDING stones.

"GREY RECUMBENT TOMBS OF THE DEAD IN DESERT PLACES, STANDING STONES ON THE VACANT WINE-RED MOOR, HILLS OF SHEEP, AND THE HOMES OF THE SILENT VANISHED RACES AND WINDS, AUSTERE AND PURE ...."

Robert Louis Stevenson ('Treasure Island')

(5) ROUND BARROWS

"A ROUND BARROW IS ALWAYS LOCATED ON ONE OR MORE POWERFUL BLIND SPRINGS (ENERGY NODES). THIS MARKS ITS MYSTIC CENTRE."

Dowser Guy Underwood

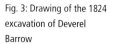here are probably in excess of 40,000 round barrows of prehistoric age throughout Britain, even this figure being a fraction of the original number. Most date from the Bronze Age, but many are also Neolithic in age. Some are chambered but the vast variety are not. In the Wessex region alone there are over 4000 Bronze Age round barrows and they commonly form prominent features on the skyline.

They quite often occur in groups and are frequently found associated with long barrows (which are usually of older age) and stone circles, which are mostly contemporaneous with the round barrows or close to it. As with the long barrows, round barrows are usually found to contain burial remains, often accompanied by a wealth of relics such as jewellery and fine ornaments. Some, however, are devoid of any remains whatsoever, suggesting that round barrows may have also served some other purpose.

The round barrows that concern us here are chiefly those which are known to have incorporated sizeable stones in their structures. Excavations by active (and sometimes over eager) Victorian antiquarians led to many accounts of huge stones covering the burial cists of barrows. A barrow on Conygar Hill, just south of Dorchester, had a 3 ton block of stone within its structure. The famous, but sadly now destroyed, Badbury Barrow had a 'massive wall of sandstone ....30ft across'. A barrow alongside the Ridgeway path north of Upwey (grid reference: 657866) had within a massive stone cist with a cover stone weighing about a ton. A bowl-barrow at Poole (047959) had, at the 1971 dig, 6 upright stone slabs.

Today we can still find vestiges of stones used in the construction of round barrows. Probably the best known, because of the rich finds it yielded during excavations in 1824, is the Deverel Barrow midway between Winterborne Whitechurch and Milborne St. Andrew. An old drawing, reproduced in Fig. 3,

Fig. 3: Drawing of the 1824 excavation of Deverel Barrow

shows 23 stones, many of which still protrude from the barrow today. Several other barrows we will visit in this book display one or multiple stones, still more evidence of early Man's close relationship between earth, spirit and stone.

We will see later that many round barrows form alignments with other barrows and a great variety of other ancient sites. The ley system employed round barrows extensively. The earth energies side of our study also touches upon several instances of strange phenomena, both in folklore and more recent, recorded in the vicinity of these round earthworks. Dowser Guy Underwood found that EVERY round barrow he dowsed had important geodetic energies.

(6) ROMAN STONES

N o survey of Dorset's ancient stones would be complete without inclusion of some of the remnants of Rome's long and significant occupation of Dorset. Vespasian landed with the 2nd Legion on the shores of Holes Bay, Hamworthy in A.D.43 and, after bloody fights to take some of Dorset's large hillforts, conquered Dorset and heralded in a period of relative peace in the region which was to last for nearly 400 years.

Many important finds have been made all over Dorset, and the area was much developed by the Romans. They built a town at Dorchester, with amphitheatre, fort and extensive aqueducts. Many villas, temples, houses and signs of fortification are scattered all over the county but we will concern ourselves here only with those that come within our brief, that is sites with visibly remaining stones.

The most impressive site described here is the townhouse at Dorchester, said by some to be the best preserved Roman townhouse in Britain. Its mosaics, heating systems and foundations are well worth a visit. Nearby is a stretch of the original wall built by the Romans around Dorchester, which was originally 20ft high.

Just to the east of Dorchester stand two Roman milestones, one at the roundabout at Stinsford, the other to the east near

Plate 6: The Roman townhouse at Dorchester.

Bockhampton. Both mark the approaches along old Roman roads from the east.

Two temples are open to general view within our area of study. The temple at Maiden Castle is only part of the total spectacular experience to be had if one climbs up to the top of this impressive hillfort. The temple at Jordan Hill is likewise rewarding. Both appear to illustrate that even as late as the 4th Century A.D. the Romans still managed a blend of pagan and Christian worship. This, I think, demonstrates that the Earth Goddess was still venerated and the earth in general treated with much more reverence than in later purely-Christian periods. The Romans thus seem to have naturally held in great regard the warm waters that issued from the ground at the village of Fifehead Neville, for they built a villa very near to it and even placed a sluice and basin near its source.

(7) STONE CROSSES

"The shape of the stone is important in establishing a link between pagan market crosses and Christian ones."

Derek Bryce

It may seem odd to some that Christian stone crosses should be included in a book on 'ancient stones'. The answer, I believe, is threefold. Firstly, how old is 'ancient'? Most of the crosses described here are over 500 years old, some even going back to Saxon times, some 1000 years ago. Secondly, and very significantly, is the FACT that many are either remodellings or alterations of early ley stones and other ancient standing stones.

But the most important reason for inclusion of these crosses is the UNQUESTIONABLE FACT that many of them occur on ley lines. This is yet more evidence for site evolution, mentioned earlier, and yet further confirmation if any were still necessary, of the actual existence of leys marking out ancient alignments of sites.

The cross as a spiritual symbol predates Christianity by a long way and many ancient pagan/aboriginal sites have carvings and drawings incorporating crosses of various designs. In these earlier ages it represented the coming together of the God and Earth, a harmonious symbol. Early Celtic crosses show a synthesis of pagan and Christian symbology and many are beautifully carved with elaborate and very artistic interlacing. The remains of these early cross forms can be seen at Todber, north of Sturminster Newton, and at Whitcombe, south of Dorchester. Derek Bryce sums up this apparent synthesis below (see quote, next page).

There is ample evidence of old stones being either replaced by crosses, or else altered in shape to incorporate the Christian symbol. The most spectacular occur in Brittany, with many examples still abounding of huge monoliths which have had crosses sculptured on the top. An obelisk at Pouance has a hole in its face which was cut to contain an image of the Virgin. It was clearly easier for the Church of the day to carve crosses on these huge stones than the immense efforts pulling them down. It also fulfilled the instructions from Gregory the Great, early in the 7th Century, to adapt the pagan sites for Christian worship rather than destroy them. Later on, things did not go so smoothly for many ancient sites, as the Church's grip on the populace became less tolerant.

So it came to pass that many stones of antiquity were either pulled down or else altered to 'Christianise' them. No fewer than 5000 Christian crosses stood in England alone prior to the Reformation, although this great religious upheaval did not cause the greatest damage to stone crosses. Most survived the 1536 and 1539 purges of Henry VIII, although the veneration of the cross as a religious symbol was greatly diminished, as well as the most valuable ones being removed or destroyed.

Queen Mary's efforts to re-establish Roman Catholicism restored somewhat the cross to a place of reverence. Queen Elizabeth I did not, it seems, desire the destruction of the out-of-door crosses and in fact issued a proclamation in 1560 against such defacing.

The death-knell for wayside stone crosses was Oliver Cromwell and the Puritans. In 1643/4 most of Dorset's stone crosses were either pulled down or broken where they stood. The only exception to this appears to have been memorial crosses, dedicated to particular individuals. This is probably why the magnificent cross at Stalbridge came to be spared.

For two centuries these crosses were left to the ravages of time until restorations began in the 19th Century, to be continued up to the present day. Many of the stone crosses we will visit have modern cross heads mounted on the top of the much older shafts. For many crosses, however, help came too late.

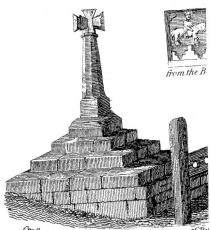

from the B.

Crofs on Gold Hill, near the West end of S.t Pet

Fig. 5: Old drawing of a cross now completely gone. This impressive cross stood on the site of the present Guild Hall, Shaftesbury. It marked a very ancient meeting place, with nearby stocks and bull ring.

"THE MODIFICATIONS IMPLY THAT SOME EARLY CHRISTIANS SAW THE SYMBOLISM OF THESE ANCIENT SACRED STONES AS NOT INCOMPATIBLE WITH CHRISTIANITY."

Derek Bryce

Having completed our brief introduction into the various types of sites, we will next delve headlong into the world of folklore, legend and old tales. For we must not despise such lore as much information can be gleaned sifting through these ancient threads of hearsay. In every tale and legend there is an element of fact. Somebody saw or heard something. Someone sensed and felt something they could not explain. One can read between the lines and pull out the beads of wisdom from the fog of the ancient past. Britain has long been held as a place of magical and legendary happenings, with a very good reason, as I hope you will discover. Let your mind be open and kick rationality out of the window for the next two chapters. You may be in for a pleasant surprise!

Crofs in Trinity Church Yard

"AND IT WAS THE WAY OF THE ANCIENTS IN THEIR RELIGIOUS BUILDINGS, TO COPY OUT OR ANALOGISE THE FORM OF THE DIVINE BEING, AS THEY CONCEIV'D IT, IN A SYMBOLIC MANNER."

William Stukeley (18th C.)

Fig. 4: Old drawing of the cross at Holy Trinity, Shaftesbury. Compare with Plate 139. This drawing shows the original taller steps, and the ornate chamfering of the shaft.

Chapter Three
FOLKLORE

"FOLKLORE TALES ALMOST ALWAYS CONTAIN SOME GERM OF PREHISTORIC FACT, MIXED WITH MUCH ACCUMULATED IMAGININGS."

Alfred Watkins, 'The Old Straight Track'

The colourful world of folklore gives us glimpses of long-gone times, times when people were less scientific and rational in their everyday lives. They led simpler lives, closer to the earth and the seasons. They had a deeper reverence for the Earth and held in great wonder, and with much respect, unusual events and unexplained phenomena when they happened upon them.

Many of the phenomena and traditions described here may seem to be absurd and illogical (and illogical is exactly what they ARE!). The Devil throwing large boulders across the countryside; stones with magical and healing powers; stones dancing at dawn; cars breaking down near to ancient stones, and so on. But, as I have said previously, all is not as it seems.

An ancient folktale originated with someone seeing something, someone telling the story and the narration being passed down orally or, better still, by way of pen to paper. The events were experienced within the context of the mental comprehension and contemporary language of that time and place. An event of the unusual would be seen as work of the Earth's mysterious forces and its entourage of underworld creatures, such as fairies and spirits. It was only relatively recently that such phenomena were laid squarely at the Devil's door, a sign of the effect of the Church's doctrine on the populace.

I think it is wise not to dismiss these old tales as stemming merely from stupid and illiterate peasants. The original observers and participants did not understand the apparitions they were privy to. One thing that is fascinating is that traditions from all over the world often share similar folklore. This perhaps demonstrates three points. First, the same processes appear to operate, regards earth energies, all over the globe, confirming for me a LIVING PLANET. Secondly, it seems to confirm Jung's 'collective unconscious', whereby all of Mankind is connected on some deep subconscious level enabling common beliefs and actions to manifest by vastly separated cultures. And lastly, it seems more feasible and 'logical' to accept the idea of earth energies than not. We should bear in mind that a vast amount of evidence now exists that stone sites, earth energies and spirits of some sort or another were observed and UTILISED by virtually every aboriginal culture, from Britain to the Americas, from Australia to Africa. Were they all just deluded savages? I think not.

As we delve into these old tales, we are reclaiming something of Mankind's birthright. We have become estranged from the Earth and its energies. These old stories can shed light on the beliefs of our forebears who lived and breathed WITH Nature, not against Her.

We will attempt here to interpret the folklore of Dorset's ancient stone sites, regardless of how fragmentary and altered they have become. We may well benefit from such insight. The types of tales and legends tend to divide themselves into groups, each component of a group linked to the others by common strands and elements. I lean heavily here on the excellent work on folklore interpretation by Paul Devereux and Janet and Colin Bord.

More information on individual sites mentioned here will be found in Part 2.

(A) The Devil's Stones

Many examples exist throughout Britain of stones being associated with the Devil. We will look at Dorset's examples and strive to interpret what we can.

The Devil threw the stones on Toller Down in an effort to block the road, whilst a group of standing stones at Corscombe is called 'The Devil's Armchair'. One of the stones is in fact shaped to resemble a chair and one can sit on a seat-like ledge. The site is also known as 'Granny's Armchair'. Other stone sites in Britain have stones which are shaped to enable seating. It has been speculated that perhaps this was where the priest or shaman sat when he was seeking to contact spirits and earth energies.

The Agglestone, that huge natural rock outcrop near Studland, is also known as 'Devil's Anvil' and 'Devil's Nightcap'. The Devil is supposed to have flung it from the Needles at either Corfe Castle or Bindon Abbey.

The Hellstone, near Portesham, is by tradition the stones flung by the Devil from Portland, some nine miles away, when he was amusing himself playing quoits. The Valley of Stones is also attributed to the Devil tossing stones.

The Nine Stones are also know as 'The Devil's Nine Stones'. They are the Devil, his wife and children. Various other folklore is also associated with the stones (see below).

There is a Devil's Stone standing next to the old Roman road on Black Hill above Bere Regis. This title of distinction is also endowed on another, this time natural, outcrop of stone near Portesham Withy Beds. An ancient earthwork at Iwerne Courtney is also called 'The Devil's Spoon and Trencher'.

The sites above would have been held in some reverence in ancient times. Even natural outcrops were seen to be magically empowered, a theme still very much in evidence in the Amerindian and Australian Aboriginal cultures of today. The Devil became associated with these sites only after the introduction of Christianity into Britain. No doubt the Church had good reason to spread tales of the Devil being associated with these ancient pagan places. It sought to stop people visiting, and having SPIRITUAL EXPERIENCES at, these sacred sites.

The Devil was created by the Church to discredit the pagan god Cernunnos, the Celtic

Fig. 6: According to the Church, the Devil lurked behind every ancient stone!

Boo!

Gemma Knight

equivalent of the classical god Pan. He was traditionally seen as a horned deity, hence Lucifer took on the horns and hooves, but his character was unhealthily changed for political purposes. Interestingly, the word Devil comes from the Persian word 'deva' meaning 'the shining one'.

(B) GIANTS AND OTHER MYTHICAL BEASTIES

".......STREWN WITH SOLEMN CROMLECHS AND HOARY CIRCLES, ALL POPULARLY KNOWN AS MEMORIALS OF THE GIANTS OF OLD."

antiquarian James Halliwell, 1860

Fig. 7: The Giant of Melcombe

Stories of giants are, of course, still very much part of the tradition of children's fairy tales. But these stories can be of great antiquity. They contain many classical and Celtic traditions, this indicating a probably prehistoric origin for this often troublesome, sometimes helpful, but always oversized character.

There is a mound at Melcombe Horsey called 'The Giant's Grave'. It is accompanied by a sarsen stone. An 1866 account informs us that two stones were then present. On the adjacent Norden Hill were more sarsens. Folklore has it that two giants held a contest to see which of them could hurl stones the furthest. They threw rocks from Norden Hill across the valley towards Henning Hill. The loser was so mortified at his failure that he fell dead on the spot and was buried beneath the aforementioned mound.

A barrow on Ballard Down, near Swanage, has been know at various times as 'The Giant's Grave', 'The Giant's Grave and Trencher', and 'The Giant's Grave and Stretcher'.

One of the sarsen stones of the Littlemayne circle was affectionately known as 'The Giant Without a Head'.

At Bockhampton Green, to the north east of Cerne Abbas, there lay a large stone said to have either been thrown there by a disgruntled giant, or else left there by villagers in an attempt to roll it up a hill to kill a giant.

The Puckstone, near Studland, literally means 'Goblin's Stone'.

'The Grey Mare and Her Colts' refers perhaps to the Celtic horse goddess Epona. Its Welsh equivalent was Rhiannon, and she was revered as a goddess of fertility and nourishment. The various prehistoric white horses carved out of chalk hillsides may also have been made in reverence to this deity.

So was there really a race of giants in these lands? It is true that some barrows have contained skeletons of men 8ft tall and more. Or are the tales referring, as Janet and Colin Bord suggest, to people with superior 'gigantic' mental abilities with the power to control the weather and earth currents, to levitate large stones and possessing ESP faculties? Perhaps we are catching glimpses of the builders of the sacred sites, as well as the shaman priesthood figures, who directed operations. Sacred sites have a multi-layering of geomantic, astronomical and geometric

Gemma Knight

wisdom. Their users would have been held in high esteem, indeed 'giants'amongst them.

A famous mythical beast is of course the dragon. We will see this beast symbolised in stone at the churches at Cattistock and Wynford Eagle.

(C) MOVING AND DANCING STONES

A great many tales exist all other Britain of stones which are restless, dance around in fields, go for drinks in nearby watering places and so on. An investigation into the folklore of these stones may reveal more insight into the phenomena and nature of earth energies.

It is perhaps relevant that most restless stones appear to become active, by tradition, at particular times of the year or times of the day. This could corroborate work done at the Rollrights and elsewhere (by Paul Devereux et al, as part of the Dragon Project) that RECORDABLE and MEASURABLE energy anomalies often occur at a specific time in a day, lunar cycle or season.

We will now look at Dorset's examples of perambulating stones and see if we can read between the lines to uncover the hidden meanings.

The members of the Nine Stones were said 'to dance at 3.00pm on certain days'. This is the time of the old noon.

The cross at Langton Herring is said to dip its head in the Fleet, the lagoonal waters behind Chesil Beach, on New Year's Eve.

The former stone halfway up the hill at Ibberton is said to have come down to the village well to drink, but only made it halfway back up!

Sarsen stones at Giant's Grave on Henning Hill used to move whenever they hear the cock's crowing at nearby Cheselborne. This tale could be a direct old interpretation of the energy 'bursts' well recorded at stones at the moment of sunrise, a time when the cocks would be seeing in the day.

Stones moving at stated times could be ancient references to those moments when the earth energies were most suited to what was required. Also, I can vouch personally that when one touches a stone to feel the energies, the stone can sometimes feel as if it is swaying or pulsating, this sensation perhaps giving birth to the moving stone tales.

Another commonly recurring tradition is that of stones, such as for a new church building, moving during the night. Dorset has some fine examples. One mile north-east of the Deverel Barrow is the church at Winterborne Whitechurch. The new building was begun in Round Meadow. Stones were laid one day, but the next morning they were found lying in another field. Villagers decided the original field must have a curse on it and built the church on the site 'shown' to them.

The church at Folke, near Sherborne, was begun in Broke Wood (grid reference: 663122). But overnight the stones mysteriously moved to the present site. Recent work by Gordon Harris (pers. comm.) shows that the wood lies directly in the path of a ley that runs from Lyme Regis up to the megalithic temple that is Stonehenge. Coincidence?

GEMMA KNIGHT

Fig. 8: Stones being moved by night must have mystified the workmen of the day.

A similar manifestation of moving church stones also took place at nearby Holnest. No details are available as to where the proposed site was.

Tales exist of workmen at Fordington Green removing a stone and taking it down to the River Frome. It later 'returned' to its original site. These stories could all represent the struggle that ensued between Christians and pagans in the era when the Church was being founded in Britain. For although Britain had been officially 'Christian' for a few hundred years when most of these church-siting tales took root, the local peasantry still carried out the old pagan rituals and utilised the earth energies. Some local 'wiseman' would be on hand to ensure that the siting of new buildings was in harmony with the landscape and the energies of it.

One last example demonstrates this well, I believe. Christchurch Priory was to have been built on St. Catherine's Hill, about 2 miles to the north of the present Saxon-dated site. Once again, every morning the stones had been moved back down the hill and south to the present site. But we have clues here to why it needed to be sited so. The present site lies on a ley line that runs from Hengitsbury Head, through the Priory, past a milestone a mile further on, over the earthworks on top of St. Catherine's Hill and onto a Tumulus at Town Common. The ley is a very compact one with the aligned sites close together. The Priory in fact fills a 'gap' on the ley. I think that the energies would have been perhaps disrupted had the building gone up at the originally intended locality. Fig.21 shows the ley line and the sites involved.

(D)THE DRUIDS

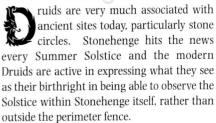

"ALL THINGS BEGIN AND END IN ALBION'S ANCIENT DRUID ROCKY SHORE."

William Blake

Druids are very much associated with ancient sites today, particularly stone circles. Stonehenge hits the news every Summer Solstice and the modern Druids are active in expressing what they see as their birthright in being able to observe the Solstice within Stonehenge itself, rather than outside the perimeter fence.

It is not surprising, therefore, that we find some stone sites in Dorset with Druidic affiliation.

The Agglestone and the circle at Kingston Russell were both regarded as 'Druidic monuments' by historian John Hutchin in 1774. He appears to have been much influenced by the antiquarian William Stukeley, himself an active revivalist of what he saw as ancient Druid practices. Stukeley visited several of Dorset's stone sites in 1723 and regarded most of them as the vestiges of antediluvian Druid culture.

J.F. Pennie in 1827 saw the circle of stones at Poxwell Cairn, near Weymouth, as Druidic. He painted a colourful picture of rituals and solemn ceremonies, a vibrantly poetic description involving naked British women and sacrifices! Unfortunately, Poxwell's stones are in fact the remains of the inner stone lining of a round barrow, not a true stone circle at all! Some sort of 'Druid mania' seems to have been prevailing in the 18th and 19th Centuries, which resulted in all manner of prehistoric (and thus PRE-Druidic) sites being assigned to the Druids. Even unto today, that erroneous belief is still held by the mass of the British public.

The stone circles of Dorset and elsewhere existed fully 2000 years prior to historical records of Druids, which place them during Celtic-Romano times. Modern Druidism goes back only to its foundations in 1833. But this is not to assume that modern Druids are completed unconnected to their ancient counterparts. For modern Druids represent religious beliefs that have affinities with their primeval brethren. There is a link between them of consciousness, a timeless cord that bonds all Mankind of all ages. Druids and other neopagans, if sincere and bona fide in their intentions, are another essential facet of Earth healing.

A link between ancient days and the modern, and proof of continuous pagan observances right through history, was at Milton Abbas. A structure called the 'Druid's Cross' formerly stood in St. Mary's Churchyard, and described by Alfred Pope in 1906. It was unlike any other cross or standing stone in Dorset, and has few parallels in the whole of Britain. Pope gave the following description in 1906, narrating a 1780 account: "It had three steps ....a large stone on top with a hole, in the middle of which there was a pyramid ......also a piece of iron in the middle." The hole and the peculiar pyramid make this an overtly pagan-orientated monument and demonstrate the survival of some form of 'alternative' spirituality in Britain.

(E) STONES OF HEALING AND FERTILITY

This aspect of ancient stone folklore has volumes of tales and traditions spreading all over the globe. Britain has hundreds of stone circles and monoliths reportedly endowed with the properties of healing, divination and the inducement of fertility. We can turn to Dorset's stones with this in mind.

Single standing stones such as the Harstone, the Broadstone, the Helstone and the huge stone at Verwood, would have certainly been visited by the local community in search of the magical and beneficial attributes of these stones. I believe that this is in fact the reason so many people are being drawn to ancient sites today. We can still feel the peace, tranquillity and healing energy of these places, our psyche connecting with benign forces.

The names Hellstone and Helstone give us surprising clues as to the sacred nature of these two sites. Antiquaries have suggested that they derive from halig, meaning 'holy', or from heal, 'to cover or conceal'. The word Hell may even have derived from the local dialect of 'heal'.

The holed stone at Men-an-Tol in Cornwall is Britain's most famous stone with a hole right through. But many others abound and it has been uncovered that Dorset, too, may have had at least one. An archaeological field trip to the Littlemayne stones in 1909 reported that one of the stones had a 1ft diameter hole right through it. The Littlemayne stones are all sarsens. This stone is very hard and it is unusual to see holes weathering right through.

A report dated 1833 tells of a stone at Wraxall which had a "hollow place ......1ft in diameter". The stone was held with 'reverence' by the locals.

Fig. 9: Stones with holes were greatly revered for healing. In India the term for a holed stone means 'gates of deliverance'.

It is worth recording here that recent work (by Devereux et al for the Dragon Project) has proved that radiation levels are MEASURABLY higher inside the holes of holed stones than the background levels outside.

The Wishing Stone of Sliding Hill undoubtedly derived its name from the locals of the area who probably named it such because they found some quality at the locality WORKED for them! It is situated halfway up a steep hill, isolated from the local villages, a place of quiet contemplation. And indeed quiet MEDITATION.

The Cross-in-Hand stone at Batcombe has no less than 8 folklore tales associated with it. It is said that a carving of a woman with crossed hands was at one time visible on the stone. The stone's phallic symbolism is also evident.

Fig. 10: Anyone can benefit from spending some time at standing stones!

At Fifehead Neville, just south of Sturminster Newton, there was reputed to be a 'strong clear stream of WARM water issuing from hillside' (my emphasis). As recently as 1901 the waters were seen to be received into a stone basin, grooved for sluice and hatch to regulate the flow. The locality is close to the Roman villa and it is well known that the Romans held in high religious regard sites where warm waters came out of the earth, most famously of course at Bath.

Standing stones and stone circles are places where Man has visited since time immemorial seeking healing. And the fact has to be faced: so many were built, so many were revered, and so many continue to be visited even today. Surely some form of beneficial effect IS there to be experienced.

It was once written of Stonehenge:

"THE STONES ARE GREAT,
AND THE POWER THEY HAVE,
MEN THAT ARE SICK, FORE TO

THAT STONE, AND THEY WASH
THAT STONE, AND BATHE
AWAY THEIR EVIL."

Layamon, 'Brut' (12th C.)

(F) PETRIFACTION

Petrifaction is the process, in legendary tales, where people and animals are literally turned into stone. It occurs in several classical tales. A whole group of tales exists of people turned to stone for various indiscretions against Christian customs and rules, such as dancing or playing music on the Sabbath. The Devil, too, has been solidified on numerous occasions. These stories were yet another subtle way of brainwashing local communities to stop them visiting stone sites, even though it was generally beneficial for them to do so! The stones of Stanton Drew, Somerset, and the Merry Maidens of Cornwall are two well-known examples of petrifaction due to violations on the Sabbath. Interestingly, this tradition of stones-once-being-people occurs across the world, even in the remotest areas.

The Nine Stones were said to be the Devil, his wife and children turned to stone. They are also said to be children who were punished by Divine retribution for playing five-stones on a Sunday.

At Littlemayne, one of the stones appeared to have been hollowed out and two small figures stood as a result, resembling 'children in swaddling clothes'. It is not known if it was said that they WERE children turned to stone.

(G) BURIED TREASURE

"THE DRAGON SHALL BE IN
THE TUMULUS, OLD, RICH IN
TREASURES."

(Beowulf)

Tales of buried treasure associated with ancient sites are plentiful. A few sites have actually yielded relics of some value, in the monetary sense, when either excavated or, indeed, pillaged and desecrated (and the line between the two is often very diffuse. Many Victorian digs were often little short of 'treasure hunts', with little regard paid to data collection or site preservation).

But most sites with buried treasure folklore have failed to furnish any rewards for those seeking the riches hoped for. We can perhaps ask ourselves in the light of this, were these ancient tales referring to something else? Janet and Colin Bord equate buried treasure stories with earth energies. Was the 'treasure' spoken of really a distant memory of the experiences with, and benefits of, the earth energies? Many tales of interred treasure are associated with ancient sites, the very structures erected to enable those benign forces to be felt and used. I think we are dealing with symbology here. The earth currents, the ancient's 'treasure' has evolved into the material sense of treasure, gold and money. Surely there is another metaphor here, with money today being held in a much higher regard than the Earth by so many people.

The Grey Mare and her Colts may well have been the barrow referred to as having buried within it a solid gold coffin. Old accounts say that the famed barrow containing it was at Gorwell, which is indeed where the 'Grey Mare' is.

The Hoarstone at Verwood had, by folklore, a golden casket buried beneath. It was said that 'any men come to upturn the stone were frightened by a large black bird, of dire omen'. Another tradition says the stone cannot be moved. Numerous other tales exist all over Britain of 'immovable' stones. But there are two ways of interpreting this piece of folklore. Does it mean literally the stones cannot be PHYSICALLY moved? Or are we being told that the stones SHOULD NOT be moved because of the detrimental effects on the earth energies?

Perhaps the ancient sites do hold within them 'priceless treasures' after all.

(h) MOMENTS IN TIME

It is not surprising that several Dorset stone sites have folklore that embrace accounts of actual historical events, whilst others hint at unrecorded episodes. Sometimes an event of some notoriety would be commemorated by the erection of a stone., Other stories relate to happenings at existing ancient stone sites. The latter remind us that standing stones and stone crosses were often the meeting place and, indeed, the very hub of village life.

The Cross-in-Hand stone at Batcombe has no fewer than 8 folklore tales associated with it and some appear to chronicle past events. Four Kings are said to have crossed hands at the stone, swearing never to fight each other again. A highway robber is supposed to have been hung at the spot. Here also, richer travellers left alms at the stone for the poor. The stone was also once a moot stone, and villagers from nearby Sydling, as recent as 1812, remembered children climbing to the top to collect halfpennies placed in a hollow at the top by Sir William Smith. This suggests that the stone was once much taller than its present 3.5ft.

The Batcombe stone also marked a place of burial where the people of Minterne, who

Plate 7: The fallen stone at Verwood. Folklore has it that a golden casket lay buried beneath it. Was this tale in fact referring to the earth energies once experienced here?

had no church, were buried within sight of Yetminster Church.

This folklore-rich stone will also be spoken of later, in terms of phenomena witnessed there.

It is recorded that men used to raise their hats when riding past the Nine Stones. The King Charles stone at Bridport commemorates the narrow escape of the future Charles II from Cromwell's roundheads. It was put up in 1901.

Several stones and other ancient sites are called 'dead men' or some variation of it. Here, as elsewhere in Britain, the 'dead' or 'dumb' character in question reveals itself as a standing stone, or at least the memory of one. The Dead Woman Stone, near Affpuddle, seems to have disappeared now after being moved from land that had been decimated by tanks. This is one site that has NOT benefited by being under the 'protection' of the MOD.

'Dead Man's Bush', on the Dorset/Somerset border, was named after the stone that lay or stood nearby. Fields at Sturminster Marshall, Wyke Regis and at Wimborne all have borne the name 'dead man'.

At Evershot, tradition tells us of a field formerly called 'Dumb Maid's Plot', mentioned in 1895 when visited by the Dorset Field Club. Three dumb sisters danced there 'to while away the time'. Are we again coming across the distant, distorted memory of stones charged with energy and feeling as if they are literally moving or 'dancing'? Later on we will see that perhaps we may be able to answer this question.

Heedless William's Stone (or even 'Headless' by some accounts!) lies just east of Dorchester beside an old Roman road. The stone is at least Roman in age but was later given its title after the name of the coachman who recklessly drove his horse and coach off the road here. The coach careered into the deep pond, still to be seen in the field to the north, with the loss of driver, his horses and the passengers. The pond is said to be bottomless. This folklore is interesting: the Celts, amongst others, held ponds, lakes and any issues of water as entrances to the Underworld.

(i) APPARITIONS AND PHENOMENA

This category is probably the most intriguing of the folklore of Dorset's stone sites. Here we have real observations of 'something' happening, including some modern, verifiable accounts of strange phenomena. I believe that most of these can be explained in terms of earth energies (perhaps those not readily interpreted are not meant to be!). They all involve some interaction between the participant/observer and energies that caused a change, I believe, in consciousness, some shift in awareness. In observing strange lights, UFO's, ghosts and the like, we are seeing perhaps some manifestation of energies and processes that are normally NON-PHYSICAL, but occasionally just 'flicker' (as Devereux coins it) in and out of physical dimensions.

Many accounts are available of unusual apparitions in Dorset and to include them all would require a whole book. Jeremy Harte's excellent 'Cuckoo Pounds and Singing Barrows' is well worth acquiring. We will just concern ourselves here with instances in the proximity of ancient stones.

The 'Burning Barrow' lies at Ridgeway Hill, Bincombe. It is a bowl barrow which old OS maps showed as having 'a circle of stones'. One night in the early Eighties, a woman had been passing the barrow as a pillion passenger on a motorbike. She witnessed an orange glow around the top of the barrow, with odd 'flames' projecting upwards, which were also seen by the rider.

Here we have a wonderful example, I believe, of the emanation of earth currents from an ancient site. Mapwork by the author has shown that it lies on an east-west ley line connecting several barrows for a distance of at least 9 miles towards Wool. Researchers on the Dragon Project have obtained infra-red photographs of glows and 'clouds' around prehistoric stones. It is perhaps only a small step between these luminosities and UFO's. A connection appears to have been made between fault lines in the earth's crust and their proximity to stone circles and UFO sightings. Are these faults places where earth energies issue? The Burning Barrow lies in the immediate vicinity of complex and major faulting!

At a recent meeting of the Wessex Research Group in Bournemouth, the group's organiser, Pat Law, told the meeting how some years prior she had visited Rempstone Circle, near Swanage, with some friends. While they went off to dowse, she settled into a meditation. "I seem to have entered an altered state of consciousness" she went on, "I saw this ribbon of light connecting all the stones and rotating very fast. I then saw a stone of brilliant white in the centre which then turned into a sphere .....figures of priests and priestesses appeared .....and then a pyramid of bright light". She remembers "a feeling of ecstasy and love". On the same trip one of Pat's companions, Anne, was lifted up and thrown back by energies just outside the circle.

The Eggardon Hill area provides us with more happenings of interest. Sites in the area are the Bell Stone, the Two Gates Stones and stones of a possible barrow at West Compton. The top of the hill itself was clearly a place of some sanctity in ancient times, with several round barrows and earthworks.

Around 1953 a man gave an account in a newspaper of being chased over Eggardon by the Devil. Was he in fact witnessing more earthlights, those displays of earth energies?

In September 1974 a man was driving past the hill when he saw a ball of bluish light in front of him. His car stalled at that instant, only to restart when the light moved off. In the Sixties, too, four cars stopped simultaneously. The cars refused to start for fully 20 minutes. This is yet more evidence of the presence of unexplained energies affecting PHYSICAL objects.

Two more stories tell of Eggardon's enigma. A certain Mr Poole was 'recently' up on the north side of the hill when he kept hearing a voice call. Every time he stopped to listen the voice seemed to come from a different direction and he could never see anyone! It was foggy and he noted a chill in the atmosphere.

At Woolcombe Farm, just east of Eggardon Hill, stones were said to actually grow in the fields, to physically increase in size. Tales of growing stones occur across Britain and could relate to the pulsing or even 'glowing' due to earth energy emission. And why not? Stones, as with everything physical, are made up of molecules of swirling energy. Do we conclude that something could not possibly exist simply because we do not (YET) understand it?

The Cross-in-Hand stone at Batcombe, mentioned previously, also has a quite dramatic apparition woven into its folklore. At the end of a rather complicated series of events, a priest in the Middle Ages witnessed a 'pillar of fire' at the locality. It is not known if it emanated from the stone, or if the stone was erected to commemorate the manifestation. It was said in the tale that cattle gathered around the 'pillar' on a stormy night. It could well be that an ancient healing stone was present and the tale was the Christianisation of the locality. The historian Alfred Pope suspected the present stone was at least Roman in age (for the full version of this old tale see 'Dorset' No.4, 1995).

Fig. 11: A standing stone is as sacred as any Church. In the open, close to the Nature and its energies; what better place to converse with the Divine?

On a January night in 1985, a breakdown recovery van was towing an impaired Ford Transit. As they were passing The Nine Stones the engine of the recovery van cut out and the lights of both vehicles failed. The electrics of the vehicles simultaneously came back on a few minutes later; they had NOT been linked! At the same time at Monkton Hill nearby, the lights of a car dulled and flashed on and off several times, only to return to normal. The local press linked the two events to a UFO at

Eggardon and the appearance of a daylight disc at Rampisham. Speculation implied a connection with the ley East Lulworth 292. I believe that most 'spooky' events such as these can be put down to spurts of earth energies near sacred sites and leys.

Ibberton resident Robert Courage has told me of a group of locals who went to dig up some large stones from a field near the village. A hollowness was felt in the ground and smoke started to issue from beneath their feet.

The site (now gone) was known as The Devil's Chimney, but it is uncertain as to whether this title already existed prior to the smoke event.

Many accounts of hauntings and ghosts exist right across the county. A great many of these occur, perhaps significantly, in the close vicinity of round barrows, Roman roads, stones and areas of prehistoric habitation. We will concern ourselves here only with those close to stone sites.

Two Roman milestones stand near Stinsford, marking the route from the east into Roman Dvronvaria, Dorchester of today. In 1969 a group of a dozen boys, under supervision of two adults, were camping in Thorncombe Wood, Stinsford. All those present seem to have observed the figure of a Roman soldier in the woods. When one of the adults approached with a torch, the figure disappeared. The soldier was said to be some height above the ground, the level of the old Roman road which passes through the woods!

This could be another example of 'earth memory', a process by which events are somehow imprinted on a locality. A sort of 'action replay' can be later displayed when conditions are right. Possibly, the participants are observing a 're-run' of an event that actually happened, perhaps a thousand or more years ago. (In Part Two, I will cite ghost stories sited within 0.5 mile of a stone.)

At Blandford, 4 sarsen stones lie in the small wooded area just south of the bridge, opposite the gates of Bryanston Park. The carved stone dogs at the entrance, either side of the gates, are said to climb down and go down to the nearby River Stour at midnight. A spectral dog is also associated with the bridge. It is recorded from Roman times that

dogs were often killed and their blood spilled on the foundations of bridges and roads.

Janet and Colin Bord (in 'The Secret Country') tell us that apparitions such as the above could be the energies at ancient sites interacting in some manner with the participant's brain processes, causing hallucinations.

In conclusion to this section, it must be added that 'apparitions and phenomena' are being experienced all the time at ancient sites. The events I refer to are dowsing and energy sensing. Dowsing energies is FOR REAL! Anyone can dowse - you, me, anyone. One has simply to be receptive and humble. The energies WILL be felt if one BELIEVES THEY EXIST. The negative doubting mind is more than able to override the subtle currents.

Dowser Guy Underwood found that most stones, and ALL round barrows, are positioned over 'blind streams', his term for energy centres. He considered that most of these sites must have been chosen for their energies by 'skilful dowsers'.

This leads me very aptly into the next chapter on Earth Mysteries. But I might add at this juncture (if I may borrow from Kahlil Gibran's 'The Prophet'): "have I spoke of aught else". For every part of this book surely IS about Earth Mysteries. Paul Devereux's definition of EM on page 4 sets the tone of the whole of this project. EVERYTHING IS CONNECTED. Man and the landscape once co-existed in much greater harmony. This sympathetic rapport is what we must strive to recapture, for the good of all Mankind and the planet. For we are one and the same.

"EVERYTHING WHICH HAS COME DOWN TO US FROM HEATHENDOM IS WRAPPED IN A THICK FOG ..... WE CAN DO NO MORE THAN GUESS."

Prof. Rasmus Nyerup, 1806

I believe we can do more than 'guess', if we have the eyes to see. The knowledge is there for the asking.

Chapter Four

EARTH MYSTERIES

Ley Lines

*"........you just keep
straight on......"*

This chapter proved the most challenging for me. Not because of lack of material. Far from it; my biggest problem was what to leave out! Dorset's wealth of sites with EM interest meant that my brief to include only stone-related sites had to be strictly adhered to. Many leys and sacred places had to be omitted and it is hoped that the reader will pursue the subject further using their own research and the bibliography at the end of this book.

Progress and discoveries on the EM front has been moving forward in leaps and bounds, and always I have striven to encompass the latest theorems and work being carried out. It is hoped that a new era for EM has been entered into, a period where we leave behind much of the 'weird/alternative/presumptuous' tag that has dogged serious studies in the past. Archaeologists, mediums, dowsers, geophysicists, ecologists, pagans, Druids, whoever, all have a part to play in unravelling the enigma of Earth Mysteries. Ancient sites are places of learning and Mother Earth is open and yielding to all-comers.

Alfred Watkins noted the above oft-used reply to someone enquiring directions, even though now it would be mostly incorrect! He used it as an example of an ancient memory of prehistoric straight tracks. In 1925, his book 'The Old Straight Track' marked the dawn of EM studies proper, and in it he expounded his theory of 'leys' as the remains of ancient trackways. Even though aeons of time may have passed since they were 'leyed' down, he argued that leys can still be followed as they incorporated barrows, standing stones, circles, hilltop enclosures and other, still surviving, features on the landscape.

He also noted the phenomena of site evolution, whereas ancient sites were later added to, and often Christianised by the erection of a church. Knowlton is a classic example of this 'site continuity'. Today we might follow a ley across the landscape and find that EVERY marker is a church, but this does in no way diminish its claim as the former alignment of prehistoric sites.

Relatively recently, leys have been more regarded as energy lines by many. Dowsing has proved that many lines of energy crossing the landscape DO coincide with alignments of ancient sites, the leys of Watkins, but many more do not.

Paul Devereux has given several examples how classical ancient sites, such as Delphi and Karnack, employ straight lines in their sacred geometry. The famous Nazca lines in Peru, and the Chaco 'roads' of New Mexico, were inscribed with remarkable straightness on the landscape.

Statisticians have proven that leys and their associated ancient sites occur more commonly than mere 'chance' would allow.

Unfortunately, for all the hype and interest in leys, most professional archaeologists still deny their existence but, as John Michell came to conclude in 'New View Over Atlantis', those whose previous beliefs tell them that leys cannot exist may indeed find them invisible!

I do not intend to be sucked into the ley debate, the limitations of space do not permit such a diversion (thank goodness!). Energy lines? Old tracks? Certainly, some leys coincide with many pre-Roman and Roman roads for part of their course and would fall under the Watkins type of phenomenon. But the latest earth mysteries theorem (pioneered by Paul Devereux and 'The Ley Hunter') seems to be going down the road of thought that many leys are 'spirit lines'. These are seen as alignments of sacred sites representing the 'paths of flight' during shamanic ecstatic trance conditions. The ancients saw the whole landscape as symbolic and would mark out the land to mark highly significant experiences.

Geometric patterns (including straight lines and grids) are produced in the cortex during early trance and these may have later been transferred onto the landscape. Devereux now appears to reject the idea of energy leys totally, but the author finds this too sweeping and simplistic considering the wide sphere of possibilities (not to mention the vast evidence of dowsers). After all, everything is ultimately connected and everything is energy!

Perhaps if the author may indulge in a hunch, the 'spirit lines' and the 'old straight tracks' may be connected. Perhaps many leys were laid out as a result of a symbolic transference of shamanic experiences onto the landscape; but what if these sites, occurring as they do in straight lines, came to be used by people to get from A to B. Some leys may have developed tracks along their course because of ritual processions which took place along them. After all, many ley markers would have already been deemed 'sacred' so it is not too unreasonable to suggest that processions and pilgrimage-type events may have ensued. Over a period of time paths would have been forged.

Fig. 12: Powerstock to Old Sarum ley. Note the varying types of marker, indicative of 'site evolution'

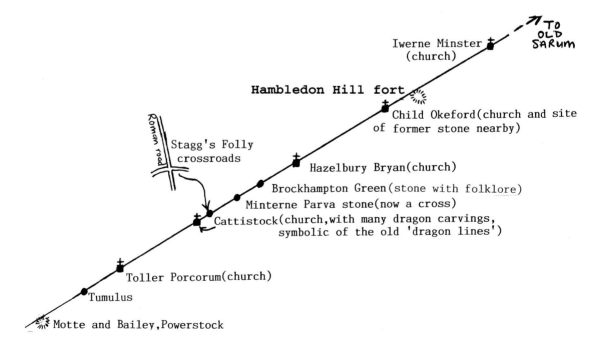

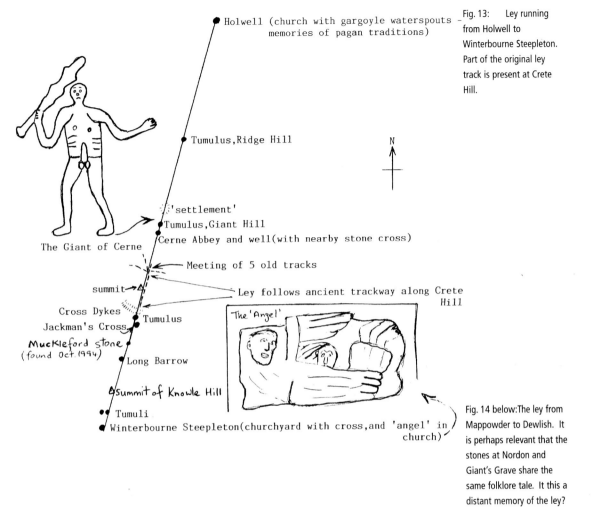

Holwell (church with gargoyle waterspouts –
memories of pagan traditions)

Fig. 13:   Ley running from Holwell to Winterbourne Steepleton. Part of the original ley track is present at Crete Hill.

Tumulus,Ridge Hill

N

The Giant of Cerne

'settlement'
Tumulus,Giant Hill
Cerne Abbey and well(with nearby stone cross)

Meeting of 5 old tracks

summit

Ley follows ancient trackway along Crete
Hill

Cross Dykes
Jackman's Cross
Muckleford stone
(found Oct.1994)

Tumulus

The 'Angel'

Long Barrow

Summit of Knowle Hill

Tumuli
Winterbourne Steepleton(churchyard with cross,and 'angel' in
church)

Fig. 14 below:The ley from Mappowder to Dewlish. It is perhaps relevant that the stones at Nordon and Giant's Grave share the same folklore tale. It this a distant memory of the ley?

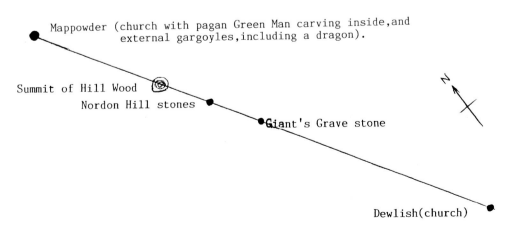

Mappowder (church with pagan Green Man carving inside,and
external gargoyles,including a dragon).

Summit of Hill Wood
Nordon Hill stones

N

Giant's Grave stone

Dewlish(church)

So you see, the different arguments of the various factions of the ley debate can all be given a chance of credence. Those who have been at each other's throats may yet find some common ground. Perhaps then, archaeologists may be more receptive to the 'lunatic fringe'.

Many leys are described in detail in Part Two. I give three examples in Figs 12-14, however, to set the scene so to speak. I lean heavily on the work of Gordon Harris, who has plotted over 30 leys radiating from Stonehenge like the spokes of a wheel.

EARTH ENERGIES

"THE TEXTURE IS ODDLY EXCITING, THRILLING TO THE FINGERTIPS, LIKE A SMALL ELECTRIC SHOCK. ONE CAN, AND, TO GET THE SENSE OF THEM PROPERLY, ONE SHOULD WALK UP AND TOUCH THESE STONES."

JRL Anderson

Plate 8: The author using dowsing rods at the Verwood Hoarstone, shortly after it was cleared, April 1994.

t megaliths, some sort of contact with benign forces was sought. Some interaction with NATURAL FORCES was achieved, and achieved successfully, for the period of megalithic building lasted thousands of years and hundreds of sites have survived even to this day.

The question, of course, is was a place of powerful energies found and then enhanced with stones, or was the place effective only after the stones were raised? I believe either could be the case, depending on locality and circumstance. Many ancient structures appear to mimic what occurs in Nature, whilst others tend to 'blend in' with the landscape. THEY ARE PART OF IT.

The siting of many circles and stones appears only too obvious, with fine views of sunrises, sunsets and other nearby sites. Others appear more enigmatic in their location. For instance, the circle at Rempstone,

the stones at Corscombe and the Helstone standing stone, all lie either in valleys or near the foot of hills. They were designed to fit INTO the landscape, not ONTO it. It was the phenomena experienced there that determined their position IN THE LIVING LANDSCAPE.

No-one really knows how dowsing works, but work it does. The rods or pendulums readily amplify the very subtle earth energies that our bodies receive. Dowsers are generally able to pick up a 'charge' from a standing stone and fluctuations dependent on the time of the day, the cycle of the moon, and the season of the year (see Fig.15).

The idea of 'energy leys' was born quite recently (causing, I might add, much confusion in the process). Tom Graves, Sig Lonegren and others have proved that energy lines can 'break out' of stone circles and travel in dead straight lines to other ancient sites.

Some leading dowsers suggest that the earth energies have been damaged by the erection of modern buildings, motorways, etc., splitting up and diverting energy routes

from their original courses.

This takes us back to the tales of church sitings, whereby foundation stones of churches were mysteriously moved overnight to new , MORE GEOMANTIC, localities. In China, a system known as 'feng-shui' attempts to choose the site for buildings, tombs and so forth, with awareness of, and regard for, the earth currents (known as 'Ch'i' or 'the breath of Nature').

Aboriginal cultures all over the world speak of these energies in the context of their own spiritualities. Is it really so strange to accept that Neolithic and Bronze Age Man of our own lands had similar awareness of the energies that flow across the British landscape?

The SACRED LANDSCAPE

> "The EARTh DOES NOT BELONG TO man, man BELONGS TO The EARTh."
>
> *Chief Seattle*

The word 'geomancy' has already been used within these pages and at this point a brief description of the term would be appropriate.

It can best be summed up as SACRED GEOGRAPHY. This encompasses many facets. It is the interaction of a living landscape with all creatures that live in and on it. The path of geomancy makes one take actions in attunement with the earth and, in the process, in synthesis with one's own spirituality.

Geomancy looks at the principles of geometry, proportion and form in the natural world around us and strives to relate them to the structures we build. To this end, sacred sites were built with the aim of letting the energies of the earth flow between them, around them and, most vitally, THROUGH them.

Ancient geomancers, such as the feng-shui practitioners in China, actually altered and engineered the landscape to redirect and balance the energies of the landscape to enable Man to live in more perfect harmony with his environment. They were conscious that any structure they built would upset the energy patterns and sought to find ways to live with these vital forces, for the good of both Man and the landscape.

Fig. 15: Energy nodes felt by many dowsers on standing stones. The movement of energy takes a spiral form.

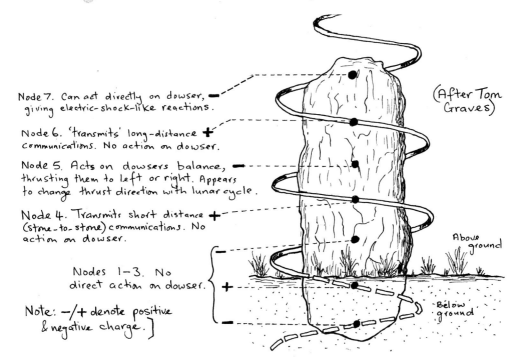

Node 7. Can act directly on dowser, giving electric-shock-like reactions.

Node 6. 'transmits' long-distance communications. No action on dowser.

Node 5. Acts on dowsers balance, thrusting them to left or right. Appears to change thrust direction with lunar cycle.

Node 4. Transmits short distance (stone-to-stone) communications. No action on dowser.

Nodes 1—3. No direct action on dowser.

Note: —/+ denote positive & negative charge.]

(After Tom Graves)

Above ground

Below ground

A good example of the above is the way stone sites seem to blend into, and look as if they belong within, the landscape. Compare the view of a barn or a house (or, more poignantly, a power pylon) stuck on a hilltop. Now picture a stone circle there. All were erected by human effort for a practical purpose. Which of them blends in with the landscape? Which of them is pleasing to our eyes and inner being? Which of them really BELONGS THERE?

The obvious answer of the stone circle is not arrived at simply because we are more 'into' conservation and preserving our heritage now (although it is undoubtedly in our psyche, thank goodness!). It is because we 'know' circles to be VITALLY IMPORTANT AND SPIRITUALLY SIGNIFICANT!

ASTRO-ARChAEOLOGY

Another key area of geomancy and the sacred landscape is the aspect of astro-archaeology. The Stonehenge alignments and astronomical features are well known and need not be repeated here. Save to say that many other stone circles around Britain also appear to have been used (probably amongst other things) for astronomical observances. What appears to be emerging is that it was not merely the function of circles and alignments of stones to record Solstices and Equinoxes, etc. per se. These calendical events were the backdrop for the vital religious rituals that no doubt took place at specific times of the year.

In Dorset we have some beautiful, and recently discovered, examples of the landscape being utilised by Man to mark key points in the pagan year. Some involve the subtle siting of ancient sites to take advantage of the skylines visible from them. Others involve barrows placed at strategic points on the horizon to enable relevant sunrises and sunsets to be marked.

Fig.16 shows the view seen looking approximately N.E. from the Nine Stones circle, west of Dorchester. The circle lies on the side of a north facing hill and in a valley next to a stream: a typical site situated thus because of the earth currents present. However, on a visit in the summer of 1994, I was looking around and tuning in to what the locality had to teach me. I turned to the relevant direction with compass in hand, and there they were: two barrows on the skyline marking the exact point of the Lammas and Beltaine sunrises.

More subtly, the place of the Summer Solstice sunrise is marked where the distant skyline is cut by the nearer hill. Further to this, the middle distance hill meets the slopes of the hill nearest the observer DIRECTLY BELOW THE TWO TUMULI! The positions of the barrows even allow for the couple of degrees difference in the point of the sunrises due to the height of the hill.

Fig. 16: The view from the Nine Stones, showing key sunrise markers. The barrows are silhouetted and slightly enlarged for clarity. From a photograph by the author.

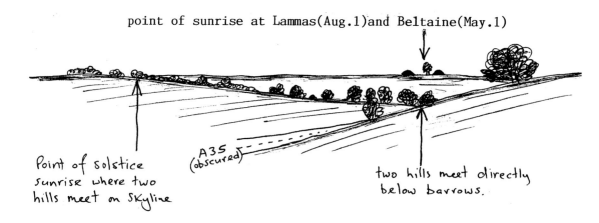

point of sunrise at Lammas(Aug.1) and Beltaine(May.1)

Point of solstice sunrise where two hills meet on skyline

A35 (obscured)

two hills meet directly below barrows.

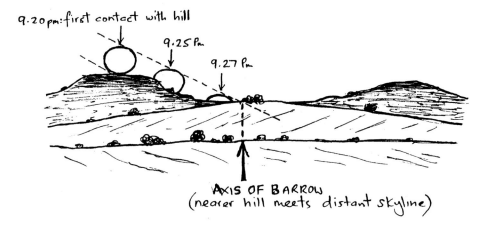

9.20 pm: first contact with hill

9.25 Pm

9.27 Pm

AXIS OF BARROW
(nearer hill meets distant skyline)

Another good example of a man-made design in synthesis with the landscape is seen with the long barrow 'The Grey Mare and Her Colts'. The axis of the mound is 130 to 310 degrees, aligning with both the Winter Solstice sunrise and the Summer Solstice sunset. Although the 'business end' of the barrow, with the megaliths, faces the Winter Solstice sunrise DIRECTION; the close proximity of skyline causes the sun to visibly rise some degrees south of the barrow axis.

Looking on the opposite direction, it was clear to me that the Summer Solstice SUNSET may be marked out by the tapered end of the barrow. The Summer Solstice of 1995 was blessed with clear skies and some beautiful sunrises and sunsets. The author observed the sunset from 'The Grey Mare and Her Colts' on June 22. Fig.17 is based on my observations.

It will be seen that at the key time (June 20-22) the sun first makes contact with the skyline at the top of a flat-topped hill. It proceeds then to skirt the slopes of the hill as it sinks. The sun finally disappears at a point where the distant skyline is cut by a nearer hill!

What is more, the axis of the barrow points directly to the VISIBLE sunset point, not the theoretical mark slightly to the right.

Researchers working on alignments between ancient sites and the stars have the added problem of having to use computers to plot the prehistoric positions of the stars, to see what positions they were in when the ancient structures were built. The question of the azimuths of prehistoric sunrises and sunsets (and moonrises and moonsets for that matter) is fortunately less complicated. The positions of these phenomena is little changed since the ancient sites were constructed. Researchers of the subject, Astro-archaeologists, tell us that combining the latitude and azimuth gives a celestial object its DECLINATION. It is this declination that determines where an object will rise and set. They conclude that in a thousand years the variance only amounts to around one-quarter of a degree! Astronomer Peter Lancaster Brown calculates that the point of the Summer Solstice at Stonehenge is only moving along the horizon by approx. one degree per 4300 years. (The solar disc is approximately half a degree in diameter.)

The barrows on the skyline at Nine Stones also help demonstrate the interconnectedness of features, man-made and natural, on the landscape. The very barrows marking the Lammas and Beltaine sunrises from the Nine Stones in fact show up on the skyline from the Winterbourne Cromlech site (grid reference: 614897), but seen from the latter they mark out the SUMMER SOLSTICE sunrise! (See fig.111.)

Gradually, archaeologists are opening up to the idea that sites are not isolated, but form an interacting network. In 1970, an archaeologist of the Commission for Historical

Fig. 17:   The author's observations of the 1995 Summer Solstice sunset as seen from 'The Grey Mare and Her Colts'.

Monuments noted that some barrow groups in Dorset

"......appear to be deliberately sited so that a complex system of intervisibility is created......

a considerable degree of control and deliberation must be postulated."

At last the penny is slowly dropping. Everything is connected. Everything. The ancients saw meaning in the skies and the earth that we can barely imagine. School has been 'out' for too long!

As well as employing them for ritual and astronomical purposes, often Ancient Man placed much symbolic importance to the placing of two barrows or the appearance of two hills on the skyline. It represented the breasts of the Earth Goddess. Examples can be seen in Figs.16,17,94 and 99.

It might assist the reader to have some information at hand to assist observing key sunrises and sunsets from ancient sites and even spotting new skyline markers and other alignments not as yet perceived. To this end, Fig.18 is reproduced. This diagram has greatly assisted myself in the field and I take it with me on every trip to an area of ancient sites, along with a compass.

It should be pointed out that the point where any celestial object rises or sets depends on several factors, not simply its astronomical direction, which is what Fig.18 basically displays. If the skyline is hilly, or even above the height of the observer, then allowances will have to be made. True, the sun will 'rise' in the predicted place, but will not be seen until it has cleared the skyline. So the sun will rise perhaps several degrees further to the south.

The latitude of the observer also greatly affects where objects in the sky rise or set. For instance, in the Shetlands the Mid-summer sun clears the horizon at an azimuth of 35 degrees, whilst at Land's End, on the same morning, the sun rises at around 51 degrees, a difference of fully 16 degrees, or approximately 30 solar diameters! Fig.18 should be accurate for general purposes for the latitudes of Dorset and southern England.

Some of the old festivals lasted several days, so the dates given in the diagram should be regarded as flexible; an aligned sunrise or sunset may be observed perhaps a few days prior to, or just after, that given here.

However, the situation is complicated somewhat by the lunar observances and alignments known to exist, notably demon-

Fig. 18: Chart for determining sunrises and sunsets at the ancient festivals of the turning year (subject to latitude variances).

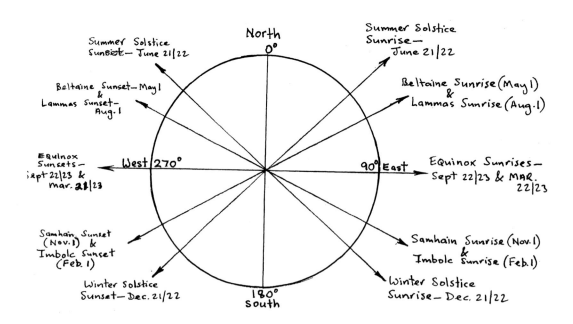

strated at Stonehenge. The moon's motion across the heavens is much more complex than the sun's, with a cycle of 18.61 years to return to the same place in the sky. So intricate are these slow changes in position that it would have taken our early ancestors many years, perhaps even generations, to plot key moonrises and moonsets accurately.

The author has not attempted to include lunar alignments and markers in this project, as it is an involved process. But it could well be that if you spot an alignment that is slightly 'off' one of the solar events, it may be one of the lunar markers. (For more details on this aspect see 'Prehistoric Astronomy and Ritual' by Aubrey Burl, or any good book on Stonehenge which deals with the astronomical side of the site.)

SEEKING OUT THE SACRED LANDSCAPE

One thing may hopefully be clear by this juncture; one cannot study and appreciate the living, sacred landscape from within your own home. Mapwork alone will never replace going out into the open spaces and experiencing the land at first hand.

The landscape is three dimensional and alignments that possess vertical dimensions, such as barrows on the skyline, can only be seen standing at a site. They need to be seen to be revealed. Devereux speaks of a sort of 'archaeological Zen', whereby we approach sacred sites with an attitude of humility, letting ourselves be open to be 'shown' what there is; to look with new eyes. We need to employ 'cognitive archaeology', to look in new ways.

We must learn to SEE. Be open to 'feel' a site. What is visible on the skyline? Using a map whilst at a site, what tumuli or stones would be visible if the plantation of trees were not now intervening? Is there a tumuli on the map which is now nearly/totally flat but would have once been silhouetted on a dawn skyline? Why would I have put this circle here if I had erected it?

But most of all, remember that ancient sites were chiefly points of SPIRITUAL FOCUS.

They exemplify moments long ago when contact with spirit was attempted and ACHIEVED. This would probably have been by a priest/shaman who may have used mind-altering hallucinogenic plants to help him/her reach states enabling divination and contact with gods and spirit.

The builders of the megaliths and stone circles were more in tune with the earth pulse and the seasons. They saw themselves as part of the landscape, not separate from it, preceding today's environmental ecologists by many thousands of years! The Earth beneath our feet is not just a lump of minerals and rock hurling through space. She is a living and aware Being and to plunder Her is the rape of our own spirituality.

A sacred site is a learning centre, a threshold where the earth can talk to us of some of its insights, wisdom and concerns. Go listen.

"WE SHALL NOT CEASE FROM EXPLORATION AND THE END OF ALL OUR EXPLORING WILL BE TO ARRIVE WHERE WE STARTED AND KNOW THE PLACE FOR THE FIRST TIME. THROUGH THE UNKNOWN, REMEMBERED GATE WHEN THE LAST OF EARTH LEFT TO DISCOVER IS THAT WHICH WAS THE BEGINNING!"

T.S. Eliot

Practical Earth healing at sacred sites is gradually being recognised. On every full moon a group meditates within Stonehenge (with the blessing of English Heritage) to help align energies and heal the earth. This is one of the ways forward out of Man's misuse of the Earth.

Much of this chapter has dealt with the new "cognitive archaeology", a new way of looking at the past with different eyes. Many archaeologists are in danger of being left behind as the Earth Mysteries snowball gathers speed. It would be a pity if they did not join the journey too.

This concludes Part One of this volume. I have striven to guide the reader through the archaeology, folklore and geomantic aspects of the ancient stone sites of Dorset. Many other admirable publications are available to enable a deeper study of anything touched upon here. The bibliography at the end of this book lists those titles I have found helpful and can recommend.

"IN CELEBRATING THE FESTIVALS AND SEEKING THE ANCIENT SITES OF THE STANDING STONES, HOLY WELLS, ETC., WE CAN CONNECT WITH THE LIVING FORCES OF THE EARTH."

Adam Mclean.

PART TWO

'THE SPIRIT OF LIFE DWELT PERMANENTLY, IT
SEEMED, IN THESE RIGID ROCKS . . . .'

Michael Harrison

INTRODUCTION TO INVENTORY OF DORSET STONE SITES

"......IT pleases like a magical spell."

William Stukeley (speaking of Stonehenge, 18th c.)

Part Two now deals in detail with each of the ancient stone sites I have so far uncovered in Dorset. Also included are former sites, folklore localities and ley lines incorporating stones as markers.

Faced with the task of listing and describing nearly 200 separate stones, crosses and associated features, I decided to divide the county into five areas.

Drawing a line from Bridport to Bournemouth, the area to the north of this border divided neatly into three regions of roughly equal size and each contained a similar number of localities.

Below this line, the area seemed to naturally divide itself in half. The eastern portion coincides with the Isle of Purbeck. The western half is the area roughly triangular in shape enclosed within lines drawn between Weymouth, Dorchester and Bridport. This is by far the smallest area in terms of square-mileage, but is the richest in terms of number of sites and wealth of interest.

Fig.19 shows how I have divided the county, enabling this book to be used more easily and sites found quickly. Each area has its own chapter with a detailed map at the start of it showing the location of individual sites.

In the case of ley lines, some of these transcend the boundaries of my areas, in which case details of them are given in the description of what is considered to be the most relevant site.

Each site has been visited personally by the author, with the exception of a small number. All photographs are by the author, unless stated and figures and drawings likewise.

I would like to list here the equipment I take with me to stone sites. A little preparation before setting out makes for a more rewarding day.

Equipment for field trips:

notebook	pen/pencil	compass
dowsing rods	pendulum	camera/ spare film
O.S. maps *	tape measure (10ft+)	relevant site books
rainwear	humility	Wellington boots
binoculars	Sunrise/set chart (Fig. 18)	

* 1:25 000 (2.5 to a mile) are essential for any serious field work. The whole of the area between Bridport and the Purbecks (Chapters 6 and 7) is covered by the excellent new 1: 25 000 Outdoor Leisure map (published in 1994, replacing the old 'Purbeck' map).

Fig. 19 (opposite) Map showing the division of the county into the various chapters

---

IMPORTANT NOTE

DO NOT STAND OR CLIMB ON STANDING STONES OR EVEN FALLEN ONES. MORE EROSION CAN BE CAUSED BY PEOPLE THAN THE THOUSANDS OF YEARS OF WEATHER.

RESPECT OUR ANCIENT HERITAGE.

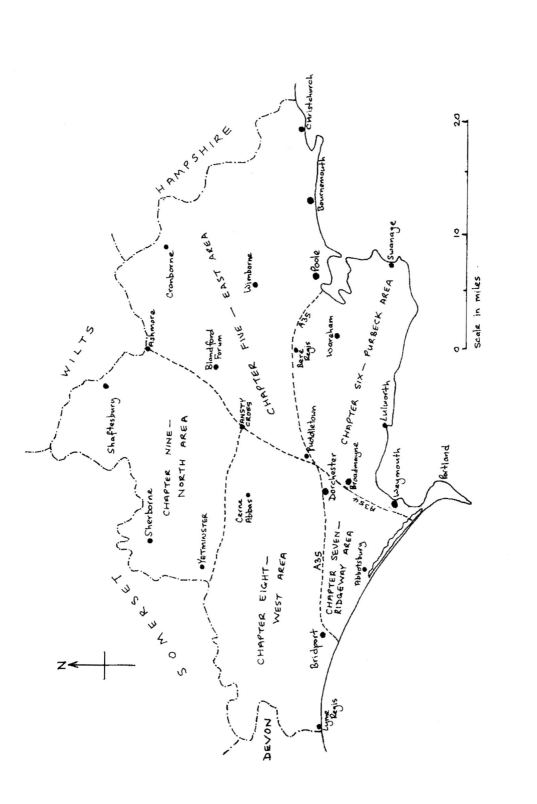

Chapter Five

EAST AREA

"SURELY NOTHING OFFERS A GREATER, STRANGER OR MORE SINGULAR SPECTACLE THAN THE ASSEMBLY OF THESE MASSIVE AND GIGANTIC MONUMENTS."

Chevalier de Freminville (1827)

Fig.20 shows the area covered in this chapter. Although this is the area of densest population, with the Bournemouth/Poole districts occupying a large portion of the southern sector, copious areas of great beauty and isolation can soon be found. Cranborne Chase spills over into the region from neighbouring Hampshire. Hurn Forest and Ringwood Forest cover dozens of square miles, whilst to the west of Wimborne, Badbury Rings and the Tarrant valley provide much beauty and solitude.

Each section commences with location details, with grid reference and map where deemed necessary. A description of the site then follows, with such items as the archaeology and dimensions, etc. of the site. Then reference is made to any folklore associated with the site, enabling the reader to recoup the details of such lore from Chapter Three.

Finally, any relevant earth mysteries, dowsing and geomancy information is presented, including any leys the site may be associated with.

Sites are listed in alphabetical order, enabling the reader to quickly locate in the text any site found on the location map.

ALMA CROSS

LOCATION: Next to the Church of St. Mary, Alma, 2.5 miles west of Sturminster Marshall. OS 1:50 000 sheet 195. Grid reference: 914989.

This fine 5ft high cross shaft protrudes above a square base, 2ft high. According to the church leaflet it dates from around 1400. It formerly stood on the south side of Alma Manor House and was moved to the present site in 1933. It was restored in 1957.

The cross is a Scheduled Ancient Monument. The Church of St. Mary is 12th Century. An old millstone lies at the foot of the cross.

Fig. 20: Location map for stone sites and leys in the east area.

Note: These are the main location headings; many more sites of interest in the neighbouring areas will be found within these sections which are not shown on this map.

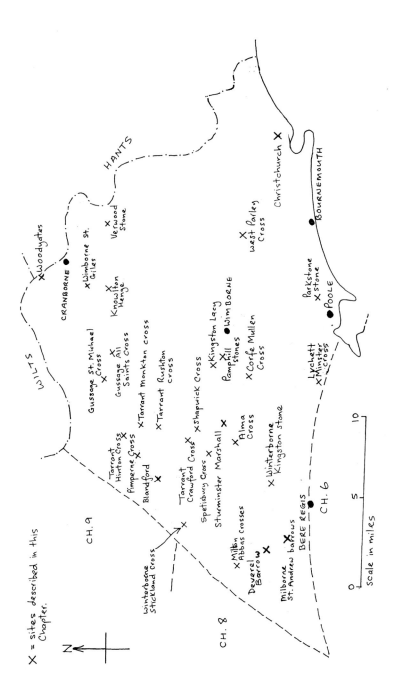

BLANDFORD FORUM STONES AND CROSS

Site 'A' LOCATION: South of the bridge over River Stour, opposite the gates of Bryanston House. OS 1:50 000 sheet 194. Grid reference: 884058.

Four hard ironstone boulders lie in the small tree-shaded area by the row of cottages. The largest is about 4ft in length. Archaeologist John Day informs me that more formerly lay in the meadows either side of the bridge.

Two folklore tales are linked with the locality (see page 26) and a ley passes through the site (see page 61)

Site 'B' LOCATION: Shorts Lane, Blandford. Grid reference: 883064.

Leslie Maskerey alerted the author of the presence of this stone in February 1996. The stone is incorporated into the walls of the old almshouse. It is 3.5ft x 2.5ft (seen) and is of a very hard ironstone, weathered smooth. It looks for all the world a classic Watkins-type markstone. A ley was plotted running from Child Okeford to Spettisbury Rings in 1994 by the author, prior to his knowledge of the

Fig. 21: The Christchurch Ley

stone. The stone lies EXACTLY on the ley! (See Fig.128 and Plate 2)

Site 'C' LOCATION: Next to the car park of the Half Moon pub, White Cliff Mill St. Grid reference: 884065.

Leslie also alerted the author to this small stone, which sits next to the wall of house no. 18. It is 2ft long, of a sandy limestone. It is not certain if this stone is ancient, or a more modern wall protector.

Site 'D' LOCATION: Market Place. Grid reference: 886063

A stone cross is recorded in the Market Place in 1644. It was probably removed after the great fire of 1731. Alfred Pope describes (in 'Old Stone Crosses of Dorset', 1906) seeing fragments piled up in a small enclosure near the then rectory. The former site of the cross lies very close to the ley already mentioned above. Alfred Watkins noted the similarity of 'market' and 'markstone', suggesting that they shared a common root origin.

Work by Gordon Harris suggests a ley running up from Poxwell, passing up the Market

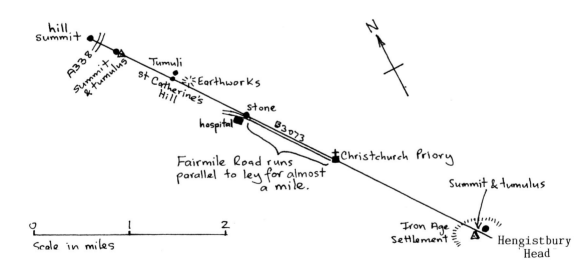

Place, then proceeding on its way, via other sites, to Stonehenge.

chRistchuRch Ley and cRoss

LOCATION: A ley running from Hengistbury Head (grid reference: 172905) to St. Catherine's Hill area (grid reference: 137962).

2ft high and about 15" wide. It is rounded at the top and is set perpendicular to the road. Despite its 'modern' appearance, the stone is not marked on any OS map as a milestone. Nor is it on a boundary, ruling out use as a boundary stone. The stone even lies on the same side of the road that the ley runs along.

Going north, the ley then climbs up the wooded slopes of St. Catherine's Hill, skirting the earthworks at the top, followed by two tumuli immediately to the NW. The path of

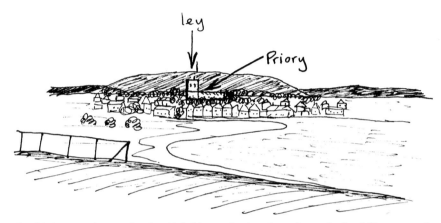

ley

Priory

Fig. 22: View from the top of Hengistbury Head along the ley line to St. Catherine's Hill. Christchurch Priory lies between. Drawn from a photograph by the author (greatly enlarged).

This is a good example of a 'tight' ley with 8 markers in 5 miles. It encompasses a variety of marker types, such as a hillfort, markstone, church, tumuli and hill summits.

The best view is from the top of Hengistbury Head. This site, now quiet, was once a thriving and very large Iron Age sea port, and its huge earthen ramparts still remain.

From here, one can look across to Christchurch Priory, and on further to St. Catherine's Hill, forming a skyline feature directly behind the Priory (Fig.22).

Christchurch Priory marks a very ancient sacred site. A Saxon crypt and altar stone are the oldest surviving relics. A Norman font dates from c1200 and a plaque tells the story of the moving stones folklore (page 20).

Leaving the Priory, the next point of interest on the ley is a marker stone. It lies at the side of the road, opposite the hospital (grid reference: 152938). Fig.21 gives its location. The stone is probably of Portland Stone and is

the ley then descends the hill, crosses the A338 and finally reaches the hilltop on the other side of the road cutting.

I am indebted to Michael Hodges, who informs me of several ghostly apparitions in and around the Priory which could be manifestations of energy associated with either the ancient site and/or the ley. Ghostly noises, smells and actual visual phenomena have all been experienced in the Priory. A mysterious figure also walks through the Castle Tavern, in Church Street. This is very close to the ley as it leaves the Priory going north.

Staple Cross is visible from the main A35 road, heading east from the Purewell roundabout. It stands under pylons at the junction of three lanes and is marked on OS maps. At the base are two steps forming a circular foundation. Above is a base stone, a 10" deep square block, 3ft wide on each face. On this rests a 1ft deep, 30" square socket stone. Into this rests the vestiges of the shaft, 24" high and 9"x12" wide at its base. The whole cross is made of a shelly fossiliferous limestone. Restoration is clearly visible.

CORFE MULLEN CROSS

LOCATION: The churchyard of St. Hubert at junction of A31 and B3074. OS 1:50 0000 sheet 195. Grid reference: 976983.

his cross may be a candidate as an older stone that was converted into a cross. Old records of 1662 tell us of alms and food being periodically distributed to the poor at the 'great stone' called 'The Cross'. What we have today could hardly be termed 'great stone', so the cross either replaced the original stone, or else is the result of remodelling it.

The Church was moved from the centre of Corfe Mullen during the Plague, so it is unlikely that we shall ever know the original location of that 'great stone'. A Roman road runs across the top of the hill in the village and the area is peppered with barrows.

The cross itself has a 14th Century base with two steps, up to a height of about 4ft. The shaft and head are modern, erected on the old base in 1925. The original cross head can be seen above the door of the Church, set into the wall. Prior to the erection of the new shaft, the mortise, which once received the original one, was measured at just 9.5" square, smaller than average.

Also in the area are two old stones at Brook Lane, Corfe Mullen (grid reference: c.982968). The first is in a hedge next to the old Brook Lane Farm. Fig.33 shows it to lie on a ley going from Holt to Tyneham. A further stone lies (mostly buried in the road) to the west, where Brook Lane meets Broadmoor Road.

At nearby Broadstone, outside the Stepping Stones pub (grid reference: 004957) are two stones. These were some of the stones used at a river crossing which gave the village its name (the 'Broadstones'). This was formerly at grid reference: 004965.

Plate 10: (left) The Corfe Mullen Cross

Plate 11: (right) The Crawford Cross. The arrow marks the join of the old and modern sections.,

CRAWFORD CROSS

LOCATION: Half mile south of Tarrant Crawford Church and half a mile north of Crawford Bridge. The cross stands at the meeting of four roads, north of Crawford Farm.OS 1:50 000 sheet 195. Grid reference: 923027.

The plinth and lowest 1ft 10" of the shaft are probably 15th Century. The shaft is 17" wide at the base, which is wider than average for Dorset's 14/15th Century cross shafts. The upper part of the shaft and the steps below the base are modern. A photograph by Alfred Pope of 1906 shows just the base and the original shaft stump. In it the stump certainly looks more like a rough stone than a fashioned cross shaft. I believe this to be another ancient stone that was later Christianised. The notable thing here is IT WAS NOT DESTROYED.

Early Christians saw the sacred symbolism of standing stones at crossroads, as symbolising the AXIS MUNDI, the world axis, the link between heaven and earth.

The material is Ham Hill Stone. The base is now very weathered and made up of a facing of small stones. The shaft is mortised with lead into the socket of the base. Close inspection reveals the join of the old and modern parts of the shaft. The cross was restored in 1914.

DEVEREL BARROW

LOCATION: 1 mile NE of Milborne St. Andrew, between Dorchester and Blandford Forum. OS 1:50 000 sheet 194. Grid reference: 819990.

Amazingly, this famous barrow, which also forms a prominent feature on the landscape, is not marked on the 1:50 000 sheet. To aid location, Fig.23 is given.

Parking at the small lay-by outside the sub-station, one can see the barrow in the field across the road, crowned with trees and surrounded by stone walling. Access is via a public footpath.

The barrow is of the round 'bowl' type, 3ft high now, and enclosed by a low stone wall. Fig.3 is a drawing of the excavation of the barrow in 1824. The excavator, W.A. Miles, is reported to have carved his initials on two large stones in the middle, but a search by the author could not locate these. Some 2 dozen stones still protrude through the barrow mound, the largest of which is on the west side, measuring 5ft x 3ft.

A cremation found near the centre gave a date of 1700-1400 BC, but later, around 1200 BC, the mound was enlarged to receive 20+ more. Some had stone slabs covering the urns.

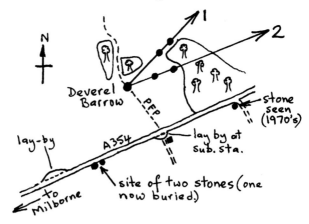

Fig. 23: Deverel Barrow. Direction 1 is the Summer Solstice sunrise, whilst 2 is the sunrise at Beltaine and Lammas sunrises. Possible outlier stones are also shown.

Mapwork and personal visits to the site in 1994 revealed to me two key sunrise alignments. These are shown on Fig.23. The barrows to the east/north-east of Deverel Barrow sit on the skyline when viewed from the latter. They proved to be indicators of the Summer Solstice, Beltaine and Lammas sunrises. Another example of five seemingly unconnected sites being an integral part of something more than the sum of their parts.

I recommend the reader to visit the mound of the barrow between November and April; during the summer half of the year the stones disappear beneath a tangled mass of nettles!

Former Milborne resident, Barry Cuff, informed the author of three stones near to Deverel Barrow which he saw and photographed in the late 70's. The two photos show two large stones south of the A354 between the two lay-bys, but a trip to the site

Plate 12. The Deverel
Barrow

in April 1996 revealed the sad sight that one stone had been buried and the other tipped up into the hedge by recent pipe-laying work.

The remaining stone is 4ft x 3ft with a depression on one side. In the hedge just to the east, the author found what may be a broken off part of the other stone. It measures 18" x 16". In the photograph supplied by Barry Cuff, the 'lost' stone appears smoother and possibly tapered at one end. It may be this end that has survived.

Fig. 24: The cross at
Gussage St. Michael (from
a photograph by the
author). The pole on the
left supports the village
post box.

It is not certain if these stones are related to the barrows in Fig.23, but the stones and the barrows are intervisible. The bearing of the stones from the Deverel Barrow is 210 degrees.

Barry also reports a stone east of the sub-station (see Fig.23) but a search by the author could not locate it in a heavily overgrown area.

GUSSAGE ALL SAINTS AND GUSSAGE ST. MICHAEL CROSSES

LOCATION: These neighbouring villages are 4 miles south-west of Cranborne. OS 1:50 000 sheet 195. Grid reference of crosses: 986114 and 999108.

The remains of the old stone cross at Gussage St. Michael are set into a bank, next to the road, some 50yds north of the Church. It lies between the post-box and a telegraph pole. Formerly (1906) 1ft of shaft, mortised with lead, rested on a base stone. Now only 5" are left, and I fear its close proximity to the road has been a factor in its demise. It is probably 14-15th Century.

Fig.24 should add location, as in summer the grass covers much of it.

This seemingly insignificant remnant

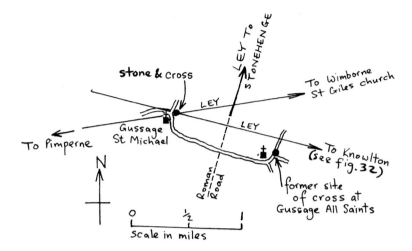

Fig. 25: The crosses of Gussage St. Michael and Gussage All Saints, with associated leys. Work by Gordon Harris suggests that the Roman road lies on a ley projecting up to Stonehenge.

marks, I believe, the intersection of two leys. The first runs from Knowlton to Stubhampton (full details under the section on Knowlton). The second passes the cross whilst running a course from Wimborne St. Giles to the Pimperne Long Barrow. The long barrow and crossroads west of Gussage St. Michael are also on the ley.

This surely means that the cross replaced a standing stone, marking out the intersection of the two ley lines. Fig.25 shows the location of the cross and its relationship to the two leys. In early 1996, James Rattue informed me of a small 1ft stone opposite the cross. Independent confirmation indeed!

In 1906, Alfred Pope spoke of 'an ancient cross' that formerly stood at the crossroads near the church at Gussage All Saints. The spot is still called 'The Cross'. Any vestiges of the cross have now gone.

KINGSTON LACY

LOCATION: Kingston Lacy House is 2 miles west of the centre of Wimborne, on the B3082 road to Blandford. Stones lie in the grounds, just south of the house. The property is National Trust and an admission is charged. OS 1:50 000 sheet 195. Grid reference: 978013.

he ancient stones included here are different from the others in this book. These ones come from ancient Egypt. I feel they should be included in this guide as they represent an ancient culture which, like the Neolithic and Bronze Age cultures of Dorset, were in tune with the Earth and celestial events.

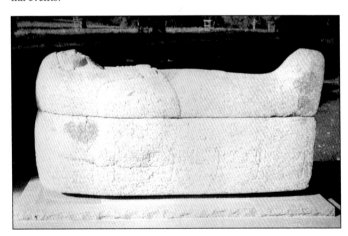

The Philae Needle (Plate 14) is a 22ft high stone shaft, which stood originally on the Isle of Philae, set up by priest/esses of the goddess Isis around 150 BC. It was discovered by Lord of the Manor William Bankes in 1815 and re-erected here in 1827.

The stone has a certain claim to fame. Study of this stone, and the Rosetta Stone, enabled Jean Francis Champollion in 1822 to decipher the hieroglyphics.

Plate 13. The Egyptian sarcophagus at Kingston Lacy house

Just to the west of the Philae Stone can be seen a sarcophagus (Plate 13). Within was found the embalmed body of an Egyptian princess.

Plate 14 also shows a square block of stone in the foreground. This, too, was brought back from Egypt by Bankes.

KNOWLTON

LOCATION: Knowlton is 3 miles south of Cranborne, on the B3078 road to Wimborne. OS 1:50 000 sheet 195. Grid reference: 024103.

Knowlton is one of Dorset's most sacred places and the classic site for demonstrating the Christianisation of an ancient prehistoric spiritual centre. It has been cited by many noted authors of archaeology and earth mysteries, and the site illustrates many aspects of geomancy such as alignments, leys, earth energies, dowsing and astronomical associations.

Visitors today generally make their way to the centre circle, the henge with the ruined church at its heart. The nave and chancel dates between the 12th and 15th Century,

having been modified at various times during that period. It now seems increasingly likely that much of the stone used in the original structure came from the demolition and reshaping of megaliths which once stood inside the henge.

R. Hippisley Cox described Knowlton (in his 1914 book 'The Green Roads of England) thus:

> "......a henge temple" and further noted "three more tumuli ......a line drawn through the middle of which leads to a break in the bank of the temple". He also thought that the material of the church "......once formed the stone circles of a sun temple".

It is recorded that meetings of the local 'hundreds' estates was held at the henge and fairs were later held there. It may have been the Church's revulsion of gatherings of the peasantry at 'heathen places' that led to the pulling down of the stones and the erection of the church.

Instances of churches replacing ancient pagan sites are plentiful. The church at Winnock, Northants, is built on top of a circular moot mound. A chapel was erected on the summit of the magnificent Tumulus St. Michel, near Carnac in Brittany. The tallest megalith in Britain, the 25ft high monolith at Rudston, Humberside, stands within the churchyard, yards from the church. Back in Dorset, the church at Church Knowle, near Corfe Castle, is built within the confines of a much older round mound.

The village of Knowlton was virtually wiped out c.1485 by the Black Death and the church fell into ruin in the 18th Century, after a new roof fell in!

The henge is a 350ft x 310ft oval. The banks are up to 6ft high and 35ft wide ditches, up to 4ft deep, lie within. The site was obviously ceremonial, not defensive, with the ditches INSIDE the banks. Only the eastern entrance is thought to be original.

Inside the church, the old altar lies on the north side of the chancel, a rectangular block of gritty heathstone, 4ft8" x 2ft6". The former 12th Century stone font is now in the Church Of The Ascension at nearby Woodlands (grid reference: 051090).

But Knowlton is much more than a henge with a church in it. Fig.27 shows the extent of ancient monuments in the area, most of which are now invisible to the naked eye but show up still in aerial photographs. Within a radius of half a mile of the church there are confirmed remains of over 40 barrows, two more earthen circles and other prehistoric

traces. Recent magnetometer/radiometry work undertaken by a team from Bournemouth University (see below also) suggests that the number of levelled barrows in the vicinity of Knowlton may have to be amended to over a hundred! This offers further evidence that the area was of major spiritual and cultural importance during the Neolithic and Bronze Ages.

The South Circle (see Fig.27) is almost circular with a diameter of about 800ft. The bank on the NW side is still well preserved and can be seen amidst the trees behind the farm. Entrances to the henge are thought to have been on the east and west sides. A trace of the bank can be seen as a low ridge in the field immediately east of the road junction. This was the spot where the team from Bournemouth University excavated during 1994. The dig uncovered a ditch 17ft (5.8m) deep, unusually deep for any henge. Dig leader John Gale added ".....the ditch is deeper than it is wide .....nowhere else to be found!" *(Lecture in Bournemouth, December 1995).*

The excavation revealed a chalk block with grooves incised on to the surface. The team also found evidence that the banks and ditches had been 'tidied up' in Bronze Age times, after a period of relative neglect.

The North Circle is now levelled but aerial photographs reveal it to be D-shaped, with a wide entrance on the south side. A ditch on

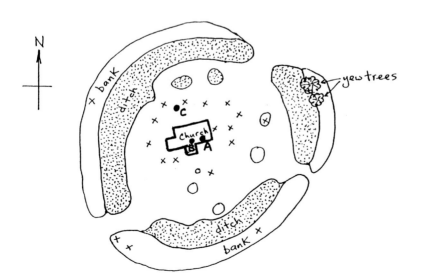

Fig. 26: Plan of centre henge at Knowlton. The stippled areas are those tracts lower than the mean height of ground level. The small crosses mark spirals of energy, possibly marking 'sites of former standing stones', according to Tom Graves (see text). A,B,C - see text.

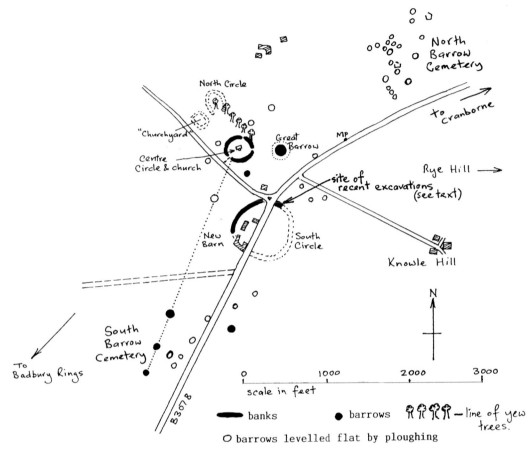

the inside of the bank is indicated here also. The circle's maximum diameter is 275ft.

The nearby site known as the 'Churchyard' is also levelled now. A ditch was at one time present on the OUTSIDE of the bank and the feature may be post-Roman in age.

200ft east of the edge of the Centre Circle is the huge Great Barrow, crowned with large trees. It is Dorset's largest barrow being 20ft high and 135ft in diameter. This feature is referred to later.

Eminent archaeologist Nicholas Thomas regards Knowlton as once having an "importance and sanctity akin to Stonehenge in late Neolithic and Early Bronze Age times". The site was in use from around 2500-1700 BC.

Knowlton is a very sacred geomantic site with many strands of earth mysteries woven into its landscape. From the energy point of view, Knowlton is still very much 'switched on'. Wessex Dowsers and Tom Graves have found complex energy patterns, including overground energies, underground water lines and spiralling lines possibly representing the locations of former standing stones.

At several points around the church the author and others have detected energies having physical effects on the human body. Fig.28 shows the buttress at the north-east extremity of the ruins. Tom Graves had located node 5 on the buttress and this was confirmed in 1994. If one stands in front of the buttress, legs together, arms straight to the stones with palms flat on the point indicated, the earth energies pull one to the left until one losses balance.

Strong energy, enough to cause unbalancing again, was felt in the SE room of the church, indicated by the small 'A' in Fig.26 (inside church).

Dowsers have commented that the energies at Knowlton are very much 'Yin', that is to say 'feminine'. Graham Cheater, a clairvoyant and 'sensitive', felt that the NE buttress was feminine in feel, the SE corner masculine and the area halfway between the two (to the left of the window in Fig.28) was 'balanced'. This spot is shown in Tom Graves' results as a spiral!

In recent years, Paul Craddock, assisted by other members of the Wessex Dowsers, has carried out a detailed study of the energies at Knowlton. He found several lines of energy flowing within the henge, most of which touched the church remains at some point. He found a particularly strong line coming in between the two Yew trees, meandering across the grass to the church, to end at a powerful spot near the church door ('B' in Fig.26). He also dowsed 'meandering, river-like' flows of energy coming into the henge from the NE which crossed at the NE buttress (see above and Fig.28).

Paul and Bob Sephton, another Wessex Dowser of high repute, found a phenomena known as a 'riser' some yards north of the church's north archway. This is marked by 'C' in Fig.26 and can be found on the ground as a bare patch amongst the grasses. What they found was a "column of energy ......very powerful ......if you find it you'll know it!"

Paul concludes by noting that Knowlton is a "strange site" and his work continues on the henge.

Plate 15: The beautiful solitude that is Knowlton

Much more work remains to be done on Knowlton's energy patterns. Work by experienced dowsers needs doing on the southern circle especially, for this was originally the larger of the two, and standing stones may have indeed been present here.

Moving outward from the circles into the immediate surrounds of Knowlton, let us see what the landscape has to teach us. A study of Fig.27 shows some aligned features.

It will be seen that four barrows SSW of the centre circle lie in a straight line leading to the henge (indicated by a dotted line). All three circles are in a straight line which is perpendicular to the Beltaine/Lammas sunrise point.

Fig. 28. Author's sketch of the NE buttress of Knowlton Church. The node 5 band is indicated (see text). From a photograph

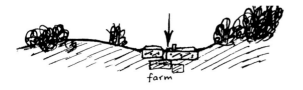

farm

Fig. 29: (Top) The point of sunrise at the Winter Solstice seen from Knowlton Church. The summit of Knowle Hill marks the spot.

Fig. 30: (Centre) The Equinox sun rising over the Great Barrow, with the summit of Rye Hill on the skyline.

Fig. 31:(Bottom) The point of Samhain and Imbolc sunrises, as seen from Knowlton's centre circle.

Seen from the south circle, the North Barrow Cemetery lies in the direction of the Summer Solstice sunrise. Seen from the centre circle the same group of barrows mark out Lammas/Beltaine sunrises. Sadly, all these barrows have now been levelled by the plough.

Seen from the centre circle, the Mid-Winter Solstice sun rises over the highest point of Knowle Hill. Fig.29 shows the view. Looking due east, one can see the Great Barrow in the next field. The summit of the barrow cuts the distant skyline, which is the summit of Rye Hill, at the point where the Equinox sunrises. This sunrise was observed by the author in 1996 (see Fig.30).

To the south-west, the mid-winter sunset is marked on the skyline by Badbury Rings, when viewed from the southern circle. Looking towards the Samhain/Imbolc sunrise point I could see no hill or skyline feature to mark it out. Then I recalled the subtlety with which early Man used the landscape for ritual observances. There before me, half hidden by

farm buildings, was a DIP on the skyline at precisely the right place (as shown in Fig.31)!

Our attention can now broaden out from Knowlton, to encompass the leys that emanate from the circles and cross the land-scape.

Some are leys in the original sense, that is aligned ancient sites. At least one has had an energy flow dowsed.

Leys radiate from Knowlton like the spokes of a wheel, too numerous for all to be included here. So I have kept to my brief to include those relating only to other stone sites, or former ones. Fig.32 shows the results to date.

The diagram shows several features not known until very recently. The huge Verwood Hoarstone was not rediscovered until late in 1993, and cleared early in 1994. The three crop circles at Gussage All Saints appeared in the field adjacent to the Inn in the summer of 1993 and warranted local press coverage. The 4 levelled tumuli next to Bradford Barrow were cited in recent Proceedings (Vols. 110 and 111) of the Dorset Natural History and Archaeological Society.

From the Earth Mysteries point of view, it may be relevant that the ghostly spectre of a white lady was seen to the north of Rye Hill (grid reference: 043108).

Regardless of what ley lines are, be they energy lines, ancient tracks, or whatever, they ARE alignments of ancient sites. Statisticians using computers have shown that the fre-quency and accuracy of these alignments far surpasses what would be expected from mere 'coincidental' chance lines on maps. Many geomancy researchers also voice the opinion that the numerous so-called 'hillforts' on OS maps were in fact the results of landscape engineering, in an effort to direct and enhance the earth currents, to help bring increased well-being and fecundity to the landscape.

"THE LAND AND THE PEOPLE ARE ONE."

Lucien Levy-Bruhl, 1935.

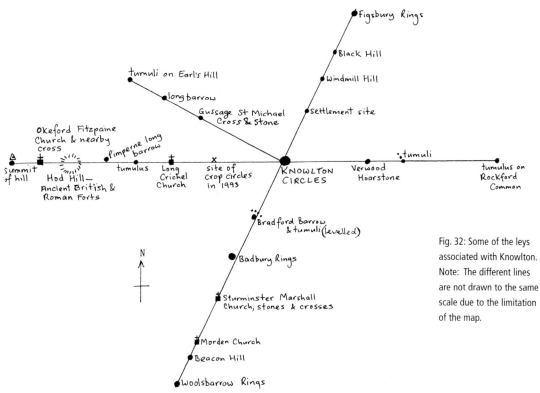

Fig. 32: Some of the leys associated with Knowlton. Note: The different lines are not drawn to the same scale due to the limitation of the map.

LYTCHETT MINSTER CROSS

LOCATION: Lytchett Minster lies 3 miles west of the centre of Poole, on the A35 Dorchester road. The cross base lies at the rear of the parish church. OS 1:50 000 sheet 195 and 1:25 000 Outdoor Leisure map 15 - 'Purbeck and South Dorset'. Grid reference: 961931.

he base of an old stone cross lies loose in the churchyard, just NW of the tower. It lies upturned on its side next to a wooden bench near the groundsman's shed. It is 2ft in diameter, square, but sloped back to an octagon on the top. The 1ft diameter socket can be seen, which used to take the now vacated shaft. It dates from the 15th Century.

Alfred Pope (1906) noted damage to the stone, surmising that considerable force had been used on it, possibly during the purges of 1643.

Map and fieldwork in 1994 enabled the author to uncover a ley running through the church on its course from Holt to Tyneham, a distance of 18 miles. Fig. 33 shows the ley and a sketch of the cross base.

Whilst in the area, one can visit a bound-

Plate 16: The church at Knowlton on a snow-covered winter's day. (Note the area of melted snow near doorway; it is energy point 'B'!!)

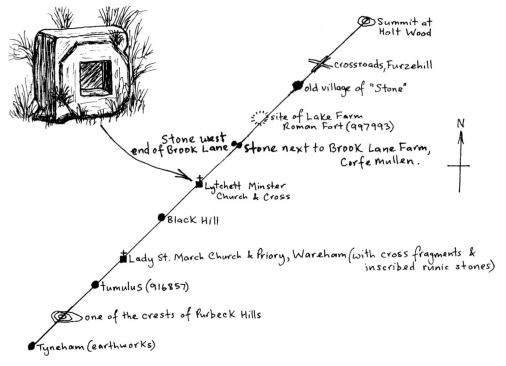

Summit at Holt Wood

crossroads, Furzehill

old village of "Stone"

site of Lake Farm
Roman Fort (997993)

Stone west
end of Brook Lane

Stone next to Brook Lane Farm,
Corfe Mullen.

N

Lytchett Minster
Church & Cross

Black Hill

Lady St. March Church & Priory, Wareham (with cross fragments &
inscribed runic stones)

tumulus (916857)

one of the crests of Purbeck Hills

Tyneham (earthworks)

Fig. 33: The Holt to
Tyneham ley and the
Lytchett Minster cross base.
(Note: The stones at Corfe
Mullen were located in
April 1996 and never
described before.)

ary stone at Halls Road, roughly halfway between Slepe and the centre of Lytchett Matravers (grid reference: 935942). Although probably 17th-19th Century, it is a fine example of standing stones being used as boundary markers. It is 3ft high, in a grass verge, leaning slightly south. The letters 'HL' are inscribed on the back.

"MAKE STRAIGHT PATHS FOR YOUR FEET"

Hebrews xii, 13

MILBORNE ST. ANDREW BARROWS AND THE 'GREAT BARROW' LEY

LOCATION: Milborne St. Andrew lies roughly halfway between Blandford and Dorchester, on the A354 road. The two barrows of interest are 1.5 miles east of the village and Fig.34 shows the locality in detail. Public

footpaths serve the area. OS 1:50 000 sheet 194. Grid references: 827968 (not marked on the present 1:50 000 sheet) and 830973 ('long barrow').

low rise on the edge of the field indicates the position of the remnants of a bowl barrow, which was excavated twice in 1840. Large sarsens lay on the top and were removed to the edge of the field in 1914.

A trip by the author in October 1993 resulted in the location of the stones. They lie behind a wire fence immediately east of a gate. They are very overgrown. A trip to them in April 1994 enabled a better view and access to measure them. Three stones appear to be present, the largest being about 6ft in length. The intermediate one is around 4.5ft square, whilst the smallest approximately 4.5ft x 2.5ft in size. They are typical hard, rounded sarsens.

In 1774, historian John Hutchins spoke of a barrow in the area with a 1.5 ton sarsen projecting out of it. One of the above stones could be the one he saw.

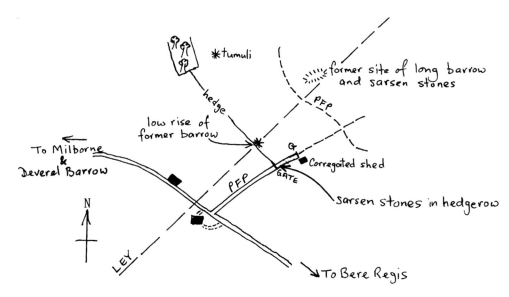

The stones are best viewed between November and April.

Not far north of the bowl barrow sarsens is the site of a 180ft long barrow. 5 sarsens formerly protruded from the mound and were considered to be the remnants of a chambered tomb. The mound was 7ft high at the east end and was aligned on a bearing of 70 degrees.

All traces of the barrow and its stones now appear to be lost.

Work by the author in August 1994 resulted in one of Dorset's finest leys being revealed. What makes it important is that every marker site is a prehistoric one, some 14 in all. Not one example of 'site evolution' is found. This may perhaps sway those sceptics who cannot accept 'S.E.'s', but who may be receptive to the possibility of the existence of leys.

Fig.35 plots its track across 23 miles of Dorset countryside. Two other interesting points come to light on studying the ley. For one, it is terminated at the northern end by the great cursus, that mysterious huge earthwork which still defies interpretation. It is actually two straight cursuses, end-to-end, extending in total about 6 miles. These huge earthworks once amounted to a massive 6.5 million cubic feet of earth.

The ley line meets the cursus EXACTLY at its southern end!

Secondly, as viewed from the cursus, the ley line follows the direction of the Winter Solstice sunset! Early Man in tune with the earth and the stars yet again.

MILTON ABBAS CROSSES

LOCATION: Milton Abbas lies between Blandford and Dorchester, 3 miles north of the A354. Two crosses formerly stood near the very magnificent Abbey. OS 1:50 000 sheet 194. Grid reference (of Abbey): 798023.

The remains of one of the finest crosses to be erected in the county can be found at the south-eastern corner of the large lawns that lie east of the Abbey. Location is aided by a small tree, under whose branches it lies. What remains is the base socket-stone, about 2.5ft high with a 14" socket for the former shaft.

These are the remains of a fine 15th Century market cross (former 'mark' stone prior to this?) which in its heyday had 30 ascending steps, a very grandiose monument indeed. Marriages and markets were held around it when it stood in its original locality

Fig. 34: The positions of the sarsen stones associated with the former bowl barrow, and the site of the long barrow with sarsens. The dashed line plots the ley line that cuts through the landscape here (see Fig.35).

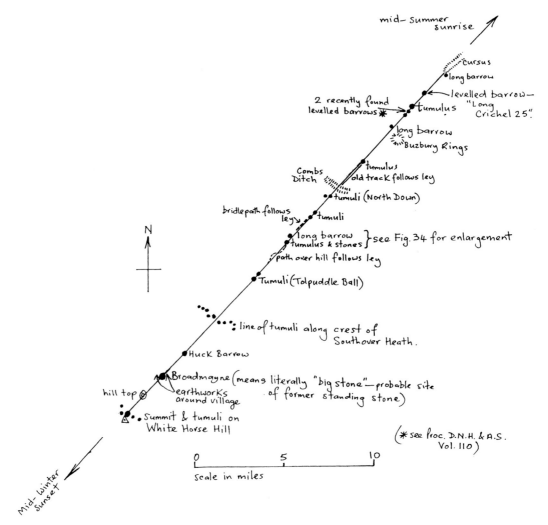

mid–summer sunrise

cursus
long barrow

levelled barrow—
"Long Crichel 25".

2 recently found levelled barrows ✳ → tumulus

long barrow
Buzbury Rings

Combs Ditch

tumulus
old track follows ley

tumuli (North Down)

bridlepath follows leys

tumuli

long barrow
tumulus & stones } see Fig. 34 for enlargement

path over hill follows ley

Tumuli (Tolpuddle Ball)

line of tumuli along crest of Southover Heath.

Huck Barrow

Broadmayne (means literally "big stone"—probable site of former standing stone)

hill top ⊘

earthworks around village

Summit & tumuli on White Horse Hill

(✳ see Proc. D.N.H. & A.S. Vol. 110)

N

Mid-Winter Sunset

0   5   10

scale in miles

Fig. 35: The Great Barrow Ley, running for over 20 miles and inscribing Solstice sunrises and sunsets on the landscape.

at the east end of Market Street. An old painting on the north wall of the Abbey chancel shows the cross. The scene depicts the village as it was prior to the demolition of the cross and the village in 1786, at the whim of the local Lord of the Manor. He ruthlessly redesigned the whole village to incorporate the lake into his plans.

The second cross in the village has already been described on page 21. This unusual 'Druid's Cross' is indeed very important in showing just how, even into the Christian era, Druidic traditions were still recorded. It may be that forms of pre-Christian rituals were still carried out there, well into the Middle Ages.

It stood 12ft south-east of the Abbey and

'perished with the churchyard' (Proc. DNH & AS, Vol. 25).

Whilst in the village, the Abbey itself is worth a visit. To the right as one enters is a display of stones of the original Norman church, destroyed by fire in 1300.

A ley line has been revealed running through Milton Abbas Abbey en-route from Tarrant Keynston to Jack's Hill, a distance of some 28 miles. The ley (Fig.36) passes through the Abbey itself and, interestingly, passes the point where the old market cross originally stood. The ley also passes the sarsen stone at Giant's Grave (see page 18).

But of most interest, I feel, is the passage of the ley through the most intriguing Cattistock

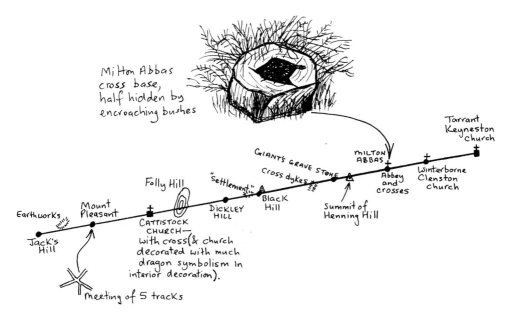

Milton Abbas cross base, half hidden by encroaching bushes

Tarrant Keyneston church

GIANT'S GRAVE STONE
Cross dykes
MILTON ABBAS

Abbey and crosses

Winterborne Clenston church

Folly Hill
"Settlement"
Black Hill

Summit of Henning Hill

Earthworks
Mount Pleasant
DICKLEY HILL

Jack's Hill
CATTISTOCK CHURCH— with cross(& church decorated with much dragon symbolism in interior decoration).

meeting of 5 tracks

Church. The interior of the church is copiously decorated with dragon effigies. These include paintings, sculpture and wood carvings. The church is not even dedicated to St. George!

The relevance is that much research by earth mysteries authors, especially Janet and Colin Bord, has led to the linking of dragon symbolism and folklore with leys, ie. 'dragon lines' and even UFOs. Old tales could have been ancient memories of earth energies experienced; did UFO sightings give rise to the famous dragon's fiery breath? The depiction of St. George suppressing the dragon was clearly symbolic of the Church overthrowing older pagan practices.

"NOTHING OF CADMUS OR ST. GEORGE, THOSE NAMES OF GREAT RENOWN, SURVIVES THEM BUT THEIR FAMES; TIME WAS SO SHARP SET AS TO MAKE NO BONES OF THEIRS, NOR OF THEIR MONUMENTAL STONES....."

Verse of tomb (dated 1086) in Brent Pelham Church, Herts.

PAMPHILL

LOCATION: Pamphill is a small village on the outskirts of Wimborne, and lies to the south-east of the Kingston Lacy grounds. OS 1:50 000 sheet 195. Grid reference: c.995003.

Several interesting features lie in the neighbourhood of Pamphill, including markstones, ancient tracks, a Roman road and ford, and place names referring to former stone(s). A ley line is also postulated. Fig.37 sets the scene.

Stone 'A' is a classic example of Alfred Watkins ley mark stone. It lies at the side of the lane, at a point where the western extremity of the school (dated 1698 and formerly an almshouse) is at its closest to the lane. The paving of the building has been cut out AROUND the stone. The stone is of hard ironstone and is just over 2ft across. It is earthfast and has been much smoothed, probably due to its proximity to the road surface, and perhaps the school also! Fig.38 is a drawing of the stone.

Stone 'B' is the only one of the three standing. According to a local man I spoke to, it was re-erected 'quite recently'. It stands on a high bank at the junction of Vine Hill and

Fig. 36: The cross at Milton Abbas and the ley from Tarrant Keynston to Jack's Hill.

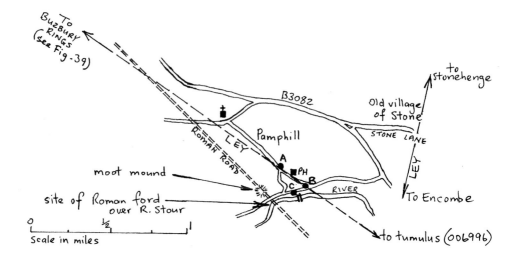

To Buzbury Rings (see Fig.39)

B3082

to Stonehenge

Old village of Stone

STONE LANE

Pamphill

LEY

Roman Road

moot mound

A

PH

C

B

RIVER

site of Roman ford over R. Stour

LEY

To Encombe

0 ½ 1
Scale in miles

to tumulus (006996)

Fig. 37: The Pamphill area. A,B & C are stones mentioned in the text.

Fig. 38:(below) Stone 'A' at Pamphill. The building behind is the school, and the post next to the stone supports the village post-box. (Drawn from a photo by the author.)

Cowgrove Road. 2.5ft of stone projects from the ground and the matrix is micaeous and sparkles in the sunlight.

Plate 17 shows the stone in October. On a visit in the height of summer I could hardly see the stone for tall grass.

I felt that these two stones were somehow linked, occurring as they do at the top and bottom of Vine Hill. Mapwork was undertaken and it became clear that they lie on an alignment with a tumulus to the east, and several more to the west, terminating in tumuli just south of Buzbury Rings. Fig.39 sets out the ley and several recently discovered barrows (not shown yet on OS maps) seem to bear out my findings. NB: Recently, experi-enced dowser Roger Sleet map-dowsed energy lines passing very close to stones 'A' and 'B' at Pamphill.

Stone 'C' lies prone in a bank next to the car park at Eye Mead, a local picnic spot, near a footbridge over the River Stour. It is 4ft long and 2.5ft wide at its maximum. It appears to be a block of worked limestone and is not earthfast. In summer, again, the stone is almost 'lost' midst a tangle of vegetation. This stone lies close to the Roman ford, but it is not clear if it lies in its original position. Plate 18 shows the stone, as exposed in late autumn.

Local archaeologist, John Day, informs me that more stones lie to the west of stone 'C', near the path that follows the river, but the author has not as yet been able to confirm this.

In the centre of nearby Wimborne, old stones still survive. One lies in the lane lead-ing west from Church St.; the other is in the lane leading to a car park north of the Albion pub. The latter has been painted black.

Further points of interest also occur local-ly. A mound at grid reference: 990002 was a Saxon moot, or meeting place. It lies on the old Roman road. On show inside Wimborne Minster is a small section of Roman tessellat-ed pavement.

The former village of Stone, centred around the aptly named Stone Lane, gives us a clue of a former stone of some standing.

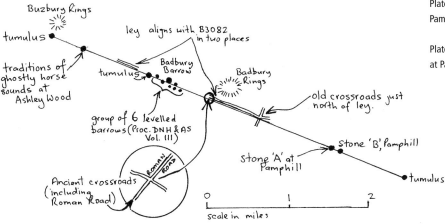

Plate 17: (left) Stone 'B' at Pamphill

Plate 18: (right) Stone 'C' at Pamphill

Fig. 39:(above) The ley running from east of Pamphill, through numerous ancient sites, westward to just south of Buzbury Rings.

The old stone is spoken of as a moot for the local 'hundred' estate. Of relevance, perhaps, is a ley found by Gordon Harris joining Encombe and Stonehenge which passes through the old village of Stone.

PARKSTONE

LOCATION: A stone lies in the grounds of Branksome Library, Poole. OS 1:50 000 sheet 195 and 1:25 000 sheet 'Purbeck and South Dorset'. Grid reference: 050922.

This stone lies at the rear of the library garden, just north of the buildings and sheltering under trees. It is 4ft 3" long and 2ft at its widest point. The matrix is very hard and irony.

It was found 8-10ft below the surface in

Plate 19: The Parkstone stone, showing the hollows (rain-filled).

So we have at least two stones originally sited at the top of a prominent hill. The view from the car park nearby is one of Dorset's finest, with a vast panorama of Poole Harbour and the Purbeck Hills beyond. Ritual fires at the Agglestone, Corfe Castle, or anywhere on the tumuli-rich crest of the Purbecks would have been visible. This locality would also have made an excellent look-out vantage point, perhaps to warn of sea-borne invaders.

We may never know why the stones were positioned where they were. But at least in the surviving stone we have a thread to link us to the remote past.

"WHETHER ISOLATED OR IN GROUPS, THEY (STANDING STONES) REMAIN SHROUDED IN MYSTERY."

Prof. P.R. Giot, (French archaeologist).

July 1909, during the construction of new sewers near the top of Constitution Hill, Upper Parkstone, 1 mile to the west of its present locality (at grid reference: c.023923). Local archaeologists and geologists were duly informed and gave various views on its matrix and possible origin. It lay in gravel but could not be confirmed as being a glacial erratic, dumped during the Ice Age. Analysis revealed it not to be a sarsen, but 'more like quartzite ......lots of quartz'.

It was formerly slightly longer and 1.5ft wider, but some pieces 'broke off on removal'. A curious feature of the stone are the two hollows on one side, which were present in a photograph dated 1909. Hollowed out areas, like the celebrated 'cup marks' adorn countless ancient stones across Britain. It is now accepted that these marks had ritual significance. Dowser Guy Underwood called such stones 'basin stones'. He found them to be energy foci.

Another stone is also reported in the same area. Its fate was to be made into a gatepost 'on the south slopes of Constitution Hill'. This has been the sad story of many stones, as we will see later.

PIMPERNE CROSS

LOCATION: Pimperne is situated 2 miles NE of Blandford, on the A354 Salisbury road. The cross is outside the entrance to the parish church of St. Peter. OS 1:50 000 sheet 195. Grid reference: 904094.

This fine 14-15th Century cross is made of Tisbury greensand and the whole structure stands some 7ft tall. The lowest 2ft of an octagonal shaft still protrudes out of a 2ft high square pedestal. The base of the shaft is 28" in diameter, larger than average for Dorset crosses. Could we have here the surviving remnants of a much older stone?

The pedestal is mounted onto three steps, 2 of which are 10" deep, the lowest one being 2ft deep, and showing traces of very worn moulding.

Two other interesting relics of antiquity are recorded at Pimperne. The 350ft Pimperne Long Barrow (shown on OS maps, grid reference: 917105) lies about a mile NE of the cross. It is orientated SE-NW and is a good example of an earthen long barrow. It lies on a ley running west from Knowlton Henges (see Fig. 32).

A unique maze known as 'Troy Town' once existed at Pimperne. It was recorded in 1686 by John Aubrey, the famed antiquarian who wrote extensively on Avebury's monuments. On each side of the paths were 1ft high ridges.

Mazes and labyrinths date back to ancient times and many European ones have been dated as Bronze Age. The spiralling patterns had ritual, perhaps even astronomical, significance and only in more modern times did mazes become degraded into the popular recreation they are today.

Work by Gordon Harris (unpub.) places the Pimperne Cross and long barrow very close to a ley that progresses from Poxwell, via Blandford, Pimperne and Barford St. Martin, to Stonehenge.

shapwick cross and barrows

LOCATION: Shapwick is situated midway between Blandford and Wimborne, to the NE of the A350. The cross stands at the centre of the village, opposite the Inn. OS 1:50 000 sheet 195. Grid reference: 938017.

Plate 21 shows the cross, but only the lower half is the original 15th Century remains. (The join of the old and the modern is level with the street sign on the other side of the road in the photograph.)

Three steps lead up to a base stone, which once held the shaft. The steps are of a red sandstone and have been regrouted in numerous places. The total height of the original stones is about 5ft. Above this, a modern war memorial and cross have been added.

A photograph by Alfred Pope, dated 1906, shows 3.5ft of shaft still sitting in its socket. The shaft was either replaced by, or surrounded by, the modern work.

The cross is directly on the route of the old

Roman road running from Badbury Rings to Dorchester, a former major artery in Iron Age and possibly older times. The cross could be yet another Christian 'take-over' of a more ancient stone (see Fig.49).

Also in the Shapwick vicinity we find remnants of barrows that were recorded as containing stones of note. The famous Badbury Barrow (now levelled but situated at grid reference: 948035) had a 'massive wall of sand-

Plate 20: The Pimperne Cross.

Plate 21: The Shapwick Cross. The top half of the monument is modern.

stone ......30ft across'. At the centre lay a 'huge block of sandstone .....half a ton' with cup marks and carvings on, 'similar to Stonehenge' it was noted.

The carvings are dagger-like, up to 12" long, similar indeed to those found on sarsens at Stonehenge. The block is now in the British Museum. Carvings and inscribed stones of pre-Roman age are rare in Dorset. Four stones with pictograms on were found at Dorchester (see Fig.96 and Proc. DNH & AS vol. 109, 1987).

Clearly, Badbury Barrow was a site of great importance, lying as it does in an area crowded with barrows (most of which have now, sadly, been levelled by the plough). A ley runs close by and Fig.39 shows the position of the barrow relative to it.

Close by to the south, the OS maps show Straw Barrow at grid reference: 946032. This barrow is now reduced to a low mound, but archaeologist Nicholas Thomas records "many sandstone blocks scattered over it today" (1960's). On field trips during 1993, the author could find no traces of any of these, the Landowner presumably having removed them.

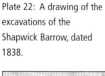
Plate 22: A drawing of the excavations of the Shapwick Barrow, dated 1838.

What is of real interest is that records of the 1845 excavation speak of a huge wall of sandstone being at the centre and carvings. Indeed, it could be one and the same barrow described above. With such a profusion of barrows in the area, confusion appears to have arisen (not for the first time!). Whether one or two barrows, large blocks of stone were incorporated into sacred structures and close to a ley at that!

My own view is that they were different barrows, for Plate 22 shows a drawing of the Shapwick Barrow excavations, and it is dated 1838, seven years prior to the opening of the Badbury Barrow. The possibility does exist that the barrow(s) were opened up more than once, a common practice in Victorian days.

Also of interest is that one of Gordon Harris' leys radiating from Stonehenge passes within a few yards east of Straw Barrow, on its way south to Lulworth Castle and Mupe Bay, via other tumuli en-route. During the winter of 95/96, experienced local dowser, Roger Sleet, map-dowsed energy lines passing through the site.

SPETTISBURY AND STURMINSTER MARSHALL

LOCATION: Both villages lie on the A350 Poole to Blandford road, in the valley of the River Stour, west of Wimborne. OS 1:50 000 sheet 195. Grid references (of village churches): 951004 and 909028.

lfred Pope, in 1906, described the socket stone of the old stone cross at Spettisbury and showed a photograph of same. He described it as being "in a garden in front of neat farm house near to the church". A search by the author led to the village rector, plus a local lady, both of whom furnished data of much use. The stone had stood under a holly tree, near the entrance to Chestnut House, just east of the church (grid reference: 909027). It was no longer there.

The search then turned to the churchyard of St. Mary's, Sturminster Marshall. West of the tower is a 14th Century cross base, 'said to come from 'Spettisbury' (Royal Comm. for Historical Monuments). The old photo of Pope enabled me to confirm it was the Spettisbury cross base. Plate 23 shows the stone in the centre of the photo, the steps and shaft being modern.

The stone is 38" square and 18" deep, with convex broaching. At least part of the former cross has regained some of its former dignity after years of sitting amidst a rockery as a receptacle for flowers!

Another old stone cross stands in the same churchyard as the above. It stands between the gates and the church. The shaft stands 6ft 6" high and is tapered, being 15" at its widest at the base. It protrudes from an octagonal socket stone which is moulded.

The remains are probably the vestiges of the old village cross, the steps having long since gone. The material is a very irony gritstone (see Plate 24).

Some small stones, of uncertain age, can be found near the centre of the village at Sturminster Marshall and their positions, along with the two crosses, are shown in Fig.40.

The stones were known to Wessex Dowser Bob Sephton and others, who provided information of interest. Apparently, quite recently, contractors were working on the road surface where the stones lie. There was a danger of the stones being dumped in a truck or buried. Bob informed the workmen of the importance of the stones to the local energy lines and they were replaced after the work had been completed.

Plate 23: Close up of the former Spettisbury stone cross base, now in the churchyard at Sturminster Marshall.

Plate 24: The Sturminster Marshall cross, shrouded by a magnificent yew.

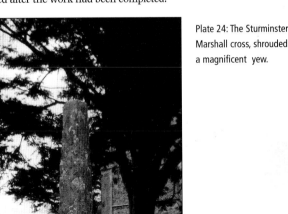

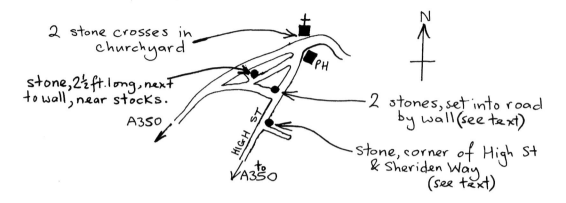

2 stone crosses in churchyard

stone, 2½ ft. long, next to wall, near stocks.

A350

HIGH ST

to A350

PH

N

2 stones, set into road by wall (see text)

Stone, corner of High St & Sheriden Way (see text)

Fig. 40: Location map for Sturminster Marshall stones

The largest of the three lies at the corner of High Street and Sheriden Way.

Plate 25: Stone at Sturminster Marshall with the peculiar hollow in its side (6" pen shows the scale).

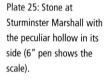

The stone stands on one edge of its long axis. This longer side is 4ft in length and the stone rises to 2.5ft above the grass. On the side nearest the wall, away from the road, a crater-like hollow is present, nearly 1ft across, as shown in Plate 25.

To the north, within view of the above stone, 2 small stones lie at the junction of High Street and Balls Lane (Plate 26). The smaller one is 14" high, the large one being almost a cube at 18" x 21".

On a visit in 1994, I dowsed an energy current running along the road, linking these two stones with the one found to the south.

Bob Sephton's timely intervention is echoed by others; old stones should not be moved. There are still many seemingly insignificant looking stones scattered across

Plate 26: Stones by the roadside, Sturminster Marshall. These were nearly lost forever by road works.

our countryside, a great many still unrecorded. They were placed where they are for good reason, and only our own arrogance and ignorance perceives them as of little consequence. Is ignorance really bliss?

"These (the stones) should never be moved ......for they may be important links in the system of megalithic alignments."

John Michell

As late as January 1995, the author received information from Gordon Harris (in a map, unpub.) that a ley stretching from Flowers Barrow right up to Stonehenge, passes up the main street at Sturminster Marshall, within feet of the stones and the church.

Surely this cannot be coincidence. The idea of 'energy leys' may be quite a recent one (as Paul Devereux explains) but does that mean that they do not exist?

"The more you find out about earth energies, the more you realise you don't know."

Bob Sephton, Wessex Dowsers (lecture, April 1995).

The Tarrant Valley

LOCATION: The River Tarrant is a tributary of the River Stour and flows south through a quite steep-sided valley from Tarrant Gunville (NE of Blandford) some 8 miles south to its junction with the Stour, NE of Spettisbury. OS 1:50 000 sheet 195. Individual site references are given in the text.

Fig.41 shows the chief sites of interest in the valley and the region illustrates well how many small, subtly 'hidden' features can be found if one has the patience and inclination to seek them out.

Working from north to south, the first site we encounter is at Tarrant Hinton. In a field behind Manor Farm House (at grid reference: 939108) lies the octagonal base and broken shaft of an old stone cross. The base is 3ft square and the base of the shaft still lies in the socket, sewn off level with the top of the socket stone. Lead grouting can still be seen around the shaft. The material is a green sandstone and Alfred Pope noted, in 1906, that the church, dated 1180, is of similar material.

The cross probably once stood at the crossroads close by to the west, and that place is still called Hinton Cross.

This is another case of something being brought back from the edge of obscurity. The Landowner was unaware of its significance and was grateful to be informed (his permission should be sought before entry). Whether one places the cross at the crossroads or its present position, both points are crossed by a ley running from Pimperne Long Barrow to Wimborne St. Giles (see Figs. 25 and 41).

The road south then crosses 2 leys before reaching the charming village of Tarrant Monkton. To the left as one enters the churchyard, the socket stone of the old village cross lies. The shaft is still in the socket, sewn off at the top of the base stone. The base is octagonal, 4ft in diameter, with worn moulding still visible. The base of the shaft is 15" across and is still secured into its socket with lead grouting. The material is Ham Hill Stone

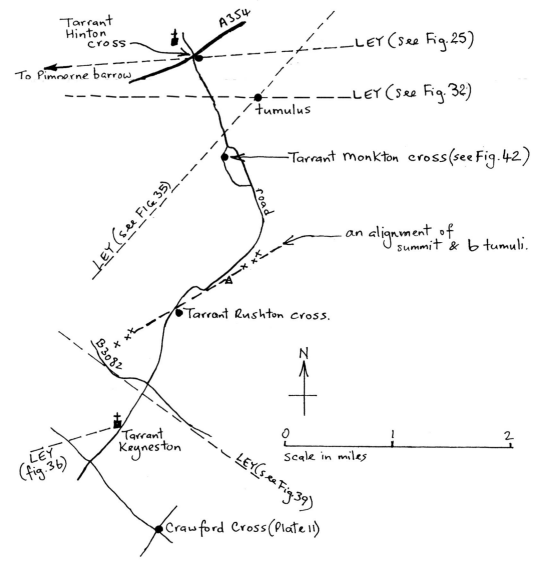

Fig. 41. The Tarrant valley, showing sites mentioned in the text, and reference to other illustrations

and it has been tentatively dated as early 14th Century. Without question, this cross once stood in the middle of the road at the crossroads, 50 yards to the NE. A drawing by Dr. E.G.R. Grant, dated 1900, shows the base (almost identical to its present appearance) at the crossroads. This is reproduced in Fig.42.

Travelling further south on the road along the valley, we pass three tumuli at the top of a steep slope called 'The Cliff'. An alignment appears to be present with three more that stand on the hill on which Ashley Wood stands.

From the intervening summit (marked by

triangulation pillar) the barrows are intervisible.

Less than a mile south of the summit is the parish church of St. Mary, Tarrant Rushton. Built into the south face of the 14th Century tower is a stone cross. It is 2.5ft long and 16" wide with a faint cross on it. Pope described it as simply 'medieval'. Over the south doorway of the nave is a sculptured lintel, dated early 12th Century: A large Agnus Dei is flanked by two figures.

At the very southern end of the valley stands Crawford Cross, which we covered earlier (see Plate 11).

Fig.42: This 1900 drawing shows the base of the Tarrant Monkton cross in its original position, in the foreground.

VERWOOD STONE AND LEYS

LOCATION: The Verwood stone lies on Forest Enterprise land, north of the centre of Verwood, a village situated on the B3081 road west of Ringwood. OS 1:50 000 sheet 195. Grid reference: 094098.

Fig.43 shows the location of the large stone, which may prove useful. The stone lies in a forest crossed by a network of paths and tracks. Parking is at the end of Stephen's Lane (grid reference: 095093), proceeding then through the gate at the north-west corner. Ignore the track going up to a prominent tumuli in front and take the path soon encountered on the right.

Fig.43: Location map for the Verwood stone.

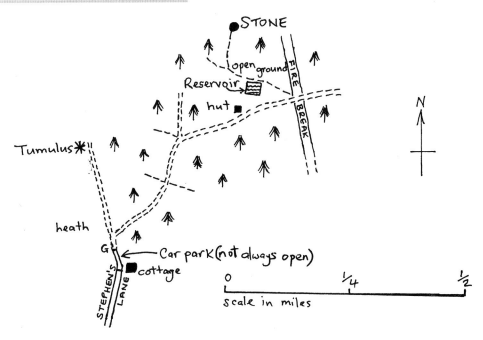

Keep to this track for about 750 yards (ignoring other paths leading off) until one sees the hut and reservoir to one's left. The stone is signposted from here.

I take some pride in describing this stone. Local people of Verwood, with the author's help, instigated location, clearing and general awareness of the stone. But more of that later. First some history.

Local folklore (see page 23) and early antiquarians spoke of a large stone on the (then) open heathland at Verwood.

A record of 1280 speaks of "le Hoarstone near the road leading to the great bridge of Ringwood" (quoted in 1841 by Wake-Smart), a 700+ year old testimony. In 1872, Charles Warne ('Ancient Dorset') described the legend of the black bird and also confirmed that it had already been 'thrown down' in his time. John Hutchins, the great Dorset antiquarian, recounts (in 1868) details of the stone, including "......the Wurstone - no doubt a hoar or boundary stone, which probably marked one of the boundaries of Cranborne Chase".

In 'A Brief History of Verwood', Pam Reeks and Jill Coulthard, of the Verwood Historical Society, mention the stone as "a block of sandstone, 20ft long, 10ft wide and 9ft deep".

Alerted by this, I contacted Pam and visits in October and November 1993 revealed the stone and liaison with the Forest Enterprise Officer, Mike Casserley, enabled the site to be cleared in March 1994.

The local press and the Guardian covered the story and a grand unveiling by the local Mayor in April 1994 heralded a new era for this once-forgotten monolith. Signposts, a bench and paths, now greet the visitor. Prior to the clearance of the site, only a patch of overgrown stone was visible above the ground, surrounded by almost impenetrable forest.

I feel privileged to have been a part of this story and wish to use it to demonstrate how enthusiastic 'amateurs' can play such a leading role in unearthing the secrets of the landscape and OUR heritage.

IMPORTANT NOTE

Please do not stand or sit on the Verwood stone. Several fragments have already broken off. Use the bench provided.

After the clearance of the stone, measurements and dowsing commenced and I visited

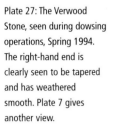

Plate 27: The Verwood Stone, seen during dowsing operations, Spring 1994. The right-hand end is clearly seen to be tapered and has weathered smooth. Plate 7 gives another view.

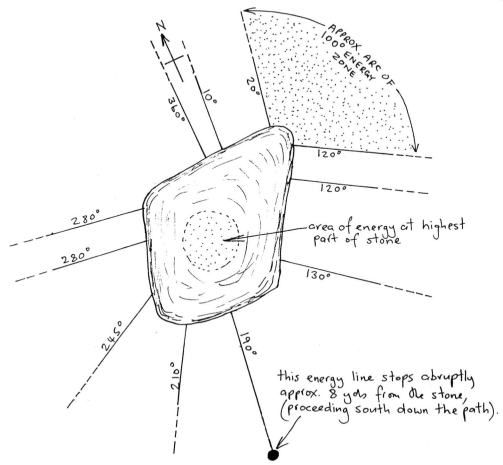

N
360°
10°
20°
APPROX ARC OF 1000 ENERGY ZONE
120°
120°
280°
280°
area of energy at highest part of stone
245°
210°
190°
130°

this energy line stops abruptly approx. 8 yds from the stone, (proceeding south down the path).

Fig.44: Dowsing results at the Verwood Stone, Spring 1994.

the stone several times in the spring/early summer of 1994, often with friends, to collect data and to confirm findings of previous trips.

The stone lies prone, elongated approximately SW-NE, being 13ft long on this axis. It is 11.5ft wide at maximum and the southern end attains a maximum thickness of 2ft. The NE end is decidedly tapered, both in width and thickness and I envisage this to be the top of the stone when it was standing. I have an overwhelming 'gut feeling' that it once DID stand. The thickest end also displays countless fresh, unweathered quartz grains, whilst the tapered end is much smoother, showing more signs of being exposed to the elements and the ravages of time. Plate 27 shows the stone's size and the tapering.

The matrix of the stone is typical Bagshot Beds gritstone, a quartz rich deposit, which was used to build the Rempstone Circle, near

Corfe Castle. No other large blocks appear to have been encountered by forestry workers. A large old quarry to the NW reveals only finer-grained sandstone.

Fig.44 shows a plan of the dowsing results obtained by the author, confirmed and assisted by Sarah Litchfield, Graham Cheater and Jenifer Oakley. Of great interest is the large wedge of energy, registered with dowsing rods, at the NE end of the site, the TAPERED END of the stone. The plan shows its extent just before new moon. On a later trip, this time just AFTER FULL MOON, the spread of the energy arc was several degrees less, the energy band having reduced in size.

The line going 190 degrees from the stone (coincidental with the path) vanishes abruptly approximately 8yds from the stone. Two separate dowsers (unprompted) confirmed this. The point is, energy bands are still active despite the present fallen aspect of the stone:

> ## "IF A STANDING STONE BECOMES PRONE THE ENERGY BANDS ARE RETAINED."
>
> *Bob Sephton, former*
> *Chairman of Wessex Dowsers*
> *(at lecture in Bournemouth, April 1995).*

A photograph taken during dowsing operations in 1995 shows a mysterious white 'cloud' floating about the stone. Similar outbursts of earth energies have been photographed at other sites across the world.

The shape of the stone may also be of some relevance. To quote Janet and Colin Bord:

> *"Apart from holed stones, there is another shape thought to have symbolised the female principle, a broad diamond."*

The stone is indeed similar to the feminine-associated stones at Avebury. Why was this great stone, one of the largest ever to stand in Dorset, placed where it was? I think the location is the key here, the actual place being of sacred importance to our distant ancestors. The whole area is now covered by plantations of pine, but study of the contours shows us that views of distant skylines, or any nearer notable features, were very limited from the stone.

The area from west, through north, right across to the east, is higher than the stone, and only the direction from east to approximately SW would have offered any distant views whatsoever. The Purbecks and Hengistbury Head may have been visible from the stone when it stood on open heath (as we know the land once was here), but the uncertainty of the visibility of these makes it all a bit conjective when thinking of astronomical observations.

I think here we have an important energy site, well known to early wisemen and shamen and used by locals for healing and 'good luck' rituals.

Fig.45: The leys associated with the Verwood Stone.

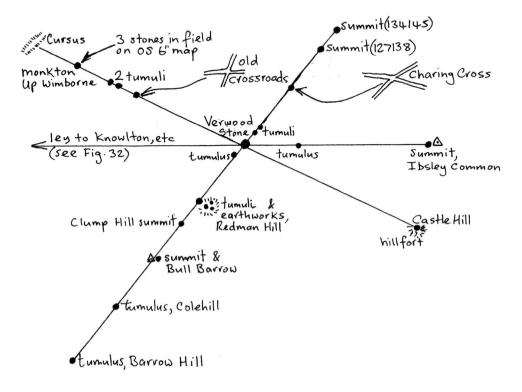

Fig.46: The author's drawing of the possible appearance of the stone at Verwood when it was standing. Its height above the ground may have exceeded 10ft.

"FOR IN THESE STONES IS A MYSTERY, AND A HEALING VIRTUE AGAINST MANY AILMENTS."

Geoffrey of Monmouth, 12th C.

We will now focus our attention on how the stone relates to the landscape regarding ley lines. Fig.45 shows the leys at present linked to the stone.

I believe that the importance of the Verwood Stone is confirmed by its connection by ley line to Knowlton and the Pimperne Long Barrow, both significant sites. In addition to this, the stone is linked to the monumental earthworks of the Dorset cursus by a ley.

An impression of the appearance of the stone, standing on the open heathlands, is given in Fig.46.

"THE STANDING STONES COMPARE WITH THE NEEDLES USED BY CHINESE ACUPUNCTURISTS."

George Trevelyan ('Operation Redemption')

WIMBORNE ST. GILES BARROW

LOCATION: Wimborne St. Giles lies 2 miles SW of Cranborne. The barrow lies just east of the village in field on the south side of the B3081. OS 1:50 000 sheet 195. Grid reference: 039123.

It lies at the far side of the field from the B3081. A large beech and a tall pine standing on the barrow aid location,. The barrow has a diameter over 60ft and is up to 5ft high. Two stones lie on the edge of the barrow, both orientated NE-SW along their longest axis. They both appear earthfast. The one nearest the beech is 4ft long and 2ft high,

Fig.47: Wimborne St. Giles barrows.

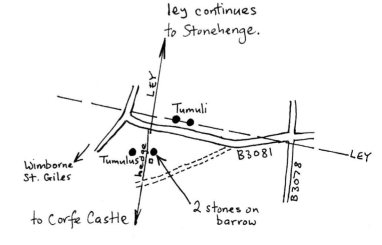

Plate 28: One of the stones on the barrow at Wimborne St. Giles, overshadowed by the huge beech tree.

Fig.48: (right) The cross at West Parley

rectangular stone stands fixed to the outside of the church porch. It is 3ft 8" high, 2ft wide and 6" thick. A cross can be seen inscribed on the stone.

A tradition exists that the stone once stood close by a roadside pond, called 'Cross Pond', in the village. The meeting of the main roads to the north is still called Parley Cross. From the shape of the stone, which is anything but traditional cross-shaped, I think we have another modification of an older pre-Christian stone. It may have marked an ancient way from Badbury Rings, past Dudsbury 'fort', to St. Catherine's Hill, and perhaps onwards to the Iron Age port at Hengistbury Head.

whilst the other, to the east, is 3ft long and 1.5ft high.

Also, at the NE edge of the barrow, the ground felt as if it concealed another stone.

The barrow lies close to three others and in close proximity to the ley traced from the cursus to Castle Hill (see Fig.45). Fig.47 shows the area in detail, whilst Plate 28 shows one of the barrow stones.

The N-S ley on Fig.47 is one plotted by Gordon Harris. It travels up from Corfe Castle, via tumuli at Arne and Barrow Hill, and passes within yards of the barrow. In Plate 28, the hedge in the background marks the course of the ley. From here the ley progresses north via Wilton to Stonehenge itself.

WEST PARLEY CROSS

LOCATION: West Parley lies just north of Bournemouth, to the west of Hurn Airport. The cross stone is at the Church of All Saints, near the banks of the River Stour. OS 1: 50 000 sheet 195. Grid reference: 087967.

WINTERBORNE KINGSTON STONE

LOCATION: Winterborne Kingston is situated 2 miles NE of Bere Regis, just off the A31 Wimborne road. OS 1:50 000 sheet 194. Grid reference: 863977.

utside the village hall, at the cross-roads, is a stone. It is 4ft x 3ft, composed of limestone and appears to have been worked. It rests solidly on the ground but is not earthfast.

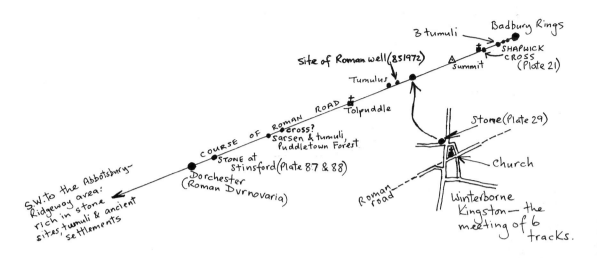

Badbury Rings
3 tumuli
SHAPWICK CROSS (Plate 21)
Site of Roman well (851972)
Summit
Tumulus
COURSE OF ROMAN ROAD Tolpuddle
cross?
Sacsen & tumuli, Puddletown Forest
STONE at Stinsford (Plate 87 & 88)
Dorchester (Roman Durnovaria)
S.W. to the Abbotsbury Ridgeway area: rich in stone sites, tumuli & ancient settlements
Stone (Plate 29)
church
Roman road
Winterborne Kingston — the meeting of 6 tracks.

Next to the stone is a war memorial (Plate 29) with several fragments of older stonework incorporated into its steps.

The stone lies at one of two crossroads in the village and, I believe, is a ley marker. A Roman road runs through the village and here we may have a good example of the Romans utilising and improving an existing older STRAIGHT TRACK. Fig.49 shows the course of the Roman road, the marker stones en-route, and the ancient sites encountered. Excavations in the village, close to the Roman road, yielded a bronze sheet with a hare figure - a cult animal.

tion of the vacated shaft. The base has been set into a modern foundation.

A sign next to the base states 'Base of Medieval Cross Excavated Jubilee Year 1977' (see Plate 30).

The village stocks formerly stood next to the cross, on its north side, and culprits sat on the base stone when confined.

Fig.49: The course of the Roman road from Badbury Rings to Dorchester: A prehistoric route?

Plate 29: The stone at Winterborne Kingston.

WINTERBORNE STICKLAND CROSS

LOCATION: This village is situated 3 miles west of Blandford, nestling in the valley of the River Winterborne. The cross lies in the centre of the village, at the junction of three roads, 50yds south of the church.

he base of this stone cross rests under a huge lime, the 'Cross Tree', and is probably 14th-15th Century. It is made of Ham Hill Stone, is 37" across and 9" deep. It is octagonal, each face being 15" across. The hollowed centre marks the posi-

Plate 30: The base of the stone cross at Winterborne Stickland.

To the north of the village, by Hedge End Farm, a cairn barrow once stood at grid reference: 826066. In 1860, 150 wagon loads of flint and stone were removed from it. Flinty cairns are common in Dorset and we shall encounter more later.

WOODYATES BARROW STONES

LOCATION: This long barrow lies to the east of Woodyates, on the Hants/Dorset border. OS 1:50 000 sheet 184. Grid reference: 039195. Access is restricted.

his is the Pentridge III long barrow and is a fine example, 95ft long and a maximum height of nearly 4ft. In 1812, Mr Colt Hoare saw "a tumulus surrounded by large sarsen stones". It is not sure if these were an integral part of the long barrow's original structure or the result of field clearance, a common problem encountered. The author could find no surviving stones in 1993.

The barrow is orientated SE-NW, the line of the mid-winter sunrise and the mid-summer sunset.

Work by Prof John North (in his book 'Stonehenge') shows that the Winter Solstice sunset occurs over the Worbarrow long barrow as seen from Pentridge III. He also shows that Sirius, the brightest star, set over the same barrow, seen from the latter at around 3250BC.

So yet another stone site has lost its sarsens. How many more do we have to loose before the tide is turned? No-one would think of bulldozing Stonehenge. But its builders were of the same contemporary culture that erected the thousands of smaller stones and countless barrows.

"HISTORY CANNOT TELL US (WHO ERECTED THE STANDING STONES) FOR ITS RECORDS DO NOT REACH BEYOND THE DAWN OF OUR CIVILISATION. BUT BEFORE THAT DAWN THERE WAS THE TWILIGHT OF ANOTHER CIVILISATION."

Dion Fortune

Chapter Six

PURBECK AREA

"PRIMITIVE TEMPLES, LIKE AVEBURY, ARE SCATTERED OVER THE FACE OF THE EARTH, WITNESSING ONE COMMON RELIGION FOR ITS INHABITANTS."

Rev. W.H.E. McKnight (1887)

This area includes a well-defined and famous region, the Isle of Purbeck. It is an area of outstanding beauty, of rolling hills and high towering cliffs. The area was well populated by prehistoric Man, with large settlements/hillforts at Flower's Barrow, Bindon Hill and Chalbury.

The area is peppered with hundreds of barrows, which show up on the skyline of the Purbeck Hills at many places. The local stone, utilised by modern Man (too ruthlessly for my liking), was also used by ancient Man for standing stones, stone circles and for cists and linings for barrows.

The Romans had settlements and mining operations in the region also and, later still, early Christians left their own ancient relics.

Many stone boundary markers and other monuments are scattered over the Ballard Down and Swanage area. I have not included these, as they appear to be post-Mediaeval in age.

AGGLESTONE AND PUCKSTONE

LOCATION: These well-known landmarks lie on Godlingston Heath, 0.75 mile west of Studland. OS 1:50 000 sheet 195 and 1:25 000 'Purbeck and South Dorset' sheet. Grid references: Agglestone 024827; Puckstone 022832. Access to the stones is via the network of public footpaths that criss-cross the heath.

The Agglestone is a famous landmark of the Purbecks and well visited. It is a huge natural rock outcrop some 80ft in circumference and estimated to weigh some 400 tons! The name may have derived from the Saxon 'halig', meaning 'holy'. It has Druidic and Devil-associated folklore, as told on pages 17 and 20. The locality was probably revered by our distant ancestors who would see such a huge rock, high up on an open heath, as having magical properties, a place to encounter the Earth spirit.

Interestingly, the great rock was capable of being rocked, formerly pivoting on an area underneath its bulk. Stones with this quality of movement are known as logan stones and many are known, most with attached folklore. Many have Druidic associations and some earlier writers thought them to be raised by the Druids using magical powers. Guy Underwood found that of the logan stones that had been dowsed, ALL were on important energy sites.

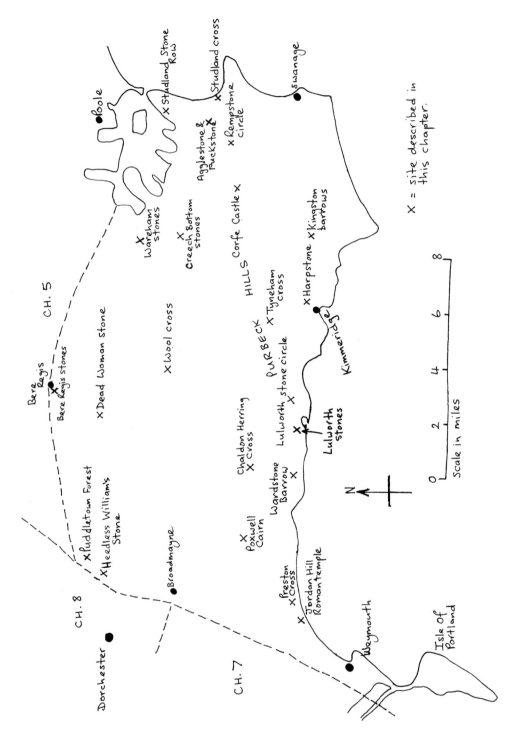

Fig.50: Location map for stone sites and leys in the
Purbeck area. (NB: additional sites can be found under
these main headings)

Plate 31: (left) The Agglestone, with the heath and Bournemouth cliffs in the background. The views from this stone are worth the visit.

Plate 32: (right) The Agglestone, from the south, capping a prominent hill.

"THE AGGLESTONE ......A RUDE DRUIDIC MONUMENT."

Philip Brannon, 1858.

Plate 33: The Puckstone

The Puckstone is visible to the NW from the Agglestone, a mound in the middle distance. The intervening ground is low and boggy and it is best to walk via a path that skirts to the south of this area, then north to the Puckstone.

The mound is in fact a rocky outcrop and the stone at its summit, shown in Plate 33, gives the locality its name (which is literally 'goblin's stone').

This stone is about 3ft tall and appears to be attached to the outcrop. It does, however, have the appearance of having been shaped. By the fairies perhaps?

"A HEAP OF STONES IN A FIELD SHOULD NOT BE DISTURBED ......FAIRIES ARE SAID TO LIVE INSIDE AND TO MOVE THE STONES WOULD BE MOST UNFORTUNATE."

Irish Roman Catholic Priest, early 1900's

BERE REGIS STONES

LOCATION: Bere Regis lies on the A35
halfway between Poole and
Dorchester. Two stones lie just to the
south of the village. OS 1:50 000
sheet 194 and 1:25 000 'Purbeck and
South Dorset' sheet. Grid references:
Devil's Stone 837941; Wool Road
sarsen 847943.

evil's Stone lies near the summit of
Black Hill next to the Roman road and
therefore probably marks an older
track.

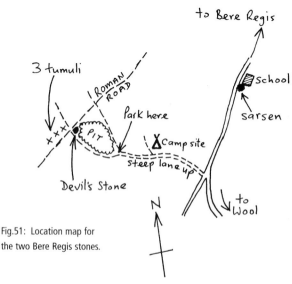

Fig.51: Location map for
the two Bere Regis stones.

It is a heathstone monolith, about 4ft high
and agreed by various writers as being erected
by human means. It was utilised by the
Romans, whose road passes within feet of it.
Since the OS map of 1888, it has been shown
as a boundary stone, separating the parishes
of Bere Regis and Turners Puddle.

Old records describe it as being 11ft long,
so the stone may have been broken at some
stage. Perhaps it was all part of the efforts of
the Church to keep people away from the
stone, aided by the endowment of the name.

Mr G. Smith of Parkstone, informs me that
local children used to call the stone a 'five-fin-
gered stone' because they used to put their
hands into a hollow on the top.

The stone lies at a crossing of two paths,
and a few yards the other side three tumuli,
arranged in a straight line, grace the open
heath.

Less than half-a-mile east of Devil's Stone
(see Fig.51), lies a large prone sarsen stone. I
was led to it via verbal information by a local
farmer at a meeting of Wessex Dowsers in
November 1993. The stone lies on the east
side of the road, outside Bere Regis County
First School. It had been there "as long as I
can remember" he said.

The stone is triangular in outline, but with
well-weathered, rounded edges. It is 4.5ft x
5ft along each side. It has the appearance of
limestone/quartzite, and is different in texture
to the typical sarsen stone (see Plate 35).

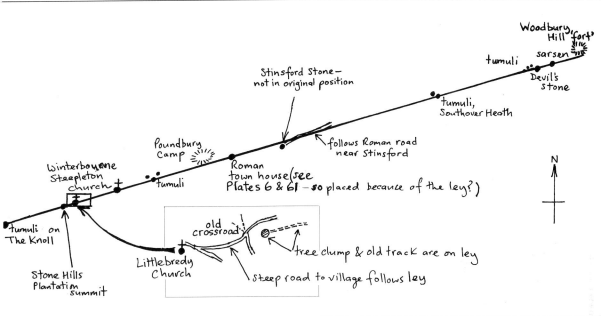

Woodbury Hill 'fort'

sarsen

tumuli

Devil's stone

Stinsford Stone – not in original position

tumuli, Southover Heath

Poundbury Camp

follows Roman road near Stinsford

N

Winterbourne Steepleton church

Roman town house (see Plates 6 & 61 – so placed because of the ley?)

tumuli

tumuli on The Knoll

old crossroad

tree clump & old track are on ley

Littlebredy Church

steep road to village follows ley

Stone Hills Plantation summit

We have already noted the Roman road passing the Devil's Stone. It probably marks a much older track. I felt that two stones as close to one another as these were perhaps also connected. Mapwork, and some field plodding, gave the ley line in Fig.52. It is a good example of a ley marked out with a variety of ancient structures, including Roman buildings and roads, stones, churches, hilltops, tree clumps and surviving tracks.

chaldon herring cross

LOCATION: Chaldon Herring (also known as East Chaldon) lies south of the A352 Wareham to Dorchester road. The cross sits on the village green. OS 1:50 000 sheet 194 and 1:25 000 'Purbeck and South Dorset' sheet. Grid reference: 792834.

his square socket-stone, of an old Medieval stone cross, is about 2.5ft square and 9" deep. The socket reveals that the base of the now-vacated shaft was about 16" diameter. The socket is circular, rather than the commoner octagon or squarish type. Curiously, the cross was not includ-

Fig.52: The ley from Bere Regis to The Knoll. (Not to scale-length of ley about 19 miles.)

Plate 36: The Chaldon Herring Cross

ed in Alfred Pope's comprehensive 'Old Stone Crosses of Dorset' in 1906.

A ley passes just north of the centre of the village (see Nine Stones in Chapter 7). But the cross actually stands exactly on ley 'East Lulworth 92', mapped by Paul Devereux, if it is extended westwards to Chalbury Camp (see Fig.65).

1.5 miles to the south of Chaldon Herring is Wardstone Barrow, at grid reference: 793813 and named on OS maps. It was opened up in 1867 and had a height then of 4.5ft. The use of 'stone' in its naming suggests that stones were encountered. Sarsen stones were reported, by Leslie Grinsell in 1959, lying to the north of the barrow, but it is not certain if these particular ones gave rise to the name. The barrow is isolated on private land and the author has been unable to gain access to the site to see if any of the stones still survive.

Fig.53: Location of the mere stones at Corfe Castle.

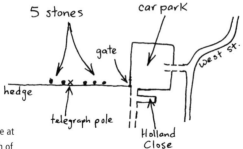

Plate 37: The stone at Peake House, south of Corfe Castle.

CORFE CASTLE CROSS AND STONES

LOCATION: The cross stands in the centre of the village, near the entrance to the castle. OS 1:50 000 sheet 195 and 1:25 000 'Purbeck and South Dorset'. Grid reference: 960822.

The present village cross was built in 1897, but has incorporated in its base and steps stones from a much older construction. The former cross is recorded in 1381 when it is mentioned in a Decree by Richard II. The present cross is of Swanage stone and topped by a Latin cross.

The cross stands close to a ley running from Rempstone Circle (see Fig.65) to Chalbury Camp. Another old ley remnant is probably the A351 road going south from the castle and leading to two tumuli (grid reference: 965807). Shrovetide football is played along this road, distant memories of past rituals (and ley energies?).

On May Day, the old pagan Beltaine festival, Morris dancing still takes place at the cross each year, vestiges of much older rituals and celebrations.

Also worth visiting whilst in Corfe are the Medieval mere stones. Fig.53 shows their location. Access is via the footpath running west from near the south exit of the car park in West Street.

They are associated with strip plots, established prior to the 16th Century, when the fields here were named 'West Hawes'. Five were found still standing in-situ in 1994, ranging from 12" to 18" high.

One mile west of Corfe is the church at Church Knowle, mentioned on page 49 as a fine example of a Christian building on a much older mound, 'site evolution' indeed.

South of Corfe at Peake House (grid reference: 967807) the owner, Mr P. Bowyer, has shown the author a fine old stone in the gardens. It is 2.5ft diameter and 10" deep, appearing at first to be a mill stone. But it has no hole and has inscribed on it a simplified representation of the Heraldic Arms of Sir John Matravers (1290?-1365), making it 14th Century (see Plate 37).

It was found in Scoles Lane in 1965 at grid reference: 966800. It may have been in transit from the stone quarries to the south when some mishap may have transpired.

At Norden, just north-west of the castle, the Romans built two altars and steps leading down to a holy well.

CREECH BOTTOM STONES

LOCATION: Creech Bottom is on a minor road, 2.5 miles south of Wareham. OS 1:50 000 sheet 195 and 1:25 000 'Purbeck and South Dorset' sheet. Grid references: Three Lord's Barrow 914847; boundary stone 918846.

he Three Lord's Barrow is named on OS maps and can be reached via entering the gate at 'The Cottage' (asking permission) and keeping on the north side of the east-west hedgerow.

This barrow marks the junction of four parishes, a good example of how ancient sites are still used for defining land divisions. The tumuli stands on a natural knoll, accentuating its height.

Older OS maps show a boundary stone crowning the summit of the barrow. It was once described as a stone arch, of unknown age. Unfortunately the mound is now a mass of impenetrable brambles and bushes and I have been unable to confirm its survival or otherwise.

To the east, back at the road, directly opposite 'The Cottage' is the entrance to Creech Bottom Lane. Next to the road sign, on the south side of the lane, lies a stone. It has been omitted from the latest OS sheet, after being marked on it previously. But it is still there, as Plate 38 testifies. It is 3ft long and of ironstone. It marks the same west-east boundary line as the Three Lord's Barrow.

The stone could also be an old track marker, possibly marking the route from Wareham, an old Saxon town, to Kimmeridge and Lulworth.

"The path has faded, and there is no means on the open downs of knowing whether the direction pursued is right or wrong, till a boulder which is a landmark is perceived."

Richard Jeffries 'Open Air' (19th C.)

DEAD WOMAN STONE

FORMER LOCATION: Evidence of a cross is reported at the Affpuddle/Turner's Puddle parish boundary, near the junction of two roads 0.5 mile north of Cloud's Hill. OS 1:50 000 sheet 195 and 1:25 000 'Purbeck and South Dorset' sheet. Grid reference: 822916.

his stone, recorded in 1839, stood near the bridlepath that skirts the MOD ranges, about 40yds from the road. It is mentioned again in 1911. Mr G. Smith of Parkstone informs the author that during WWII the Canadians moved the stone into the garden of one of the cottages at the crossroads in Briantspuddle, a mile to the north. The author spoke to several residents on a trip in April 1996, but to no avail. Any information would be appreciated as it could

Plate 38: Stone at Creech Bottom.

be that the stone survives, albeit in someone's rockery!

Tradition has it that the stone is associated with a woman hung at Gallows Hill, to the east. There are certainly other cases of stones and crosses being linked with burials. But as we have already seen (page 24) stones were often given personalities and named in bygone days, was the woman 'dead' because she was made of stone? The term 'dead man' crops up commonly in folklore of stones.

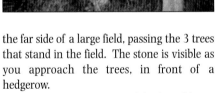

> "THE INTERPRETATION OF SINGLE MENHIRS (STANDING STONES) IS ONE OF THE ARCHAEOLOGIST'S NIGHTMARE."
>
> P.R. Giot, 1960.

THE HARPSTONE

LOCATION: 0.5 mile NE of Kimmeridge, named on OS maps. OS 1:50 000 sheet 195 and 1:25 000 'Purbeck and South Dorset' sheet. Grid reference: 922805.

This fine standing stone, a Scheduled Ancient Monument, is easily accessible via a public footpath (see Fig.54). Take the footpath, descend a slope and cross to the far side of a large field, passing the 3 trees that stand in the field. The stone is visible as you approach the trees, in front of a hedgerow.

This stone stands over 7ft high and has a maximum width of approximately 3ft. It is cut by long vertical grooves. In 'The Old Straight Track', Alfred Watkins noted many

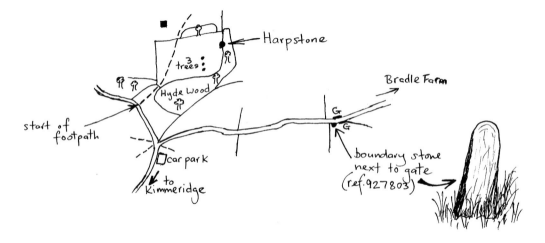

other standing stones in the area reveal themselves from surviving place names. The heathland around grid refeence: 895834, west of Creech, is still known as King's Standing. Many standing stones are bestowed with royal names. There is King Arthur's stones and circles in Cornwall, and elsewhere. Likewise, the stones of the Rollright Circle are known as the King's Men. There is a King Stone on Bredon Hill, Worcs. Land to the west of Kimmeridge is known as Stonehips. There is also Brimstone Bottom at West Chaldon.

The Harpstone stands in a river valley, orientated east-west near the river itself and not on exposed ground. Similar 'secluded valley' or 'slope-sites' can be found at the Rempstone Circle, Nine Stones, Devil's Armchair (at Corscombe) and the Helstone standing stone.

Tom Graves, and other dowsers of renown, has suggested a link between stones and water. Many see the underground flow of water as being an integral part of the transference of earth energies. Recent research (by Paul Devereux for instance) suggests a close link between stone circles and faults in the earth's crust. Coincidence?

Fig.55: Drawing (from an old photograph) of the Harpstone, showing the now-vacated top part of the stone.

"THESE BUILDERS OF STONE UNDERSTOOD STONE IN A WAY WE SIMPLY CANNOT CONCEIVE OF, THEY WERE THE GREAT MASONS, THE MASTER MASONS, IN FACT, OF THE WORLD'S MOST ANCIENT SCIENCE."

J. Foster Forbes, 'The Unchronicle Past' (1938)

ley markstones which displayed vertical grooving.

On a visit to the stone in October 1993, 4 days before full moon, the author felt a distinct warmth emanating from about halfway up the stone when his hands were placed on it. This was felt several times, being repeatedly experienced after taking the hands off and then trying again.

Was this band 5 of the stone? The day was chilly and the stone had not been warmed by the sun.

Fig.55 is a drawing of a photograph taken earlier this Century of the Harp Stone. Comparing it with the present view in Plate 39, it will be noticed that the top 4-5" have been lost. It is not known how this came about. Perhaps a search through the undergrowth during the winter months may reveal it.

The place named Herpston is mentioned hereabouts in 1340 and probably refers to the stone. There is a Hurpston on the present OS map, just to the east of the stone. Hints of

About 0.25 mile SE of the Harpstone is a fine boundary stone, close to a gate on the south side of the road to Bradle Farm. The stone is of local limestone and about 5ft tall. It is shaped with a rounded top (see Fig.54 for position and drawing). The age is uncertain, but again illustrates Man's utilisation of stone to mark out the land.

About 0.5 mile to the south, on the slopes

of Smedmore Hill, a 3ft high stone formerly stood at approximately grid reference: 924793. A recent search by the author proved negative, and it appears 'lost'. It did not lie on any known boundary.

ḣeeOless william's stone

LOCATION: 2 miles east of Dorchester, on the minor road linking Stinsford and Tincleton, south-east of Pine Lodge Farm. OS 1:50 000 sheet 195 and 1:25 000 'Purbeck and South Dorset' sheet. Grid reference: 732913.

Plate 40: Heedless William's Stone

his stone is still proudly upright next to the road, immediately west of Pond House. It stands on the north-south running boundary of Stinsford and Puddletown, yet is amazingly not shown as a boundary stone on the latest OS sheets despite being one of Dorset's finest examples of an ancient stone boundary marker. Older OS maps have even shown the stone as a cross, which it never was.

Its height above ground is about 5ft and has a circumference of about 4ft. It is shaped and has a matrix of coarse, reddish, quartz-rich sandstone. It is a cemented grit, having many smaller fragments incorporated in the general stone. The matrix is thought to be Tertiary in age.

It has been considered to be Roman in design, and indeed does bear a resemblance to the stone of Roman age at Stinsford, 1 mile west of here. The lane next to the stone is on the course of a Roman road which ran from Lake Farm, near Poole, to Dorchester. The stone may be in its original locality, the Romans either erecting a new stone or remod-elling an older one. The stone may therefore be the remnant of a much older 'straight track'.

C. Sinclear Williams (in Proc. DNH & AS Vol. 110, 1988) considers the stone to be pre-historic, similar in appearance to the statue menhirs of Brittany. The idea that many Roman roads were simply built on existing prehistoric STRAIGHT TRACKS is gaining acceptance. For instance, the tracks are extensive in Ireland, a land the Romans did not conquer.

A report of 1372 speaks of a rogation, or 'beating the bounds' ceremony taking place at the stone.

The name 'Heedless William' (or indeed 'Headless William' of some accounts) derived from an old piece of folklore whereby a coach-man, renowned for the reckless driving of his horses, left the old coach road one night and plunged into the adjacent pond in the field to the north of the stone. The pond bears his name to this day. Horses, passengers and William himself were all drowned.

Several other folk stories around Dorset deal with hauntings and phenomena associat-ed with stream and pools. Perhaps we are dealing with the survival, in much altered form, of a belief held by the Celts that wells and pools were entrances to the Otherworld.

Perhaps, long ago, the stone marked out a holy place to our distant forebears. NB: Of interest is that the stone lies EXACTLY on an energy line map-dowsed by local dowser Roger Sleet (Pers. comm.). He was unaware of the existence of the stone at the time of dowsing!

The area is rich in tumuli and two other stones are known just to the north (see Puddletown Forest Stones). Just over a mile to the south-west lies the once mighty henge at Mount Pleasant, and the stone is linked to the henge by a clearly defined ley which runs on to Langton Herring (see Fig.98).

The Rev. G. Moule reported in 1940 the possible remains of a cross base in the garden of a cottage at Higher Bockhampton.

JORÖAN HILL ROMAN TEMPLE

LOCATION: 2 miles NNE of Weymouth, above Furzy Cliff overlooking Bowleaze Cove. It is an Ancient Monument and is signposted from the A353. OS 1:50 000 sheet 195 and 1:25 000 'Purbeck and South Dorset' sheet. Grid reference: 698821. A public footpath passes the site gate.

This temple is typical of the Romano-British type of the 3-4th Century AD. Although noted as early as 1842, excavations on a scientific level did not take place until 1932. Coins found at the site date from AD 72 to AD 395, indicating a very long period of usage.

The ground plan can be made out, some 25ft square with 3-4ft thick walls, of which the footings are still to be seen. The most extraordinary discovery was a deep shaft, 14ft deep and up to 4ft across, at the south-east corner of the temple. Its sides were lined with clay and stone slabs. The layering of the shaft gives us clues to the rituals of the users of the temple. Alternating layers of clay with birds, coins, ashes, swords and other artefacts were found, some sequences being repeated for more than 16 layers. At the base of the pit was a cist, containing spearheads, a 21" sword, a knife and other remains.

A high degree of ritualistic activity is indicated. The birds found were crows, ravens, buzzards and starlings, all of which have well documented magical and mythological pagan associations.

The site was possibly still in use as a religious centre even after Christianity arrived. The superb view from this site (now unfortunately marred by obtrusive houses) also lent the site to be used as a lookout post. Many sunrises and sunsets of significance would

Fig.56: The Roman temple at Jordan Hill, looking NNW.

route of possible ley to maiden Castle marked by tumuli on Bincombe Hill

Chalbury Hillfort

have been visible from this site. Six tumuli stand out on the skyline almost due NNW, with 2 more at about 30 degrees. These may have played some part of the ritual activities of the site, perhaps well before the Romans arrived to build their temple. Once again, intervisibility of ancient sites seemed of vital importance to their builders. A ley is suggested linking the temple, several tumuli in the Bincombe Hill area and the eastern end of Maiden Castle.

KINGSTON BARROWS AND STONES

LOCATION: The village of Kingston lies at the top of the steep scarp that leads up to a limestone plateau that stretches from near Kimmeridge to Swanage. The nearest town is Corfe Castle, 1.5 miles to the north. Four sites are grouped together in this section for convenience of location, and individual locality details are given in turn below. OS 1:50 000 sheet 195 and 1:25 000 'Purbeck and South Dorset' sheet.

Fig.57: Sites at Swyre Head, near Kingston.

The first site of interest is a round barrow at grid reference: 966785. It sits prominently on the hill to the west of Swanworth Quarry, almost midway between Kingston and Worth Matravers. A good view can be had walking south towards it from Afflington Barn (grid reference: 968793) along the bridleway. The barrow stands out on the skyline, crowned by a tree.

The barrow is 6ft high even now, despite being damaged by ploughing. Old records speak of it being of the cairn variety, and on excavation part of a circle of upright stones was uncovered. Today, several large stones, up to 2.5ft long, litter the barrow, though it is not clear how many of these are from field clearance.

Officially, the barrow has been dated as 'Romano-British', much younger than the more common 'Bronze Age' barrows. Stone was much utilised in the Purbeck area, due to the local availability of thin-splitting limestones. As early as 1881, antiquarian J. Pleydell stated "Most of the interments in the Purbeck barrows are in cist-vaens, lined with slabs of stone, the abundance of the stone favouring this mode of sepulture".

We now move 1.5 miles to the west, to the vicinity of Swyre Head. Fig.57 shows the area of interest with 3 sites to be looked at. There is parking as shown. One then proceeds through the stone gate posts, turning right to follow the public footpath to Swyre Head.

After crossing an open field, a gate is encountered, at the point where the wood changes direction (grid reference: 941789), and a group of prone stones can be seen to the east of the gate, either side of the field fence.

The largest of the half dozen or so stones

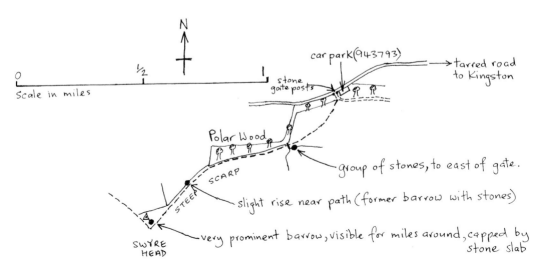

is approximately 3.5ft x 2.5ft in size. They are all of local limestone and some appear to have been shaped. It is not certain if they are prehistoric; no records exist about structures at or near this spot. The view from here is certainly a commanding one, with a view down into the Encombe Valley and on to St. Aldhelm's Head. A key may lie, perhaps, at the next site.

This is situated about 0.25 mile further west along the public footpath to Swyre Head. Old records speak of a possible bowl barrow 'at west end of Polar Wood' at grid reference: 936787. It had a height of only 1.5ft remaining but had 'many stones visible'. I believe the remains of this barrow are still visible today, as a low rise, just west of the path, and cut short by the stone walling that runs parallel with the path.

Could it be that the stones already mentioned were cleared from this barrow? Or were they placed there as a separate structure? There are certainly enough of them to have formed a small stone circle. Perhaps we may never know the answer for certain, as is so often the case. The lesson may simply be to open our minds to the POSSIBILITIES of such alternative ideas and speculations. Unconfirmed evidence does not mean it is valueless.

At Swyre Head itself, at the end of the ridge that takes the path past the above barrow, stands a very magnificent barrow, visible from miles around (grid reference: 934784). The height of the barrow is still about 8ft, despite erosion due to paths to its crown. Modern stone blocks provide seating at the top, but beneath can just be made out much older stones. Stone slabs protrude from the foot of the newer blocks and were recorded some time ago, their age being 'uncertain'.

The views from this barrow are amongst the finest the reader will encounter following this book. To the west, the Isle of Portland rises from the sea. To the east, the Isle of Wight looms on the skyline. Incredibly, the buildings of Bournemouth stand out despite the intervention of the Purbeck Hills.

Certainly, early Man would have utilised such an outstanding and inspiring locality as

the barrow testifies. Later on, the British or Romans may have used such a prominent vantage point as a look-out post. So it is not possible to date the stones of the barrow accurately. Some form of ritual observance may be speculated, however. At the time of the Equinoxes, the sun rises over the prominent back of the Isle of Wight and sets directly behind the Portland promontory.

Our distance ancestors held the sun in great reverence and marked out its rising and setting at thousands of sites all over the world.

"......they not only worshipped the light, but they knew how to draw the rays of the sun into their very being."

Olive Pixley, 'The Trail' (1934)

In 1960, a 14" high Roman Altar stone was found near the village of Kingston. It is now housed in Dorchester Museum. Also in the area is the 12th Century St. Aldhelm's Chapel (grid reference: 961755). It has a pyramidal roof supported by a central pillar. It is perched at the top of 350ft cliffs and the scenery is isolated and grand.

Lulworth Stone Circle

LOCATION: Uncertain. The area is covered by OS 1:50 000 sheet 194 and 1:25 000 'Purbeck and South Dorset' sheet.

Records by J.F. Pennie in 1827 and Charles Warne in 1872 speak of a stone circle near East Lulworth. Jeremy Harte (Folklorist and author of 'Cuckoo Pounds and Singing Barrows') informs the author (Pers. Comm. 30.4.94):

"......it was near Whiteway Farm in the general SY 87.82 area, and the stones were removed to form gateposts and a bridge over a rivulet, which they may still be doing today."

The stones were removed by a farmer called Bower prior to 1872. The area between East Lulworth and Povington Hill is peppered with tumuli and earthworks. Warne gave the locality as ".......between East Lulworth and Povington". The latter is still named on OS maps and small streams and bridges do occur in the vicinity of Whiteway.

This story is another sad one to relate. Another sacred site desecrated on the mere whim of an individual.

On an unpublished map sent to the author, Gordon Harris maps out a ley line running from Stonehenge down into the Purbecks via several sites (which include the Sturminster Marshall stones - see Fig.40). It crosses Povington Heath and passes Whiteway before crossing the road at grid reference: 870812 and ascending Rings Hill to Flowers Barrow.

The destroyed circle may have lay on or near this ley. Perhaps dowsing and fieldwork may reveal more. Much of the land is MOD and care should be taken to observe warning notices.

It may be relevant that just 150yds west of where the ley crosses the road, Jeremy Harte records a tale of a large black spectral dog.

Lulworth Stones

LOCATION: See Fig.58. Stones A,B and C are grid reference: c.829815; stone D is at the edge of field, grid reference: 824800.

Local residents, Sheila Cutts and Diane Coade, reported these sarsen stones to the author. They may or may not be in their original positions due to possible field clearance by farmers, but they need to 'go on record'.

Stone A lies at the foot of the footpath marker stone at the intersection of the paths. Some 3ft of flinty stone is visible.

Stone B lies to the south next to the path. It has two holes in its side, one which is very deep. The stone is 6.5ft long and tapered at one end (see Plate 1).

Stone C is further south on the same path, next to a hawthorn clump. It is quite overgrown but is again flinty with a tapering end.

What is interesting is that if we look due 120 degrees from these stones, we get a visual alignment of Arish Mell, Worbarrow Tout and the Chapel on top of St. Alban's Head. This is the line of the Samhain/Imbolc sunrise!

Fig.58: Stones at West Lulworth. The sketch of stone B shows the holes in its side.

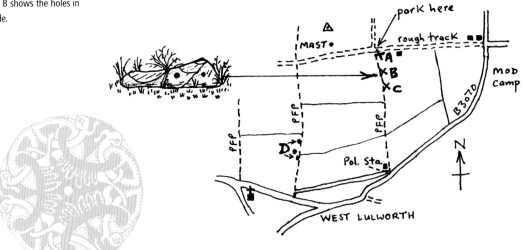

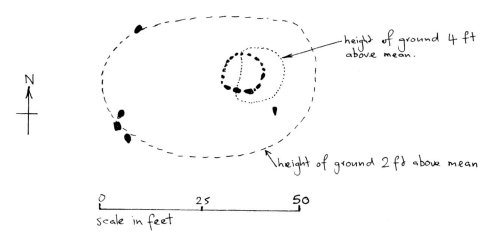

height of ground 4 ft above mean.

height of ground 2 ft above mean

0   25   50
scale in feet

Site D is north of the church in a field flanked by public paths. Near the footpath on the east side of the first field (going up the hill) are two large smooth sarsens. Over the fencing nearby can be seen a depression and more stones lie within it. Further north along the path, another stone will be encountered.

It is not known if these stones are associated with ancient Man. More fieldwork remains to be done.

POXWELL CAIRN AND SARSENS

LOCATION: Poxwell is situated on the A353 road, NE of Weymouth, and some 5 miles SE of Dorchester. The cairn is marked and named on OS maps as 'Cairn Circle'. OS 1:50 000 sheet 194 and 1:25 000 'Purbeck and South Dorset' sheet. Grid reference: 744836.

The folklore associated with this site has already been discussed on page 20, with all the erroneous Druidic links envisaged. The circle of stones was still called the 'Pokeswell Druid's Temple' by the eminent Alfred Pope as late as 1906. As we shall see yet again, all is not as it seems!

Fig.59 gives the plan of the cairn. Taking the bridlepath that skirts an old quarry, one goes east for about 300yds, at which point the east-west ridge is ascended. Arriving at the top, the cairn stones will be seen. The stones are isolated and the place feels strange.

Fig.59: Site plan of Poxwell Cairn.

Fig.60: Charles Warne's 1872 view of Poxwell Cairn, showing the barrow mound and some of the outlying stones.

"CRAGS, KNOLLS AND MOUNTS, CONFESEDLY HURDLED, THE FRAGMENTS OF AN EARLIE WORLD, AND MOUNTAINS THAT LIKE GIANTS STAND TO SENTINEL ENCHANTED LAND."

W.H. Hamilton Rogers (1888)

The circle of stones is in fact the inner stone lining of a round barrow, most of which has been destroyed. Over 20 stones form a circle 14ft in diameter. Most of the stones are less than 2ft long and were once seen to have the spaces between them packed with limestone rubble. All the stones now lie in a prone position, but a glance at Warne's 1872 drawing (Fig.60) shows that at least two of them were once 'standing'.

The drawing also shows a clearly defined mound with the remains of a ditch, as well as outlying stones to either side. These stones, or ones that appear to be them, can still be seen today. The three stones to the west are easily seen from the circle and are probably associated with the original mound. As the site plan in

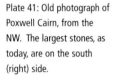

Plate 41: Old photograph of Poxwell Cairn, from the NW. The largest stones, as today, are on the south (right) side.

Fig.59 shows, the obvious rise in ground level in the immediate area of the circle of stones is surrounded by a subtler rise. This is about 2ft above the general hilltop contour, approximately 63ft from E-W and 44ft across from N-S.

Warne, in 1872, describes 'avenues' of stones running from the cairn both easterly and in a westerly direction. And indeed, a trip by local archaeologists in 1900 (Proc. DNH & AS, Vol. XXI) speaks of 4 large stones, up to 4ft in HEIGHT, (although probably meaning 'LENGTH') lying around 'in confusion', some 200yds NE and E of the cairn circle. Today, odd stones can be found on the grassy hillside, but no pattern or structure can be discerned.

So it could be that any one of three situations occurs at Poxwell. Firstly, the stones outside the main circle could be natural sarsens. Secondly, they may have been removed from the cairn at some point in its long history (the cairn has been dated at around 1500 BC using cremation remains found at the site).

Or thirdly, the 'avenues' spoken of by Warne did exist. Confirmed cases of rows of stones leading to barrows in Dorset is nil. But certainly many cases occur elsewhere in Britain, most notably on Dartmoor. Some rows there run for miles, passing near to, or ending at barrows.

The stones of the cairn are low and practically disappear during the spring/autumn grass growing season, so a winter visit is recommended. Plate 41 is a photograph taken on a field trip earlier this Century. The rubble infilling between the stones is visible.

PRESTON CROSS

LOCATION: The cross lies within St. Andrew's Church, Preston, on the A353 road NE out of Weymouth. OS 1:50 000 sheet 194 and 1:25 000 'Purbeck and South Dorset' sheet. Grid reference: 706829.

This old stone cross lies on the window ledge of the south-west window, near the organ. It is about 18" high and has a circular top with a cross inscribed in its centre.

A plaque near it suggests that it came from an 'ancient burial ground' but no other details are forthcoming regarding a locality.

The cross is thought to be c.1100.

Also in the area is the mysteriously named 'Boiling Rock' (shown on 1:25 000 maps) at grid reference: 694835, along Combe Valley Road. I have been unable to ascertain the origin of the naming of this natural rock, but could it be another ancient folklore memory of phenomena/earth energies at the locality? The prominent Chalbury 'hillfort' with associated tumuli is immediately to the north.

At nearby Osmington, a 3ft flinty stone lies at the village crossroads, north of the church. Any ancient connections are unproven, but the stone needs to go 'on file' as it were.

"The most wonderful thing we can experience is the mysterious."

Albert Einstein.

PUDDLETOWN FOREST STONE AND CROSS

LOCATION: A boundary stone, on bridlepath linking Pine Lodge Farm and Hardy's Birthplace, on the western extremity of Puddletown Forest, 2.5 miles SE of Dorchester. OS 1:50 000 sheet 194 and 1:25 000 'Purbeck and South Dorset' sheet (shown as BS on the latter). Grid reference: 731922.

A report in 1957 mentions a small sarsen stone near the path, half covered by the roots of a holly tree. But a trip to the area in 1993 was to no avail. The author was unable to locate the stone and would welcome any information regards its present whereabouts.

Records exist of another stone, to the east of the sarsen, still within Puddletown Forest. Alfred Pope records, in 1906, a stone cross "in the vicinity of three barrows (Rainbarrows) where the trackway north intersects the Roman road". He is probably referring to the area around grid reference: 734923, where these conditions all meet, to the north of the four 'Rainbarrows' he mentions.

He describes a stone 1.5ft high x 1ft wide, with sculptured figures. He further states that the stone was formerly 4.5ft high as late as the second half of the 19th Century. He regarded it as a wayside cross.

As with the other stone, fieldwork has failed to yet locate it. Forestation of the area makes location of both stones much more difficult than if they were on open ground, as they once were.

It is interesting that both stones appear to lie on or near to the Roman road. We could have two more examples here of old ley stones being used/altered to suit both Romans and Christians alike.

Nearby, St. Mary's in Puddletown houses a beaker-shaped Saxon font of pre-Conquest age.

REMPSTONE

LOCATION: Rempstone Stone Circle is situated in a wood, beside the B3351, Studland to Corfe Castle road. Access is easy into the woods at several points over broken wire fencing. The public is allowed full access to the wooded area, but the surrounding arable fields should not be violated. All the stones mentioned under this heading can be seen via public footpaths or roads. OS 1:50 000 sheet 195 and 1:25 000 'Purbeck and South Dorset' sheet.
Grid reference: 995821.

Fig.61: An old sketch of Rempstone Circle.

The stone circle at Rempstone is nestled within a very atmospheric wood and even the close proximity of the road does little to detract from the ancient 'feel' of the place.

This Bronze Age circle had an original diameter of around 85ft. The stones are of local Bagshot Beds, a deposit of irony, gritty sandstone.

Incredibly, this Scheduled Ancient Monument was not recorded until 1900. It was not until 1908 that it was surveyed and Fig.61 is a sketch of the site made at the time.

The sketch shows 9 stones remaining on the north side of the circle, the stones on the south side having been removed. A map shown in the Inventory of the Commission of Historical Monuments of Dorset (1959) shows 12 stones. Trips by the author in 1993 and 1994 produced the results shown in Fig.62. This can be compared with the 1908 sketch. I have given the stones the corresponding letters to Fig.61 and it will be noticed that stone J of my survey is not on the older sketch. Stones K and L were small and not earthfast. However, they could be the ones marked on the 1959 map that were lying in the places marked by 'X's' in Fig.62. None were found in these positions by the author, so we may have here a recent attempt to 'bridge' the vacated part of the circle.

Dowsing by the author, in May 1994, gave results indicating that a further stone may have stood midway between E and D. At the very least, energy was strongly experienced at that point. The reader is also referred back to Page 25 for more reported phenomena.

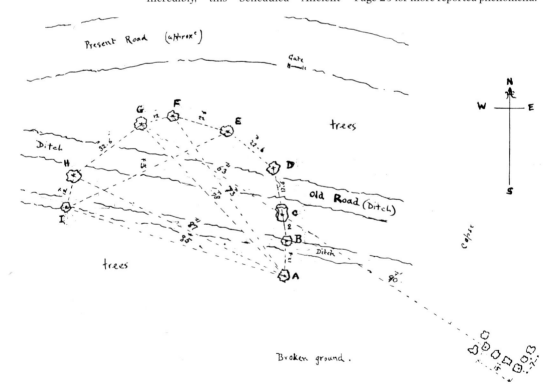

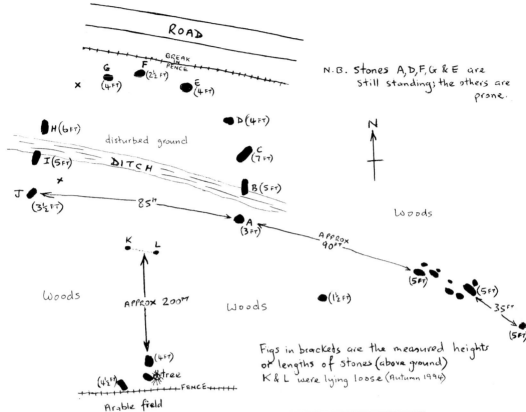

ROAD

BREAK IN FENCE

G (4 FT)   F (2½ FT)

x   E (4 FT)

D (4 FT)

H (6 FT)   disturbed ground

I (5 FT)   DITCH

C (7 FT)

J (3½ FT)   85"   B (5 FT)

A (3 FT)   APPROX 90 FT

K   L   Woods

(5 FT)

Woods   APPROX 200M   Woods   (1½ FT)   (5 FT)   35"

(4 FT)   (5 FT)

(4½ FT)   tree

FENCE

Arable field

N.B. Stones A, D, F, G & E are still standing; the others are prone.

N

Woods

Figs in brackets are the measured heights or lengths of stones (above ground). K & L were lying loose (Autumn 1994)

Fig.62: Sketch map of Rempstone Circle (1994)

Few photographs are recorded from the circle, due I suspect to the poor lighting of the woods in which the stones stand. Plates 42-44 will hopefully redress the situation somewhat. Late autumn to early spring is the best time to view and photograph the stones as the smaller ones can be obscured by vegetation during summer months.

Both sketches show outlying stones to the east of the circle, whilst still more are found to the south at the very extremity of the woods. It is uncertain as to whether these outlying stones were taken from the circle or formed avenues leading from/to the circle. We need at this point to expand our attention out to the landscape around the circle. Some discoveries have been made that may show that Rempstone was once much more than a solitary stone circle. Fig.63 shows the area around the circle, with the sites mentioned in the text.

We will look at the sites of interest from east to west (right to left in Fig.63). We first find an outlying stone at grid reference: 003817, on the south side of the road from

Plate 42: Stone E at Rempstone.

Plate 43: (left) Looking from stone E, towards stones C and D. The area to the left of the stone in the foreground (E) gave energy emissions during dowsing, possibly indicating the position of a former stone (see text).

Plate 44: (right) Stone D at Rempstone.

Fig.63: The overview of the Rempstone area.

Studland to Rempstone. It appears to have been exposed or moved due to adjacent drainage work. The block of gritty sandstone is 4.5ft long and 3ft wide. It is not earthfast.

The next stone is at grid reference: 996819. It lies some 8yds east of the bri-

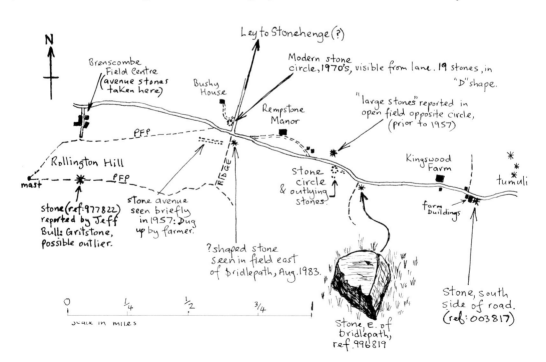

Ley to Stonehenge (?)

Modern stone circle, 1970's, visible from lane. 19 stones, in "D" shape.

Brenscombe Field Centre (avenue stones taken here)

Bushy House

Rempstone Manor

"large stones" reported in open field opposite circle, (prior to 1957)

PFP

Rollington Hill

PFP

mast

Kingswood Farm

tumuli

Stone circle & outlying stones

stone (ref:977822) reported by Jeff Bull: Gritstone, possible outlier.

stone avenue seen briefly in 1957: Dug up by farmer.

farm buildings

? shaped stone seen in field east of bridlepath, Aug.1983.

Stone, south side of road. (ref: 003817)

0   ¼   ½   ¾

scale in miles

Stone, E. of bridlepath, ref.996819

dlepath going up to the top of Nine Barrow Down. The stone was described by Ian Hewitt, of the East Dorset Archaeological Society, in August 1993 and a trip to the site by the author in February 1993 confirmed its survival. Two sides of the stone are clearly shaped and the one end is tapered and very smooth.

From this stone, Rempstone Circle would clearly have been visible before the woods grew, and vice versa. Looking due east from the stone, a prominent hill with a crowning obelisk can be seen. A tumulus sits on the skyline as viewed from the circle and stone. Notwithstanding the height of the hill, its top marks the sunrise at the Spring and Autumn Equinoxes. In fact a line drawn from the circle to the tumulus/obelisk passes directly through the eastern-most stone, described earlier. More subtle placing of ancient sites on the landscape.

To the north of the circle, across the other side of the road, large stones were seen in a field, prior to 1957. I have been unable to find any on two searches of the fields and the woods opposite the stone circle. A large field stretches west from the woods in which the circle rests, and at the far end of it is where our next stone was seen. In 1983, Ian Hewitt saw a 'possibly shaped' stone lying close to the bridlepath, in the field, at grid reference: 987823. Gordon Harris has plotted a ley (unpublished) running from Winspit right up to Stonehenge. The ley passes within feet of the stone Hewitt saw!

In August 1957, Mr J.B. Calkin described two parallel rows of small stones crossing a field, from west to east, at grid reference: 986823 (approx.). He recalls (in DNH & AS Proc. Vol. 81) of how the local farmer, Eric Best, dug up the stones whilst field clearing. At least 26 stones were seen and they formed a 'double avenue at the east end'. The direction of the row gave a heading that pointed 12 degrees N of the circle (perhaps to the stones reported to be north of the circle?, above). Fig.64 is a sketch by the author taken from Calkin's photograph.

Calkin states that most of the stones were 2.5ft high when stood up, but that some were larger. In the sketch the stone in the distance must have been over 3.5ft in height.

Study of old tithe maps shows no walls crossing the field, nor any old buildings. Ian Hewitt surmises that the stone he found just to the east of the row (Fig.63) could have been an extension of the row nearer to the stone circle.

Standing in the field where the row stood, one cannot see the circle due to an intervening ridge, and an extension of the row eastwards would enable one to see it. In fact, standing on the crest of the ridge, on the bridlepath, one can look eastwards down the slopes to the stone circle and see that the Equinox sunrise point discussed previously aligns with it on the skyline.

I think that some sort of processional avenue, such as at Avebury, may have been present here at Rempstone, perhaps even more than one. One can envisage, perhaps,

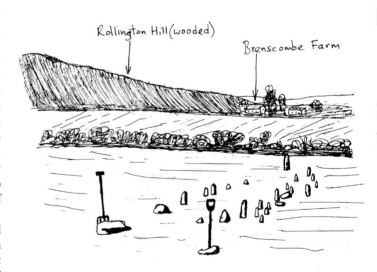

priests/wisemen proceeding along the avenue towards the circle, with the growing glow of the Equinox dawn sky in the distance.

Dowsing of surviving stone avenues, such as on Dartmoor, has shown that the avenues mark geodetic energy lines, each stone having a small energy loop.

The stones forming the avenue were removed almost immediately by the farmer and Calkin describes seeing them piled up in a heap 'behind Brenscombe Farm'. A conversation with the then farmer, Eric Best in May 1994, yielded the sad news that the stones

Fig.64: The stone avenue west of Rempstone Circle (Aug. 1957). Drawn from a photograph by J.B. Calkin.

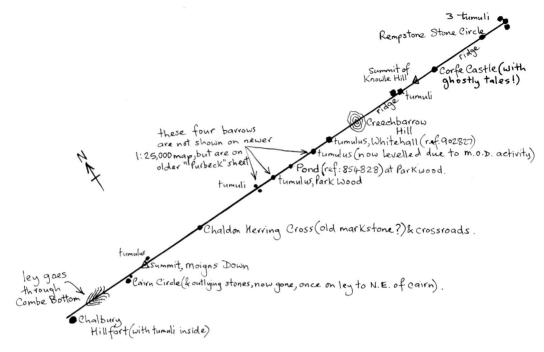

3 tumuli

Rempstone Stone Circle

ridge

Summit of
Knowle Hill

Corfe Castle (with
ghostly tales!)

ridge tumuli

Creechbarrow
Hill

tumulus, Whitehall (ref. 902827)

tumulus (now levelled due to m.o.D. activity)

these four barrows
are not shown on newer
1:25,000 map, but are on
older "Purbeck" sheet

Pond (ref: 854828) at Parkwood.

tumuli

tumulus, Park Wood

N

Chaldon Herring Cross (old markstone?) & crossroads.

tumulus

Summit, Moigns Down

ley goes
through
Combe Bottom

Cairn Circle (& outlying stones, now gone, once on ley to N.E. of cairn).

Chalbury
Hillfort (with tumuli inside)

Fig.65: The ley from
Rempstone to Chalbury.
(Sites may not be in exact
positions due to limitations
of scale.)

had been used for walls, etc. around the farm. A sad end indeed to a prehistoric stone row. How many more stones will be lost before Man realises that the symbology, the energies and the very structures themselves, are all part of our very nature and, ultimately, part of the Earth's healing.

───────── ◌ ─────────

"YOU ASK ME TO DIG FOR STONE? SHALL I DIG UNDER HER SKIN FOR HER BONES?"

Sioux Indian, 1890

───────── ◌ ─────────

Fig.63 also shows the position of a modern stone circle, erected in the 1970's by Major Rider of Rempstone Hall. Nineteen stones form a 'D' with fine views of Equinox and Summer Solstice sunrises. One stone is shaped like a chair.

Paul Devereux and Ian Thomson in 1979 described a long ley running from the tumuli east of Rempstone (the group of 3 in Fig.63) some 10 miles west to West Lulworth. I believe, however, that the line can now be extended to the Chaldon Herring Cross (see page 79) and

even further to the Poxwell Cairn area (page 89). Fig.65 plots the ley across the landscape. The ley contains some interesting points worthy of further comment. Firstly, it follows the course of the ridge of the Purbeck Hills. Does this mean, to apply Alfred Watkins' interpretation, that it marks out an ancient path? Or, to lean towards more modern thought, does the ley follow faulting (and earth energies?) that run the length of the Purbeck Hills? Perhaps BOTH points are relevant.

The ley passes close to or through tumuli not on the latest 1:25 000 OS sheet. This highlights one of the problems of ley hunting, inasmuch that more modern printings of maps do not contain what WE HAVE LOST from the landscape.

The pond near Parkwood is perhaps relevant. Watkins and others have found quite frequently that ponds, small lakes, springs and wells can be seen to be ley markers. It was suggested by Watkins that these watery markers would reflect the light of the sun and sky, giving a 'ley walker' a distantly visible pointer.

Many, if not most, leys are difficult to follow on foot for anything other than short distances. This particular one does enable one to follow the ley for several hundred metres at several places. Twelve of the ley markers can actually be reached on foot, to enable the reader first hand to visually trace the 'ley on the land'. But do they record a track? Or a shaman's symbology? Or something else? To quote one interpretation:

"thus it looks as if the supposed 'trackways' may compare with our pylon lines for carrying energy across the country from the spiritual generating plants'.

George Trevelyan

STUDLAND CROSS AND STONE ROW

LOCATION: The village of Studland lies at the very eastern end of the Purbeck Hills, nestling under the protection of Ballard Down.
(A) The cross is situated just south of the Norman Church in the village. Grid reference: 037824.
B) The stone row crosses the Ferry Road about 2 miles north of Studland. Grid reference: 026853.
OS 1:50 000 sheet 195 and 1:25 000 'Purbeck and South Dorset' sheet.

At the crossroads, just south of the church, stands the village cross. The shaft and head date from 1976, but the base has been dated as 'Saxon' in age. It is mentioned in a text in 1882, and before the modern shaft was erected a mortise was visible which once took the old shaft. The base is round, unusual for Dorset's stone crosses, and is of red, irony heathstone. It is approximately 4ft in diameter and over 20" deep.

Stocks once stood next to the cross and this spot would at one time have been the focal point of much of the village gatherings.

Plate 45 shows the old stone base, with part of the delicately carved modern shaft above.

An article in 'Antiquity' (Vol. XXXVII, 1963) alerted the author to the possible survival of a stone row north of Studland village. It described 6 small standing stones on the heath either side of the ferry road. They were reported alongside the discovery in the same area of over 70 earthwork circles and mounds. Fig.66 shows the area in question and the results obtained in 1993 and 1994.

A trip to the site by the author in November 1993 resulted in 3 stones, all earthfast and standing, being found. They were intervisible and clearly aligned in a well defined order. The tallest is only 2ft high but I was interested by the fact that they seemed to be of different material. Stone 1 is a Jurassic limestone. Stone 2 is a block of irony-heathstone. Whilst stone 6 is sandstone.

In conversation with Paul Craddock of the Wessex Dowsers in October 1993, it appears

Plate 45: The cross at Studland village.

that he had already dowsed stone 2, which is easily seen from the road, and found it to be on at least one energy ley. It later transpired that in early 1994 he located stone 5 (by means of dowsing) which had not been found by the author; Plates 46-48 show three of the Studland stones.

The purpose and age of the stone row is still a mystery, and has only been tentatively dated (presuming contemporarity with the earth mounds) as between the Iron Age and 1700. But perhaps we can apply once again an approach of looking at stones as an integral part of the landscape and not just 'plonked on it'. Fig.67 shows the alignments associated with the Studland stones and one

can once again see how seemingly insignificant small stones fit into something much larger when the whole GEOMANTIC picture is perceived. The main axis of the row can be extended to the Fishing Barrow, 2 miles to the south (grid reference: 018822).

A line drawn through the two northernmost stones (1 & 2) extends in one direction to the King Barrow (grid reference: 046820) on the slopes of Ballard Down. In the other direction, a line-of-sight effect is achieved. One can stand at stone 2 and look in the direction of stone 1 (which in reality can only be seen now when closer to it due to the vegetation) and directly behind can be seen the westernmost tip of Brownsea Island. In the distance Round

Fig.66: The stone row at Studland.

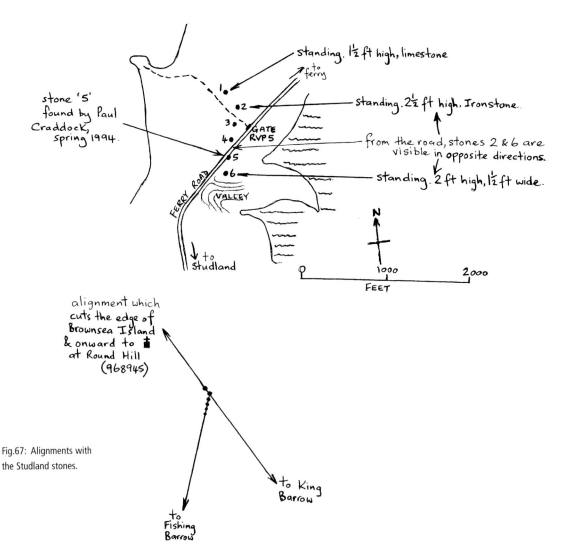

Fig.67: Alignments with the Studland stones.

Plate 46: (left) Stone 2 at Studland.

Plate 48: (right) Stone 1 at Studland, resembling, in miniature, some of the Avebury sarsens!

Hill and Beacon Hill stand on the skyline, crowned by a church.

TYNEHAM CROSSES AND STONES

LOCATION: The deserted village of Tyneham lies on MOD land, between Kimmeridge and Lulworth. Access is usually possible at weekends and longer periods during the summer: telephone 01929 462721, ext. 4819 for opening times. OS 1:50 000 sheets 194 and 195. 1:25 000 'Purbeck and South Dorset' sheet. Grid reference (of church): 882803.

n the vestry of Tyneham Church is a stone cross, about 2ft in height. It dates from the 15th Century and could be either a memorial or wayside cross. Other stone cross fragments lie loose in the church.

Earthworks occur in the fields to the SE of the church. Stone blocks have been found in them and they are probably Medieval mere stones.

In 1906, Alfred Pope described (in his 'Old Stone Crosses of Dorset') a stone 'of some antiquity' to the NE of Tyneham. The position was said to be "......in an angle formed by the

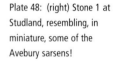

Plate 47: Stone 6 at Studland.

meeting of the roads from Tyneham, Corfe and Wareham". This could be the junctions at either grid references: 894815 or 902817. The author favours the latter locality from Pope's description. A visit by the author to the spot in June 1994 failed to reveal anything. Pope measured the stone, which he regarded as the base stone of a cross, as 2.5ft square and 9" deep. A winter or early spring visit, when the grass is short, may yet reveal its survival.

The stone cross may have 'evolved' from an older stone marking out the prehistoric path along the ridge. The views from the locality make it well worth a visit. Any cross or stone at the site would have been visible for some distance. A ley plotted by Gordon Harris (unpub.) passes within yards of the locality on its way from Tyneham to Stonehenge.

Fig.68: Inscribed stones in Lady St. Mary, Wareham. Drawings by the author, from his own photographs.

WAREHAM STONES AND CROSSES

LOCATION: Several stone relics can be found within the Church of Lady St. Mary, Wareham. Church opening times: summer 10-5pm; winter 10-3pm. OS 1:50 000 sheet 195 and 1:25 000 'Purbeck and South Dorset' sheet. Grid reference: 925872.

Several interesting and unique stones form part of a permanent display next to the organ and pulpit.

First and foremost are 5 inscribed stones. As well as the use of Latin characters, Runic figures are also inscribed on the blocks. Runes were the old north European alphabet, used extensively in Saxon and Viking lands before

A. 7th century. In vestry.

B. late 7th Century. On floor display

C. 7-8th Century. Mounted on wall by pulpit steps

D. late 8th Century. On floor display.

E. 8-9th Century. Mounted on wall above display.

Plate 49: 7-10th Century stones in Lady St. Mary, Wareham.

Plate 50: Inscribed stones B and D, Lady St. Mary, Wareham.

the oncome of the Christian-Latin official text.

But the runes were, and still are, more than an alphabet. Each rune represents a magical and symbolic potency and can be used for divination and ritual purposes. Many large standing stones in Scandinavia are still covered in runic characters.

On the Wareham stones we see a mixture of Latin, Old English and Runic characters, suggesting not only a fusion of languages but also the coming together of the old and the new spiritual ideals. In Romano-Saxon times, pagans and Christians seem to have found common ground. This state of affairs seems

to have existed for a long period and was only ended when Papal/political doctrines crept insidiously into religious life.

Fig.68 shows the 5 inscribed stones. Four are on display, whilst block 'A' is housed in the vestry and permission is needed to see it.

The stones were all found in 1840 during the demolition of the old nave. Four fragments of 10th Century cross shafts are also in the display in addition to a Saxon font found in the churchyard. An iron age saddle quern is also displayed (see Plates 49 and 50).

The church site is obviously a site of great and ancient sacred significance, probably predating Christianity. It may be recalled that the church lies on a ley line running from Holt Wood to Tyneham (Fig.33), a sure sign to me of an original prehistoric site.

On the north side of the town, the Church of St. Martins is also pre-conquest and has some interesting historical features such as the Saxon nave.

Gordon Harris (on an unpublished map to the author) plots a ley that runs from Tyneham up to Stonehenge. It passes through Wareham on the north side of the River Piddle.

To the east of Wareham stands the village of Arne. The Church of St. Nicholas (grid reference: 972881) is worth a visit. The altar stone has been dated as 'Medieval'. The slab has on it 5 inscribed crosses. It was found outside the church.

"WHEN THOU DOST BUILD ME A TEMPLE OF STANDING STONES, THOU SHALT NOT LAY THY TOOL UPON IT NOR ANY IMPLEMENT OR IRON ACCORDING TO THE LAW."

Old Testament.

WOOL CROSS

LOCATION: In the churchyard of parish Church of Holy Rood, Wool. OS 1:50 000 sheet 194 and 1:25 000 'Purbeck and South Dorset' sheet. Grid reference: 847865.

This Medieval cross lies just west of the tower of the church. The socket stone is 2ft square, resting on a low base stone. The empty socket hole, which would have housed a stone or wooden shaft, is only 8.25" across, smaller than most Dorset examples.

Plate 51 shows the cross, with the church behind.

Two leys end at Wool (see Fig.71) and the cross may be the remnant of an older stone, as we have seen elsewhere. Jeremy Harte (in 'The Ley Hunter', No. 121, summer 1994) lists two ghostly apparitions in Wool. Modern research very much links supernatural sightings with earth energies and ley lines. We have already seen this connection at Stinsford (page 26).

Nearby Quarr Hill is crowned by two tumuli and the crossroads to the south-west is called 'Woodman's Cross'. Earthworks lie immediately to the east of the church and further east stands Bindon Abbey, another sacred site.

Plate 51: The Wool Cross.

Chapter Seven

Τhe RIDGEWAY AREA

In terms of square-mileage, this is easily the smallest of the five regions I have incorporated into this guide. However, it is probably the richest in respect of the number and quality of sites, with many amassed in a relatively small area.

The area is defined by lines drawn roughly between Bridport, Dorchester and Weymouth. The enclosed region is roughly triangular in shape and one of the most beautiful and, in terms of our study, one of the most instructive areas regarding earth mysteries.

Fig.69 shows the region and the locality of the sites mentioned in the text.

The region is dominated and overlooked by the Ridgeway, with the famous path running along its crest. The path is followed almost continuously by ancient sites, particularly tumuli. Many were utilised as markers on the skyline, as viewed from other sites. This ancient prehistoric way and its sites can be summed up thus:

"GREAT STONES ON THE
UPLANDS AND GREEN WAYS
WINDING ACROSS CHALK
BEAR WITNESS TO THE WORKS
OF AN ANCIENT PEOPLE
LONG SINCE FALLEN ON
SLEEP."

Dione Fortune

ABBOTSBURY AREA

LOCATION: The Abbotsbury area has several sites of interest in and around this picturesque village. Fig.70 shows the whereabouts of the sites we will visit. The text has grid references for each one. OS 1:50 000 sheet 194 and 1:25 000 'Purbeck and South Dorset' sheet.

Plate 52: The churchyard cross at Abbotsbury.

The first object of interest is outside the parish Church of St. Nicholas. Next to the wall of the south aisle are the remains of the Medieval stone cross. Its square to octagonal base is about 3ft across with a central socket. The stone at present occupying the socket is probably not the original shaft remnant, as it is loose and ill-shaped. Plate 52 shows the cross remains.

Nearby, next to the path, lie several fragments of medieval moulded stones. Some show weathered carvings on. All, however, are in a poor state and are slowly being overgrown.

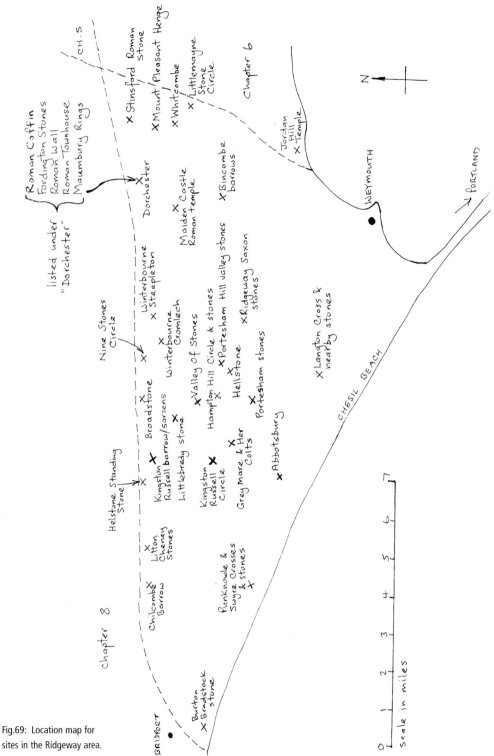

Fig.69: Location map for sites in the Ridgeway area.

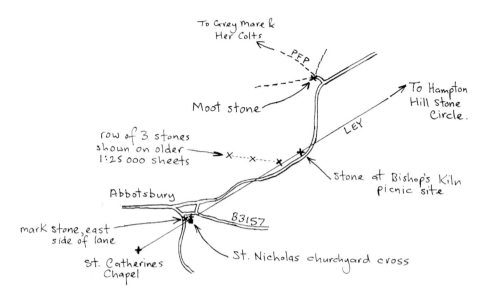

To Grey mare & Her Colts

- PFP

Moot stone

To Hampton Hill Stone Circle.

LEY

row of 3 stones shown on older 1:25 000 sheets

X----X----+

Stone at Bishop's Kiln picnic site

Abbotsbury

B3157

mark stone, east side of lane

St. Nicholas churchyard cross

St. Catherines Chapel

We shall return to the church later as it has been found to be associated with a ley line

To the south of the church can be seen the scattered remains of the Abbey and the manor house, both destroyed after the Reformation. The fine Abbey House, nearby, houses four 12th Century carved stones, depicting a zodiacal crab, a seated figure, flowers and a man's head. A 12th Century door head can also be seen.

Lying next to the north-south lane that goes down to the Abbey Barn is a markstone. It can be found due west from the church tower, on the east side of the lane. Plate 53 shows the stone. It is earthfast, composed of limestone and around 4ft in length. The stone is close to a ley crossing the lane a little to the south.

The next site of interest is at the Bishop's Kiln, about 0.75 mile NE of the village centre, besides the steep road that goes on to the Hardy Monument. A stone lies on the north side of the car park (grid reference: 588858, marked as 'picnic site' on new 1:25 000 sheet).

The stone is a squarish block of Portland limestone, around 4-5ft wide. It actually lies on a north-south parish boundary line, separating Abbotsbury and Portesham (see Plate 54).

At first it looks like the common practice of using stones as parish boundary markers took place here. But perhaps the stone was

used for a much different and much more ancient use. A glance now at Fig.70 may reveal some interesting insights.

Fig.70: Location map for the Abbotsbury area.

It shows the course of a ley line which crosses the area from bottom left to top right. The ley starts on top of Chapel Hill, crowned magnificently by St. Catherine's Chapel. From here it crosses the fields downhill to the lane west of the church. The ley crosses the lane betwixt a gate with a cattle grid and the arched stone gate of the Abbey grounds. Dowsing by the author detected a band of

Plate 53: Stone by side of lane west of church, Abbotsbury.

Plate 54: Stone at Bishop's Limekiln car park, north of Abbotsbury.

the gate. This may have further implications. I believe the stone formerly marked out the passage of the Ridgeway track, lying as it does between the Hampton Stone Circle and the Grey Mare and Her Colts. Further evidence submitted on page 116 (Fig.76) seems to suggest perhaps a processional route leading to the Kingston Russell Stone Circle.

Once again we see the importance of the survival of these seemingly insignificant stones that exist in our landscape. Still further, the stone near Gorwell Farm may be a possible ley marker too (see Fig.82).

> "NO ONE CAN INVESTIGATE LEYS IN THE FIELD FOR LONG WITHOUT BEING CONVINCED THAT THE WAY WAS PLANTED AT INTERVALS WITH STONES ......"
>
> *Alfred Watkins, 'The Old Straight Track'* *(1925)*

energy some 15ft wide crossing the road at an angle, heading towards the church.

The ley cuts through the church at the altar end (a phenomena commonly found elsewhere). The altar is the centre and focus of energy in holy places and leys and underground water courses seem attracted to these foci.

The ley then proceeds uphill to the stone at Bishop's Limekiln (Plate 54). From there it travels NE, to pass very close to the Stone Circle at Hampton Hill (see Figs.70 & 79) before ending (for now anyway!) at Black Down, site of Hardy's Monument, a high point formerly crowded with tumuli.

Last on our Abbotsbury itinerary is a stone 0.5 mile N of the Bishop's Kiln stone. Turn off onto a track signposted 'Gorwell Farm'. The track quickly forks at the gate to the farm, and the stone lies half-hidden to the left of the gate. It measures approximately 5ft x 4ft, one end being tapered. During the summer half of the year the stone is practically lost in the hedgerow.

Sandra Harding, former Head Teacher of Portesham School, informed the author in 1993 that she regarded the stone as a moot stone, and indeed it does lie on the parish boundary. A drawing supplied by her shows the stone STANDING on the OTHER side of

BINCOMBE BARROWS AND LEYS

LOCATION: Midway between Weymouth and Dorchester, either side of the A354, lies a high area richly endowed with barrows, many of which have stones and leys associated with them. OS 1:50 000 sheet 194 and 1:25 000 'Purbeck and South Dorset' sheet. Grid references are given individually below for each site of interest.

Fig.71 shows the area in question and immediately it can be seen as a region thickly blessed with barrows and several leys.

Barrow 'A' (Figs.71 & 72) is at grid reference: 673858. It can be reached by parking at the area of cleared ground to the west of Down Farm, on the south side of the road just before the bend in the road. The barrow lies

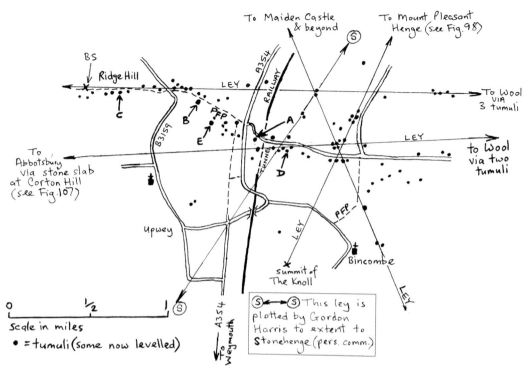

To Maiden Castle & beyond

To Mount Pleasant Henge (see Fig.98)

BS
Ridge Hill

A3354
RAILWAY

LEY

C
B
PFP
E
A

B3159

To Abbotsbury via stone slab at Corton Hill (see Fig.107)

TUNNEL
D

To Wool VIA 3 tumuli

LEY

to Wool via two tumuli

Upwey

LEY
PFP
Bincombe

summit of The Knoll

LEY

0   ½   1   (S)

Scale in miles

• = tumuli (some now levelled)

A3354
To Weymouth

(S)←→(S) This ley is plotted by Gordon Harris to extent to Stonehenge (pers. comm.)

Fig.71: Location map and leys in the area of Bincombe.

just the other side of some disused rusty farm implements. Look for the two hawthorn bushes that crown the barrow.

This barrow is the famed Burning Barrow, and we learned how it acquired this title earlier (see page 24). This alone makes it a site of interest. But the author was alerted to the possibility of stones on the barrow when a study of the OS 6" map revealed 'circle of stones'!

It is a bowl barrow about 4ft high and was excavated in 1922. An inner retaining dry stone wall was found, around 25ft in diameter.

A trip in September 1993 enabled the author to confirm that stones are still visible on the barrow. Some 15 stones, of local limestone, protrude from the mound at several places, the largest of them approaching 3ft in length.

Looking around the landscape from the barrow shows that some key astronomical events are imprinted on the landscape by some of the neighbouring barrows. Fig.72 shows the barrow in the foreground, with some of the stones visible, and the view looking west to north west. The barrow exactly on the skyline (E in Fig.71) marks the spot of the Beltaine and Lammas sunsets.

At Beltaine, May 1995, the author was

Fig.72: Bincombe Barrow A, showing some of the stones and the barrow on the skyline marking out Beltaine and Lammas sunsets (arrowed).

observed sunset point, May 1st, 1995.

able to witness the sun going down behind the barrow in a clear blue sky. A wonderful moment. Just 2 days later the sun was already setting three solar diameters further north along the skylines.

In the opposite direction, we look towards woods on the skyline, past Bincombe Barn. Tumuli, now levelled or obscured, would have marked out Samhain and Imbolc sunrises.

Barrows B,C and D in Fig.71 also have records of large quantities or large stones associated with them. Barrow B (grid reference: 665864) lies to the south of the public path joining the A354 and B3159. Excavations revealed a circle of 22 stones, 10ft in diameter, with an 8ft wide gap on the SE side.

Barrow C (grid reference: 657866) lies in a field immediately west of the mast on Ridge Hill, on the track of the ancient Ridgeway. Old records of the excavations show that a massive stone cist was found, with a cover stone weighing around one ton.

Barrow D (grid reference: 675858) was excavated in 1963. Skeletons and vessels were found and a secondary grave was stone slab-lined. The barrow was a stony cairn, and these features are repeated many times in Dorset, ancient Man utilising the local stone for ritual means, a practice that continued to the present day.

Plate 55: Sarsen stone to the east of the Broadstone, behind lay-by. Did this stone once belong to a stone circle?

THE BROADSTONE

LOCATION: 1 mile west of Winterbourne Abbas, on the south side of the A35. It lies in the vegetation, to the west of the AA phone box lay-by (the only safe place to park when visiting this stone). Look out for the 4 black and white reflector posts, for the stone lies behind these at road level. A late autumn to spring visit is recommended due to the obscuring nature of the roadside brambles. OS 1:50 000 sheet 194 and 1:25 000 'Purbeck and South Dorset' sheet. Grid reference: 595903. The stone is marked and named on OS maps.

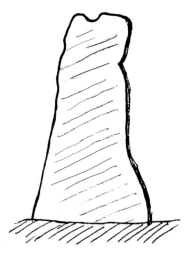

Fig.73: John Aubrey's 1687 drawing of the Broadstone

This once-great stone now lies almost completely covered next to the busy A35 road. Its length can still be measured at over 9ft and its width of 4ft can be made out with a little clearing of vegetation. Excavation earlier this Century showed a thickness of about 2ft. A photograph taken at the time shows a thinner, tapered end (at the east end of the stone as it now lies) and a notch.

Antiquarian John Aubrey, in his 1687 classic 'Monumenta Britannia', gives us a drawing of the stone STILL STANDING. And (lo and behold) he shows a clear notch at the top! Notches such as this are quite common on standing stones, perhaps being used for phallic symbolism and ritual observances. Fig.73 shows his drawing.

What is interesting is that he also saw two more stones at this site, and he considered the three to be the possible vestiges of a stone circle. On a trip to the site in 1993 the author found an isolated sarsen stone in the field behind the AA phone box lay-by. 3.5ft protrudes above the ground and it leans to the south. Plate 55 shows the stone looking east.

Dave Freeman, of Bournemouth, informs me of a conversation with a farmer whose workers sat on the Broadstone during breaks when the stone was less sunken.

heritage. The stone is actually a Scheduled Ancient Monument and it is disgraceful that it should have degenerated to such a sorry state.

Charles Warne summed up the situation regards the Broadstone in 1872:

"One cannot but regret that this fine stone has not been restored to its erect position,a work easy to be accomplished at a trifling expense."

As with previous practice, we will now broaden our horizon to look at the relationship of the Broadstone with the surrounding landscape. The stone lies almost due west of the Nine Stones stone circle, 0.75 mile distant. Plate 56 shows the view looking east through to south-east from the Broadstone.

Point A in the photo is the point of the Equinox sunrises, in March and September each year. Two things need pointing out here.

Plate 56: The view from the Broadstone towards key sunrise points (see text for details of A and B. (A montage of two photographs.)

I feel that the Broadstone is one of the strongest candidates of Dorset's fallen megaliths for re-erection. The stone is intact, large and, from what we can tell, at or close to its original position. At the moment it lies next to a very busy road, getting more overgrown by the year. Only enthusiasts know of it and can even find it!

Should the stone be re-erected a few yards to the south, with the appropriate path and information sign, many more people could then see it and experience a bit more of our

Firstly, the sunrise point is where the nearer hill meets the distant skyline (reminiscent of the situation at Nine Stones, shown in Fig.16). And secondly, the Nine Stones circle sits directly under the arrow (out of sight).

Plate 56 also shows (just!) a group of barrows on the skyline to the south-east (marked 'B'). This group marks the sunrise at the Mid-Winter Solstice. The compass bearing is a few degrees south of the theoretical sunrise point, allowance having been made by the ancients for the height of the close skyline!

Plate 57: The Chilcombe
barrow stone.

To the west of the stone the skyline is masked by a clothing of trees which obscure present day key sunsets. However, map work and field trips revealed that several tumuli would be visible from the stone were the forestation not there.

So although the Broadstone would appear to be lying in a valley with little chance of astronomical observation, the opposite once again turns out to be the case.

BURTON BRADSTOCK, EYPE AND SHIPTON

LOCATION: Near the Triangulation pillar, at the highest point of North Hill, NW of Burton Bradstock (SE of Bridport). OS 1:50 000 sheet 193. Grid reference: not available.

Fig.74: Location of the
stone at Chilcombe Hill.

n page 60 of the 'West' Vol. of 'Inventory of Historical Monuments in the County of Dorset', reference is made to the 'probable remains of a barrow'. A mound up to 3ft high is reported, much disturbed. 'Large stones in and around the mound may indicate mound material', it is reported.

The mound is on the crest of the hill. The author has been unable to gain access to the fields in question, and no public footpaths cross the relevant land. I would welcome any news on possible remaining stones.

In 1935 a stone displaying an inscribed face and phallic symbolism was found in a garden at nearby Eype. At neighbouring Shipton Gorge two ancient carved stone heads were found around 1960. All three stones are now in the museum at Dorchester.

The orientation of Shipton Hill and Chilcombe Hill 'forts' enables Equinox sunrises and sunets to be marked on the landscape.

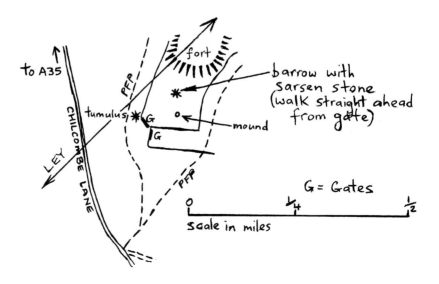

CHILCOMBE HILL BARROW

LOCATION: Chilcombe Hill is a fine vantage point, capped by an ancient enclosure about 5 miles east of Bridport. Access is via a minor road south from the A35. Fig.74 shows the location in detail. OS 1:50 000 sheet 194 and 1:25 000 'Purbeck & South Dorset' sheet. Grid reference: 528916.

A large prone sarsen stone caps this barrow. It measures 5ft long, nearly 3ft in width and is around 1ft thick. It is a block of limestone, which is noticeably squared at the west and rounded at the east end. It lies orientated at 115 degrees. Plate 57 shows the stone from the south.

Fig.74 shows a ley running very close to the barrow stone, before passing through the heart of the hillfort. The ley is detailed in Fig.120.

Incredible views are obtained standing on the barrow. Shipton Hill and the Devon coast can be seen to the west. Hardy monument stands out to the east. A fine vantage point indeed for the site of an ancient settlement that crowns the hill.

DORCHESTER

The town of Dorchester has become famed as the Roman town of Dvrnovaria, with countless remains of buildings, walls and other relics. The town was a thriving centre of commerce and military activity. Clues exist, however, to tell the tale of life prior to the Romans' arrival. In this section we shall look at stone structures and solitary monoliths in the area. OS 1:50 000 sheet 194 and 1:25 000 'Purbeck & South Dorset' sheet cover the area.

(A) MAUMBURY RINGS

LOCATION: On the A354 Weymouth road, just south of the Brewery and Dorchester South railway station. Grid reference: 690899.

This fine henge is thought to be early Bronze Age (c.2020 BC). The structure we see today was built up and extended by the Romans for use as an amphitheatre.

The site was clearly ritualistic as remains with phallic symbolism were found. Parallels in the use and structure of Maumbury can be found at Knowlton and Mount Pleasant.

However, our interest in this site is chiefly concerning the reports of a large stone which formerly stood there. In the 17th Century a monolith used for bull-baiting was moved to Maumbury from the centre of Dorchester. It was erected on the west side of the entrance. In 1846 it was lowered to a depth of 3ft below the surface, as it was impairing agricultural equipment. But this seems to be the last we hear about it. Excavations in 1879 failed to recover it. Extensive further excavations in 1908-1913 likewise found no stone or even any traces of it.

So somewhere along the line we lost another of Dorset's large standing stones. My own gut feeling on the stone is that it was in fact RETURNED to the henge in the 17th Century from, perhaps, whence it originated. Stones at the entrances of henges are well documented. Plate 58 is a view of the henge looking at the west entrance, where the stone once lay and possibly once stood guarding the entrance.

Fig.98 shows a ley associated with Maumbury and other ancient sites. NB: Wessex Dowser, Roger Sleet, has recently dowsed 'powerful' energy lines passing right through Maumbury (pers. comm.).

Plate 59: The stone at Fordington High Street.

(B) FORDINGTON STONES

LOCATION: A stone lies on a corner, opposite the green, outside 74 High Street, Fordington opposite Church Acre Road. Grid reference: 6908905.

Plate 58: (below) The aerial view of Maumbury Rings, once the locality of a stone of 'considerable dimensions', according to old reports.
(Reproduced, with kind permission, form "Goddess of the stones", by George Terence Mearden.)

It is a very smooth limestone block, 3.5ft x 3ft across. Plate 59 shows the stone, and it has all the hallmarks of a ley marker. One is referred back to page 20. Is this the stone that returned to its original spot after workmen had moved it?

Also at Fordington, we turn our attention to the Church of St. George (grid reference: 698906). A Roman settlement is suggested here by remains, and the early parts of the church show Saxon geomancy.

As one enters the porch, above the church door can be seen a fine early 12th Century

Plate 60: The Roman wall at Dorchester.

tympanum. It depicts a battle in 1097, and on the left can be seen thankful soldiers and St. George on a horse (this interpretation by the Rector).

As one enters the church proper, a Roman capital can be seen at the base of the column nearest the door. Directly in front of you is an inscribed stone. It is 2nd Century Roman, and commemorates the Roman Carinus inscribed by his family at his death. It was discovered face down in 1906 in the church grounds.

(C) ROMAN COFFIN

LOCATION: Outside the premises of Wyvern Fireplaces, Grove Trading Estate (grid reference: 685911).

his fine Roman coffin is made of Ham Hill Stone and was found in the 1970's near its present site. The surrounding area was once one of the largest Roman cemeteries in the south-west. 1100 burials were excavated

(D) ROMAN WALL

LOCATION: A section of Roman wall can be seen just south of the top-of-town roundabout, on the east side of the road. It lies behind railings and a plaque gives information on it. Grid reference: 689906.

his Scheduled Ancient Monument is our only view of the wall that once enclosed the Roman town. It is dated c.300 AD. It was excavated in 1951 and excavations revealed that it was up to 9ft wide and 20ft high.

At present we can see some 8ft of Roman wall, with a modern section attached along the top. Plate 60 shows the view today, a testimony to Roman engineering and modern conservation. The section preserved is about 28ft long.

(D) ROMAN TOWN-HOUSE

LOCATION: At the rear of the council buildings, adjacent to the Fire Service HQ. The site is signposted and an information plaque is present. Grid reference: 690910.

his splendid site shows the remains of a Roman townhouse, reported to be the best townhouse of the period visible in Britain. The general aspect is seen in Plate 6. The plan can be made out by the foundations of the walls present.

Windows, underfloor heating systems, columns and a mosaic are all to be seen at this pleasant locality.

Plate 61 shows the underfloor heating system of one of the rooms. The whole house

Plate 61: The hypocaust at the Roman townhouse, Dorchester.

was clearly a grand affair, the town equivalent of the rural villa.

The reader is referred back to Fig.52 where it can be seen that the townhouse lies exactly on a ley running between Woodbury Hill and The Knoll. Is this mere chance?

Dorchester Museum, close by, is well worth a visit with notable archaeological displays of local interest (tel: 01305 262735).

GREY MARE AND HER COLTS

LOCATION: 1.5 miles NW of Portesham, and is marked and named on OS maps. Fig.70 shows its position relative to Abbotsbury. One takes the path marked 'Kingston Russell Circle', just past the start of the road to Gorwell Farm. After following the edge of a large field, take the footpath that heads off to the left (often half-hidden by the hedgerow). Bear right and soon a gate is seen to one's left, and the barrow and stones are seen through it. OS 1:50 000 sheet 194 and 1:25 000 'Purbeck & South Dorset' sheet. Grid reference: 584871.

his site is Dorset's best example of a megalithic chambered long barrow. It is a Scheduled Ancient Monument, and is well deserving of that honour as it has a relatively well preserved earthen mound with, at the eastern end, large megaliths, some still standing.

Fig.75 shows an old plan of the barrow and the site is very much the same today. The mound is roughly triangular, about 75ft long and around 35ft at its widest (although formerly wider than this). Posts have now been erected to stop further agricultural erosion. The maximum height of the mound is around 4ft and the axis of the barrow is NW-SE.

The monoliths, and nearby smaller stones, once guarded a chamber. The area of the chamber measures 7ft x 7ft. The capstone has collapsed into the chamber, although some of the vertical small stones that clearly formed the tomb wall can just be glimpsed beneath it. The capstone is over 8ft across, squarish and 1.5ft thick. The monoliths are flinty sarsens and very hard.

Two stones stand next to the capstone, both over 7ft tall. One is squarish, the other noticeably diamond shaped. One may recall the situation at Avebury, where alternating pillar and diamond-shaped stones are thought to represent the male and female principle.

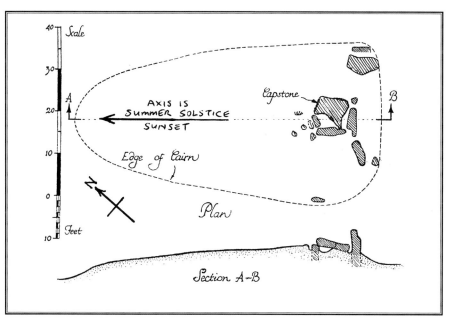

Fig.75: Plan of Grey Mare and Her Colts long barrow.

A third large stone lies just north of the standing duo. It is thought that originally the trio would have formed a crescent-shaped forecourt in front of the tomb chamber. The plan is similar to West Kennet (near Avebury) and many Cornish and Welsh megalithic barrows.

Smaller stones around the periphery of the mound may represent the remains of a peristalith, or retaining wall of stones. Some, however, may be from field clearance. Plates 62 and 63 show the megaliths at the east end of the barrow. Plate 3 shows a closer view of the stones.

On a visit to the barrow in Autumn 1994, the author and his wife, Gemma, both felt the energy emitting from the diamond-shaped stone with their hands. Band 5 of Mitchell (see Figs. 15 and 28) was presumably located, about 0.75 the way up the stone, and both present were pulled around to the left.

The axis of the barrow is aligned to the Summer Solstice sunset/Winter Solstice sunrise and observations by the author were outlined on page 33, and Fig.17. Jeremy Harte (in 'The Leyhunter' no. 121, 1994) lists two ghostly apparitions near the barrow, perhaps a sign of active earth energies.

I also believe that a processional way existed involving The Grey Mare and Her Colts and adjacent stone sites. Fig.76 shows the relevant area and an instant alignment of sites, all adjoining the ancient ridgeway path, can be seen. Some of the stones are described here for the first time.

Plate 62: The megaliths at the east end of Grey Mare and Her Colts. The view is east, looking from the barrow mound.

"WE SHOULD GO TO SACRED SITES WITH THE RIGHT INTENTION."

Pat Law-Ibison, Wessex Research Group

Plate 63: Grey Mare and Her Colts, from the South.

A clue was first revealed when it was clear that the sites shown all lay on or very close to the ancient path, and fieldwork in 1994 uncovered two stones between The Grey Mare barrow and the Kingston Russell circle. The stone nearest The Grey Mare lies in a ditch (the ancient path itself?) next to the hedgerow that follows the present path. It lies just south-east of the intersection of a N-S running field hedge (grid reference: 583873).

It is a rough triangle in shape, 6ft across each edge, and 1ft thick. Why was such a stone, positioned as it is, not regarded as important by archaeologists in the past? We have come across this puzzle before.

A further stone lies south of the Kingston Russell stone circle, on the left of the path, before you enter the field containing the circle (when coming from the direction of The Grey Mare barrow). It is about 3ft long.

Fig.76: The proposed processional route associated with The Grey Mare and Her Colts

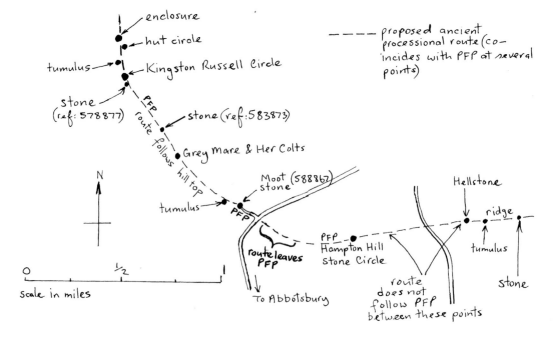

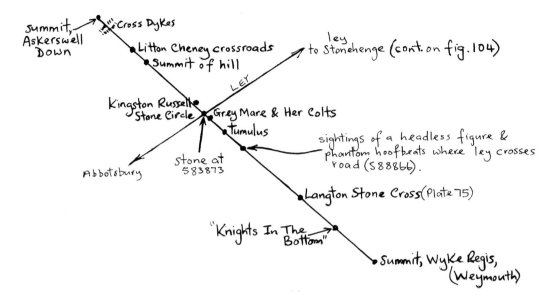

Summit, Askerswell Down

Cross Dykes

Litton Cheney crossroads

Summit of hill

ley to Stonehenge (cont. on fig. 104)

LEY

Kingston Russell Stone Circle

Grey Mare & Her Colts

Tumulus

sightings of a headless figure & phantom hoofbeats where ley crosses road (S 88866).

Abbotsbury

Stone at 583873

Langton Stone Cross (Plate 75)

"Knights In The Bottom"

Summit, Wyke Regis, (Weymouth)

Fig.77: Proposed ley between Askerwell and Weymouth. Some sites are not plotted in exact position due to the limitation of scale.

Plate 64: Sunset over The Grey Mare and Her Colts.

Archaeologists G Children and G Nash (St David's University College) propose a similar 'procession route of the dead' leading from Grey Hill stone circle (Gwent) to a nearby barrow cemetery ('3rd Stone', No. 24 1996)

A further confirmation of the antiquity of the stone at 583873, south of the Kingston Russell stone circle, is that it may also be a markstone for a ley that goes from near Abbotsbury right up to Stonehenge (Fig.104 for more details).

A ley line has been uncovered associated with The Grey Mare barrow and is shown in Fig.77. It is interesting that it includes two features in the Fleet area, not an area renowned for megalithic archaeology. The Langton Cross lies on the ley (see Plate 75). To the SE, an area know as Knights In The Bottom may be relevant. Many standing stones around Britain are called Knights, Knight, or else named after a particular knight. Could this reference on this ley be giving us a clue of former stones?

row. According to archaeologist Leslie Grinsell, the long barrow was aligned E-W and may have been +54ft long. Traces of the mound can still be made out today, as a slight rise in the field to the west of the stones.

The two stones lie 5yds apart, the western one being 10 x 4ft (shown in Plate 65) and the easterly one measuring 7.5 x 3ft. Old records speak of a capstone stone 'tilted on other stones' being present. Sadly, this has now either gone, or else the larger stone here is the said capstone, now settled to ground level.

This site is a sad reminder of what can happen to a megalithic chambered long barrow. It has not faired the centuries, or Man, as well as the nearby Grey Mare and Her Colts, which was of similar design.

Near the entrance to the field, to the west of the barrow stones, is a solitary prone stone on the left as one enters the field. It is not clear if this was once part of the barrow structure or not.

Whatever the case, it should be left there.

Plate 65: One of the fallen megaliths at the Hampton Hill long barrow.

HAMPTON HILL BARROW STONES

LOCATION: 0.75 mile NW of Portesham, west of Hampton Barn. Fig.78 shows the location and access to the stones. No gates need be opened and all fields crossed are grazing only. On the 1:25 000 map a solitary 'boulders' symbol marks the spot. OS 1:50 000 sheet 194 and 1:25 000 'Purbeck & South Dorset' sheet. Grid reference: 596868.

"......THE STONES WERE NOT ONLY SYMBOLS, BUT ACTUAL TOOLS CAREFULLY PLACED FOR VERY GOOD REASON."

Janet and Colin Bord

Fig.78: Location map for Hampton Hill stones.

Two large sarsen stones probably represent the megaliths that once stood at the east end of a Neolithic long bar-

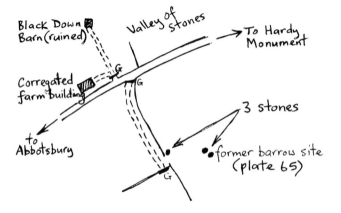

HAMPTON HILL STONE CIRCLE

LOCATION: Approximately 0.5 mile NW of Portesham, SW of Hampton Barn, reached via the Coast Path, which passes a few feet from the circle. its position is not too clear on the 1:25 000, but in fact lies just to the left of the 'H' of 'Hampton Stone Circle'. A stile gives access to the circle. OS 1:50 000 sheet 194 and 1:25 000 'Purbeck & South Dorset' sheet. Grid reference: 596865. The site is a Scheduled Ancient Monument.

lthough in itself one of Dorset' smallest stone circles, and very overgrown too, it is one of the most instructive from the earth mysteries point of view as we shall see shortly, with several aligned sites and landscape features marking key sunrises and sunsets. An incredibly subtle inter-relation between the circle and the nearby Hellstone is described here for the first time

Fig.79 is a plan of the circle drawn at the 1965 excavation of the site.

The excavations proved 28 stones, although some difficulty was experienced in defining circle stones from those cleared from nearby fields, which had been dumped there. A Bronze Age ellipse of stones was proven, around 20ft x 19ft in size, and a track roughly 4ft wide stopped t the north perimeter. The public footpath, itself following an ancient track, appeared to pass right through the circle. Three stones were found, earthfast, on the north side of the track, the opposite side to the main cluster.

Plate 66 is a 1909 photograph of the circle and this view cannot be found today, owing to the encroachment of vegetation, and a surrounding fence. The circle is as difficult to photograph as Rempstone Circle, but this time the problem is the small size of the stones and the brambles.

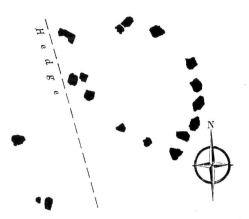

Fig.79: Plan of the Hampton Hill Stone Circle

Over half a dozen stones are usually visible, depending on the vegetation, and most are 3-4ft long and prone. One stone at the SW corner is still standing, about 2.5ft of stone showing above the ground. The stones are typical hard, flinty conglomeratic sarsens.

On a trip to the circle in October 1994, the author turned his attention to the inter-relationship between the circle and the many nearby sites, as well as checking for key sunrise/set markers. I was not disappointed and, in fact, a wonderfully subtle and incredibly delicate connection was found between the circle and the nearby Hellstone cromlech (for more details of this structure see page 121).

Plate 66: A 1909 view of Hampton Hill stone circle.

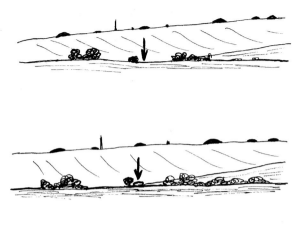

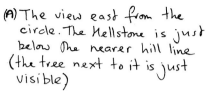

(A) The view east from the circle. The Hellstone is just below the nearer hill line (the tree next to it is just visible)

(B) 50 yds east of the circle one can clearly see the Hellstone.

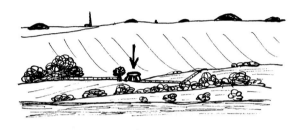

(C) 150 yds east of circle the view is thus. Note the numerous tumuli on the Ridgeway skyline, one of which aligns with the Hellstone.

Fig.80: The 'rising' of the Hellstone above the hill line as seen from the vicinity of Hampton Hill Circle. From photographs, using slight telephoto enlargement.

East of the circle can be seen a line of barrows on the skyline, marking out Equinox sunrises, and probably the limits of the Equinox moon-rises also, which constantly move in an 18.5 year cycle.

I knew that the Hellstone lies east from the circle and found it curious that it was not visible from the circle. I walked east along the path from the circle until the Hellstone became visible (about 100yds from the circle). I then kept looking at the Hellstone whilst walking backwards to see at what point the capstone stone was obscured by the nearer intervening hill. After several yards (and several stumbles!), the capstone dipped below the edge of the hillside.

I stopped and turned around. To my astonishment I found I was standing just a few yards from the Hampton Hill stone circle!

Such is the subtlety of this arrangement. The capstone aligns with the ground level when visible from the circle. It is possible that the capstone once exactly matched the nearer hill and that the rise in the land level due to agriculture means one has to step a few yards to the east now before the appearance of the Hellstone.

We can only guess what happened at these sites at certain times of the year. But it is clear to me that a fire or torch lit on the Hellstone would have been visible from the circle, perhaps as part of an Equinox sunrise or even SUNSET ritual. For don't forget, from the Hellstone the Equinox sun indeed sets behind the stone circle!

Fig.80 shows the views from the circle to the Hellstone.

Other astronomical events are impressed upon the landscape, as viewed from the Hampton Hill circle:

The summit of the prominent hill crowned by the Hardy Monument (that brick monstrosity) lie at a heading of 60 degrees when viewed from the circle. This hill marks the point of the Beltaine and Lammas sunrises. Similarly, standing at the Hardy Monument we see the sunset over the Hampton Hill stone circle at Samhain and Imbolc festivals. The circle, although not visible, IS exactly on the skyline from the Hardy Monument.

The location of the circle enables the Samhain and Imbolc sunrises (119 °) to be incredibly marked by the point where the White Nothe cliffs cut the sea horizon.

Woods due west of the circle contain tumuli, which mark out the Equinox sunsets.

The ley line associated with the circle has already been described (see Fig.70). Save to say that St. Catherine's Hill, at the south end of the ley IS visible from the Hampton circle. So here we have a ley, the entire length of which can be viewed from a single site, the Hampton Hill stone circle. Recent map dowsing by experienced Wessex Dowser member, Roger Sleet, suggests the circle stands on a powerful energy line (pers. comm.).

ÞELLSTONE BARROW

LOCATION: This well known monument stands about 0.5 mile north of Portesham and is signposted and accessible (see Fig.105). The nearest parking is a lay-by east of Hampton Barn, on the east side of the road down to Portesham. The Hellstone is signposted from here. OS 1:50 000 sheet 194 and 1:25 000 'Purbeck & South Dorset' sheet. Grid reference: 606867.

Plate 67: The Hellstone; a close-up of the huge capstone from the east.

his fine site is Dorset's last surviving Dolmen with the capstone and chamber stones intact, even though they are not in their original positions. The folklore associated with this site has already been covered in Chapter 3. John Hutchins, in 1774, described the stones and, interestingly, a 60ft long terrace leading to them from the NW.

By 1860, the stones had nearly all collapsed and in 1866 an attempt was made to reconstruct the chamber and capstone to some of their former glory. Despite the somewhat inaccurate rebuilding, the site is the original, as are the stones used. Fig.81 is a 1790 drawing showing its collapsed state.

The dolmen is Neolithic in age. It may have been erected as long ago as 4000 BC,

Fig.81: A 1790 drawing of the Hellstone.

Nine vertical stones, or Orthostats, hold up the huge capstone. These stones reach up 6ft above the ground and reach 2ft in thickness in places. The capstone measures 10ft x 8ft and averages a thickness of 2ft. Its estimated weight of 20 tons makes one wonder all the more the feats of engineering achieved using only the most primitive of tools coupled with, of course, the human spirit.

The present chamber, beneath the capstone, measures 9ft x 5ft and the roof is about 5ft above the floor. Sitting or crouching within these ancient stones is a memorable experience to those wishing to let their minds and spirits tune in with the place. The solitude and wild setting of the dolmen adds to the atmosphere. A night trip with a bright moon is highly recommended!

Some 50yds east of The Hellstone is a mound, dissected by a wall. it was described in 1959 as a 'possible prehistoric long mound'. The author recorded two stones on the edge of the mound on a trip in February 1994. It is not clear if these are the result of field clearance or part of the mound. Other stones can be seen in the vicinity of the Hellstone and may represent former barrow peristaliths. A field trip in 1920 by local archaeologists speaks of 'several large stones lying about, one of which especially seems to

Plate 68: The Hellstone from the south-east, showing the entrance.

making it probably the oldest manmade structure still standing in Dorset. The chamber of stones stands at the SE end of a mound which was formerly 88ft long and up to 40ft in width. The mound is aligned to approximately 130-310 degrees, with the Mid-Winter Solstice sunrise/Summer Solstice sunset directions.

Plate 69: The Hellstone dolmen from the south. The isolated windswept trees aid location, as well as adding to the atmosphere of this sacred site.

resemble a menhir'. (For other stone sites near The Hellstone, see Fig.120 and Fig. 80).

The Hellstone's relationship with the Hampton Hill stone circle has already been described (see pages 119-120 and Fig.80), but the site also connects with other sites in terms of ley lines. Fig.82 shows the leys found to be associated with The Hellstone.

To me, The Hellstone gives an isolated reminder of the splendour and grandeur that was sprinkled in profusion all over Dorset in prehistoric times. Let us be ever determined not to let sites like this go the way of the rest of Dorset's other chambered tombs.

"The dolmen symbolises a stone grave, the cave through which the dead must pass on their journey to the otherworld, and the womb through which the living may achieve rebirth."

Joseph Campbell (1960)

---

helstone standing stone

LOCATION: Approximately midway between Dorchester and Bridport, next to the busy A35. The stone stands in a field on the north side of the road, and access if via a farm track (see Fig.83) with a walk across an arable field. No attempt to visit the site should be made when crops are growing in the field without prior permission from the adjacent farm. OS 1:50 000 sheet 194 and 1:25 000 'Purbeck & South Dorset' sheet. Grid reference: 573915. The stone is marked and named on OS maps.

The Helstone is Dorset's finest solitary menhir that is still standing. Over 10ft of stone still rises above the ground, although its height is less due to a pronounced lean to the south.

The shape of the stone is interesting. The diamond-come-lozenge outline is reminiscent of the Verwood stone and many of the Avebury stones. This shape is thought to be symbolic of the feminine principle. Tall long stones, such as the Broadstone and the alter-

Fig.82: Leys associated with The Hellstone. The two stones east of The Hellstone are described under 'Portesham' in this chapter.

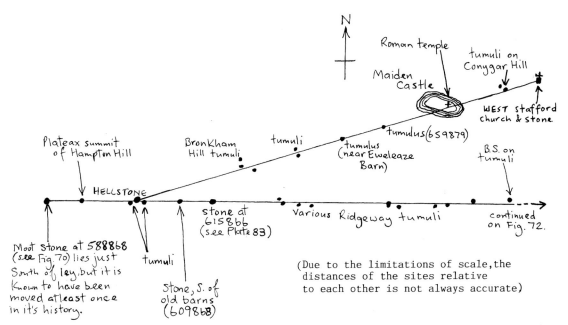

N

Roman temple

tumuli on Conygar Hill

Maiden Castle

WEST stafford church & stone

Plateax summit of Hampton Hill

Bronkham Hill tumuli

tumuli

tumulus(659879)

tumulus (near Eweleaze Barn)

B.S. on tumuli

HELLSTONE

stone at 615866 (see Plate 83)

Various Ridgeway tumuli

continued on Fig. 72.

Moot stone at 588868 (see Fig.70) lies just South of ley, but it is known to have been moved atleast once in it's history.

tumuli

Stone, S. of old barns (609868)

(Due to the limitations of scale, the distances of the sites relative to each other is not always accurate)

Fig.83: Location of the Helstone Standing Stone.

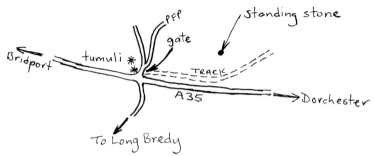

Plate 70: (Top) The Helstone, from the south.

Plate 72: (right) Sunset at the Helstone standing stone.

Plate 71: Close up of the Helstone stone, from the NE. The pointed top and lozenge-shape may be significant.

nating stones at Avebury, probably represent the male principle.

The Helstone stands in a broad low-lying valley. Despite its low position relative to the surrounding landscape, one key sunset is still marked. To the SW two tumuli stand on the skyline. These show the position of the sunset at Samhain and Imbolc. These tumuli lie on a ley associated with the Nine Stones, as shown in Fig.104. The east side of the stone is shaped so as to enable one to be seated. A shaman's seat of old?

During summer months the field around the stone is ablaze with poppies.

KINGSTON RUSSELL STONES

LOCATION: Kingston Russell lies on the A35, about 7 miles west of Dorchester. Three stone sites occur within 0.5 mile of the village. Individual details are given in the text. Fig.84 shows the area. OS 1:50 000 sheet 194 and 1:25 000 'Purbeck & South Dorset' sheet.

map. Sarsens shown as 'Hangman's Rocks' were on the map. Hutchins in 1863 referred to stones west of the Broadstone, which these are. He saw 4 upright stones, two of which were 'large'.

Bailey has little doubt that the sarsen found in the hedge today is one of the 'lost' stones. He notes that the 'Old London Road' used to run 50yds north of the A35, its course still marked out by the hedge. The stones once stood very close to the old road, a road which in turn evolved from an ancient track. The

Fig.84: Kingston Russell Localities.

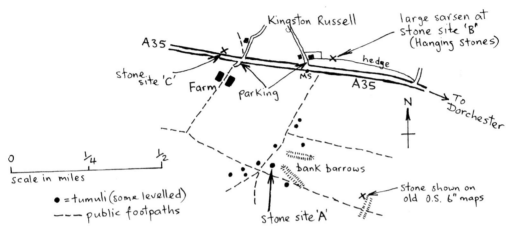

First stop is Site 'A' on Fig.84. A stone sits on the top of 'Kingston Russell 5' barrow. The barrow sits prominently immediately NE of the meeting of 5 paths. The barrow is 5ft high and shows signs of excavation, so the stone may have been part of the original structure. It is a flinty sarsen, nearly 4ft long and 2ft showing above the mound. The stone may have been shaped. Plate 73 shows the stone.

The barrow stands amidst a rich barrow area which includes the long earthen bank barrows. Seen from here the Summer Solstice sunset occurs over Eggardon Hill. Samhain and Imbolc sunsets are marked by the prominent tree-covered Knoll Hill to the SW.

Stone site 'B' lies just east of a cottage near the eastern turning to Kingston Russell. The stone lies in the north side of the hedge bank at grid reference: 583911. In March 1984 the sarsen was located by C. Bailey (see Proc. Dorset Nat. Hist. Soc. Vol. 106) after he had found stones at the locality on a 1765 estate

stone itself lies half buried in the bank of the hedge. It appears to be about 9ft long and a width of some 4ft is visible. The matrix is the hard, flinty sarsen type.

The locality certainly lends itself to the idea that it was positioned with care. To the SE (heading of 120 degrees), the Poor Lot

Plate 73: Stone on barrow at Kingston Russell (site 'A').

group of barrows can be seen in the middle distance. From the stone, these mark the Samhain and Imbolc sunrises. Barrows visible on the skyline west of the stone mark out Equinox sunsets. On the hillside due east of the stone, one can see in the field some beautifully preserved barrows.

In March 1984, C. Bailey also located a 4.5ft long sarsen to the west (site 'C' in Fig.84). He also found 2 greensand blocks nearby. They were moved to the edge of the field. A search by the author in March 1995 resulted in the greensand fragments being located, but no sarsen.

———————— ⊙ ————————

"I HAVE COME TO THE CONCLUSION THAT THE TEMPLES AMONG THAT PEOPLE (THE BRITISH) SHOULD ON NO ACCOUNT BE DESTROYED ......"

Pope Gregory, 601 AD

———————— ⊙ ————————

KINGSTON RUSSELL STONE CIRCLE

LOCATION: 2 miles north of Abbotsbury and shown in Fig.76. The site is signposted from several directions. The circle is just south of a beech and pine coppice that is visible for miles around. OS 1:50 000 sheet 194 and 1:25 000 'Purbeck & South Dorset' sheet. Grid reference: 577878.

his Scheduled Ancient Monument has appeared in some of the earliest antiquarian records. Hutchins in 1774 regarded this as a Druidic temple. More recently the celebrated Prof. Alexander Thom, whose pioneering work of surveying hundreds of stone circles across Britain was so important in pushing forward the boundaries of our knowledge of them, paid a visit to Kingston Russell circle.

According to Thom, the circle is not an ellipse, as popularly supposed, but a flattened circle (his type 'B') like the circles at Castlerigg and Long Meg. The dimensions are approximately 90ft x 80ft and the plan is shown in Fig.85.

Fig.86 shows Charles Warne's 1876 drawing of the circle, and he described 18 stones 'lying around in their original positions'. The plan bears out his total.

In a recent lecture in Bournemouth, Bob Sephton, former Chairman of the Wessex Dowsers, told the audience that the energy fields of individual stones of a circle overlap. This has the effect of 'sealing-in' the space within the circle of stones. it also appears, he added, that straight energy lines develop 'kinks' as they pass through a circle. The effect appears similar to how light is refracted as it passes through water, or a prism.

The stones are of a hard conglomerate and at least one was still standing in the last

Fig.85: (right) Plan of Kingston Russell stone circle.

Fig.86: (below) Drawing, published in 1876, of the circle.

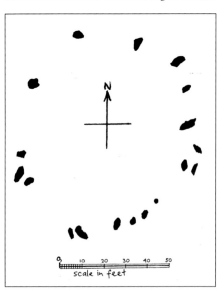

scale in feet

Plate 74: The Kingston Russell Stone Circle, from the SE *(Reproduced, with kind permission, from "Goddess of the stones", by George Terence Mearden.).*

Century. The largest stone is around 8ft long, now prone, as are all its companions.

Plate 74 shows an aerial view of the circle, viewed from the SE. Some gaps are clearly visible, whilst some stones appear bunched together. It is not clear if some of the bunched stones are those missing from the gaps.

We will now turn our attention to the immediate vicinity of the circle. In the next field east from the circle, one can see (vegetation permitting) a stone, close to the dividing hedge. It is south of the footpath, about 3ft long and prone. This could be a former circle stone, or else another stone marking out the track from the east (another stone further along the track is shown in Fig.76).

On older 1:25 000 sheets, two stones are shown at the edge of the field, to the south of the circle. I have not yet been able to find these. They may have been more stones removed from the circle.

Standing in the centre of the circle, let us see what we can detect on the landscape. To the SE, in the direction of the Winter Solstice sunrise, the Grey Mare and Her Colts would at one time have been visible, before the intervention of hedges and trees.

In an easterly direction, the Hardy Monument marks a prominent hill crowned with tumuli, marking out the Equinox sunrises.

Looking approximately SW from the circle, the view shown in Fig.87 is seen on the skyline.

Subtle positioning enables the moon, at its most southern Equinox node, to set where the line of a nearer hill cuts the very distant skyline. Likewise, the Samhain and Imbolc sunsets are marked out on the landscape by

Fig.87: The view SW from Kingston Russell Stone Circle.

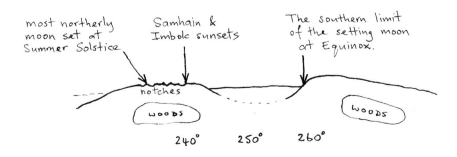

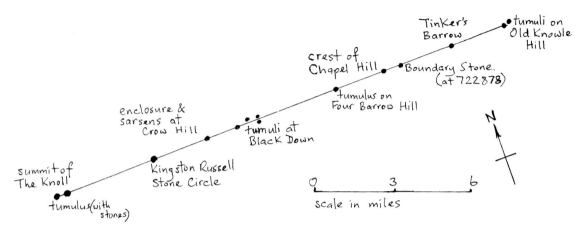

Tinker's Barrow

tumuli on Old Knowle Hill

crest of Chapel Hill

Boundary Stone. (at 722878)

tumulus on Four Barrow Hill

enclosure & sarsens at Crow Hill

tumuli at Black Down

N

summit of The Knoll

Kingston Russell Stone Circle

0   3   6

tumulus (with stones)

scale in miles

Fig.88: Ley plotted by Ward (with amendments by the author) associated with the Kingston Russell stone circle.

another prominent hill to the left (south). A possible mid-summer moonset limit may also be marked by the same hill.

⸺○⸺

"WE SHALL SHOW THEM OUR SIGNS ON THE HORIZONS AND WITHIN THEMSELVES UNTIL IT WILL BE MANIFESTED UNTO THEM THAT IT IS THE TRUTH."

Koran (XLI, 53)

⸺○⸺

The reader is referred back to Fig.77 for the proposed ley on which the circle stands. Another ley, suggested by Peter Ward in 1984, is shown in Fig.88. The Chapel Hill and boundary stone markers are additions by the author to Ward's results.

Whilst in the area, the reader is urged to visit the Celtic chapel of St. Lukes (grid reference: 557879). The ruins stand at a very atmospheric spot, deep within woods. An energy line has been dowsed by the author between the arch and the altar.

The latter was found to 'tingle' when touched. This sacred site is probably much older than the present ruins.

LANGTON CROSS

LOCATION: The cross stands on the south side of the B3157, approximately halfway between Weymouth and Portesham. It stands behind a low fence at the turn-off to Langton Herring. The cross is named and marked on OS maps. OS 1:50 000 sheet 194 and 1:25 000 'Purbeck & South Dorset' sheet.
Grid reference: 625824.

ley line associated with Langton Cross is shown in Fig.77. This suggests that the stone, or at the very least the SITE, is more ancient than the present Christian monument.

The cross is dated at 14th Century and is made of local Portland Ridgeway stone. It is 3ft 2" high and a further unseen 1ft 7" lies below the ground. The shaft is 11" square and lichen-covered. The two arms of the cross are still present, if weathered, but the top is missing.

The stone is said in folklore to dip its head in the waters of the Fleet on New Year's Eve. Later in its history, the stone may have marked the route for pilgrims journeying from the port at Weymouth and the monastery at Abbotsbury.

James Rattue informs the author of a 1ft high stone in Langton village, just south of the church, on the opposite side of the road.

A scarp crossing E-W across the enclosure had six exposed limestone blocks. The enclosure was tentatively dated as 'Medieval'.

The chapel at nearby Corton is worth a visit. It contains a rare pre-Reformation altar that survived (probably by being hidden) the Act of Edward VI, early in the 13th Century, that declared "......all altar stones used for saying Catholic mass should be destroyed". The fine structure is in Purbeck Marble.

Plate 75: The Langton Cross

LITTLEBREDY MARKSTONE AND LEY

LOCATION: 150yds NW of village church, at the junction of two lanes. The stone lies just in front of a wooden shelter. OS 1:50 000 sheet 194 and 1:25 000 'Purbeck & South Dorset' sheet.
Grid reference: 587891.

Some other sites of interest occur in the area of the Langton Stone. At East Shilvinghampton, a mile to the north of the cross, an irregular block of limestone once lay near the junction of the four footpaths, just below the crest of the hill. Fig.89 shows how the position of the stone may mark a ley.

To the east, along the same ridge, a 1923 field trip by Dorset archaeologists reported (at grid reference 643842 on Hewish Hill) a square ditch that enclosed an area of 0.5 acre.

his stone has been described by John Michell in 1976 and Jeremy Harte, a decade later. It was found by the author in June 1994.

The stone lies on the side of the road and some 3ft of limestone can be seen above the grass. Plate 5 shows the stone.

Map and fieldwork by the author may have revealed a ley associated with this stone. Fig. 89 plots the proposed ley across

Fig.89: Ley associated with the Littlebredy markstone.

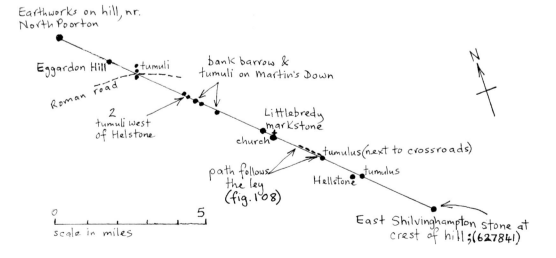

Earthworks on hill, nr. North Poorton

Eggardon Hill • tumuli

Roman road

bank barrow & tumuli on Martin's Down

2 tumuli west of Helstone

Littlebredy markstone

church

path follows the ley (fig. 108)

Hellstone

tumulus(next to crossroads)

tumulus

East Shilvinghampton stone at crest of hill ;(627841)

N

0   5
scale in miles

the landscape. The ley cuts through Littlebredy Church. Neil King, of Bournemouth, reports several sarsen stones scattered around the churchyard, some of which appear shaped.

"AND JOSHUA SET UP TWELVE STONES IN THE MIDST OF JORDAN ...AND THEY ARE THERE TO THIS DAY."

Joshua 4:9

LITTLEMAYNE STONE AND LEYS

LOCATION: Littlemayne is 2 miles SE of Dorchester, on the A352 road to Wareham. The stones lie on the land of Littlemayne Farm, but access is usually given and the residents have given the author help in locating several of the stones. OS 1:50 000 sheet 194 and 1:25 000 'Purbeck & South Dorset' sheet. Grid reference: 723870.

Fig.90: Overview of the Littlemayne area. The numbered dots are stones found in 1993/4.

circle of stones is described in the Doomsday Book. In his book 'Ancient Dorset', Charles Warne tells of the following account he had received:

"April 1728. A mile SE of Dorchester at Prior's Maen, was a circle of stones lately broke to pieces by the owner, called Talbot."

In 1841 John Sydenham wrote (in Baal Durotrigensis) of stones at Littlemayne "......scattered over several fields ......a complete but small circle is to be seen (on south side of road) ......composed of 10 or 11 stones ......the circle is about 30ft diameter ......an exterior circle is also indicated. In the field on the other side of the road are many large stones ......to the SE are several large stones reared edgeways in a direct line, forming an avenue leading to the circles."

In 1847, a 30ft diameter circle of 10-11 stones could still be traced south of the A352. Charles Warne describes a visit to the site in 1868, in which he confirmed the destruction of the circle. But he did see a stone with a hole through the centre, 18" in diameter and 6ft deep! This stone, for certain, was fashioned by Man. He also describes two avenues of stones leading up to the main assemblage.

A trip in 1909 by the Dorset Natural History & Archaeological Society found 16 stones at the edge of a field, on the south side of the A352. One was reported to have a 12"

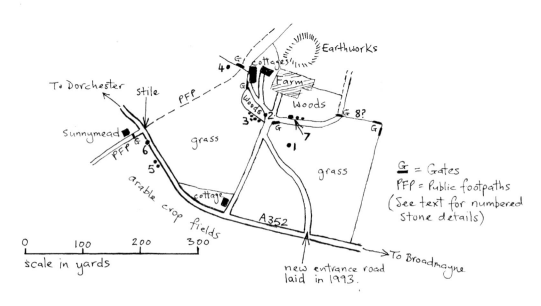

Plate 76: Stone 1 at Littlemayne (see Fig.90).

diameter hole through it and two were described as 'large at the NE end'.

Fig.90 shows the stones found by the author on a number of trips in 1993/4. Some stones were also seen built into walls and farm buildings.

Site 1 is the easiest to locate. It lies in the field east of the newer approach road. Plate 76 shows the stone. It is 6ft long and displays several hollows and craters (see site 3 below). Barry Cuff, of Milborne St. Andrew, has forwarded to me a copy of a c.1940's postcard showing this stone and another close by. The latter has now been either moved or destroyed.

Stone 2 lies half sticking out of a muddy bank on the west side of where three tracks meet. Some 3ft of stone is visible.

Site 3 is a group of 8 stones lying at the edge of a field, immediately south of a small wooded area. Plate 77 shows some of the stones. They are visible over the hedgerow from the lane to the farm. The largest stone is 6ft long and is tapered at one end and has depressions (often rain filled, as in Plate). Dowser Guy Underwood found such 'basin stones' to be centres of energy.

Stone 4 is a small stone, 2ft across but earthfast, next to a furze clump just west of where the PFP leaves the large field.

Site 5 is 2 stones that lie on the south side of the A352. They lie in the hedgerow and are best seen from the field side. The largest shows some 3.5 x 2.5ft of stone. Stone 6 is close by, to the north. It is seen protruding from the roadside verge. Some 5.5ft of stone is visible.

Site 7 is of special interest. Three stones lie at the edge of the woods, next to the track, but only visible from the track during the winter half of the year. Access to the woods can be made at the meeting of the tracks. The westernmost stone is the largest known to the author at Littlemayne to date. It is nearly 8ft long and 3ft in thickness. Nearby to the east is another large stone, some 5ft x 3ft. A third smaller one lies close by. All three stones are clothed in ivy and moss. A clean-up of the stones may repay the effort.

The farmer also informed me of a stone lying in the vicinity of '8' in Fig.90, but the author has been unable to confirm this.

So, some 19 stones are plotted to date. No doubt more may be uncovered in the woods, but it is difficult work. But the question is, do all these stones represent the remains of one circle or two? And what of the avenues Warne spoke of in the last Century? We may never know the answers, but one thing is certain:

Plate 77: Site 3 at
Littlemayne

potent and relevant today as they were over a hundred years ago:

> "......it seemed difficult to realise the fact that I was standing on hallowed ground. The few lichen-covered stones around me were all that the ignorance and destructiveness of men had left of a temple, within whose enclosures, in ages far beyond our ken, their forefathers had been accustomed to worship."

Originally, any ancient site positioned at Littlemayne would have had excellent views of distant skylines. However, woods, buildings and hedgerows now hinder research into past sunrise and sunset observances.

One marker, however, is still to be seen to this day. Looking to the south-west, from the field west of the farm approach roads, there are tumuli at 240 degrees on the distant skyline. These mark out on the landscape the Samhain and Imbolc sunsets.

It was of no surprise to find that two leys can be found associated with the Littlemayne circle(s). These are plotted in Fig.91.

The first runs from the village of nearby Broadmayne to two tumuli on Conygar Hill. One can see Broadmayne church to the south-east from Littlemayne. The view in the other direction is now impeded.

Another important ancient site has been ruined, due to ignorance and just a little greed. Charles Warne wrote these words after his visit to Littlemayne, and they are just as

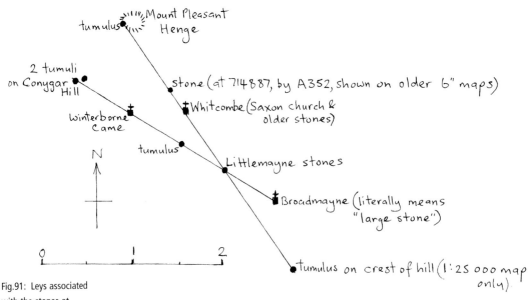

Fig.91: Leys associated
with the stones at
Littlemayne

The other ley runs from the once mighty henge at Mount Pleasant SSE to a tumulus south of Broadmayne. (This tumulus is not shown on 1:50 000 maps.)

"I HAVE FOUND THAT EVERY STANDING STONE IN THE BRITISH ISLES IS POSITIONED IN DIRECT ALIGNMENT WITH TWO OR MORE OTHER PREHISTORIC SITES."

John Williams

LITTON CHENEY STONES

LOCATION: Litton Cheney lies some 7 miles west of Dorchester, just south of the A35. Two sites lie north of the village, alongside the A35 (see Fig.92). OS 1:50 000 sheet 194 and 1:25 000 'Purbeck & South Dorset' sheet (see below for grid references).

Records exist of two sites of some antiquity that still had stones on site as late as the post-war period.

The diagram below shows the sites and although no stones appear to have survived agricultural activities, the localities are still worth a visit for they have some clues as to why the megaliths were erected.

The eastern site is on a prominent rise in the landscape, which gives excellent views of distant skylines. The word 'Earthwork' on OS maps marks the spot. Only a slight rise in the ground is now visible (grid reference: 556917).

Two circles could formerly be traced here, within 150ft of each other. The western one had a ditch, with a bank on the inside. It had a diameter of 125ft and 4 depressions on top of the banks suggest stones may have originally been present.

A second circle consisted of a shallow ditch 70ft across surrounding a flat area nearly 50ft in diameter. One sarsen was formerly to be seen on the south side and 3 more were seen scattered to the south, nearer the A35. It is not clear if the stones were from the circle, or an avenue leading to it.

The site has been dated as between 2200-1400 BC.

The views from the field of the earthworks are spectacular. Very distant horizons can be seen from the south right around to the north. Western views are obstructed, however. To the south, the prominent notches on the skyline are Abbotsbury Hillfort. The hill on which the Hardy Monument stands, as well as numerous tumuli, marks out the Winter Solstice sunrise as seen from here.

Fig.92: The location of two former stone sites near Litton Cheney.

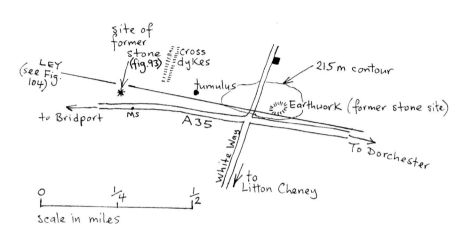

Scale in miles

(A)Enlarged view through telephoto lens. The small hillock or tumuli in the middle is only visible on clear days.

(B) Note how the nearer horizon cuts into the distant one at the key place to mark the sunset.

Fig.93: Samhain and Imbolc sunrises (A) and sunsets (B) marked out on the skyline seen from the western site NNW of Litton Cheney (see Fig.92).

To the left side of Fig.92 can be seen the second site. The view from this locality is uplifting, with a complete 360 degree horizon visible. In the field here was formerly seen a fallen stone, measuring 8ft x 7ft, thought to be a megalith from a chambered long barrow. Early OS maps marked it 'cromlech'.

The incredible number of key sunrises and sunsets marked out on the skyline testifies to the degree of precision that the stone was placed on the landscape. Fig.93 shows the views to 120 and 240 degrees and how the Samhain and Imbolc sunrises and sunsets are marked out by landscape features.

To the north-west, the Summer Solstice sunset is marked on the skyline. The sun sets in between two sharply defined summits, as shown in Fig.94. Incredibly, this view is only possible because of a DIP IN THE NEARER HILL!

To the SE, the Hardy Monument crowns the barrow-rich hill that marks out the Winter Solstice sunrise. To the west the bulk of Golden cap rises out of the sea and marks, from here, the Equinox sunsets.

A trip to the site in late July/August is recommended. At that time the field is full of beautiful small purple flowers.

Both Litton Cheney sites lie close to a ley line going to the Nine Stone circle, and beyond (see Fig.104 for details).

MAIDEN CASTLE TEMPLE AND LEYS

LOCATION: Maiden Castle is a huge earthwork overlooking Dorchester. Parking is available, with information boards to the north (marked on OS maps). OS 1:50 000 sheet 194 and 1:25 000 'Purbeck & South Dorset' sheet. Grid reference (of the temple): 672884.

Fig.94: Two prominent hills on the skyline mark out the Summer Solstice sunset seen from west stone site at Litton Cheney (Fig.92). A dip in the nearer hills makes this possible. Ancient Man saw twin peaks such as this as symbolic of the breasts of the Earth Goddess.

A trip to the top of the huge ramparts at Maiden Castle is always worth the steep walk up. This Iron Age hillfort was overcome in a bloody siege by the Romans, who then erected a temple within the old enclosure. Traces of older Neolithic structures on the hill, however, suggest a very ancient usage of the site. The Romans may have merely continued to use an already existing sacred place.

The temple was erected, along with an adjoining hut and house, between AD 350-

Plate 78: The Roman temple at Maiden Castle, from the south.

380, and was uncovered by Sir Mortimer Wheeler during 3 years of major excavations in 1934-37. The foundations of the temple are still visible today and are shown in Plate 78.

In the plate the inner cella, 16ft square, can be made out with an entrance to the right. An outer veranda had low walls originally sporting short pillars. The walls of the veranda were plastered and a brick floor was present. A wooden fence surrounded the whole temple and a path led to the east facing entrance.

A fine model reconstruction of the temple can be seen on display at the County Museum in Dorchester.

Recently, members of the Wessex Dowsers have dowsed a powerful spiral of energy in the centre of the temple.

The temple seems to represent the phase in Romano-British history were the Christian and pagan belief systems seemed to find common ground and recognised their similarities. Small bronze figures of the goddesses Minerva and Diana were found, along with a three-horned bull figure.

Various leys criss-cross and pass close to Maiden Castle. Two pass within 200yds of the temple itself. Fig.71 shows the course of the one coming up from Bincombe. Fig.82 shows the ley plotted from the Hellstone area, which passes just south of the temple. A ley plotted by Paul Devereux (in 'The Ley Hunter's Companion', 1979) passes just north of the temple and is shown in Fig.95 with amendments by the author. As a result of recent trips in the field, I have extended the ley to Owermoigne. An almost straight path follows the ley, between gaps in the woods, over the intervening hill between Warmwell and Owermoigne. I find that the ley only passes close to the long barrow by Maiden Castle, not, as Devereux cites, through it.

Fig.95: A ley from Owermoigne to North Hill, passing close to the Roman temple at Maiden Castle (not to scale, length of line 9 miles).

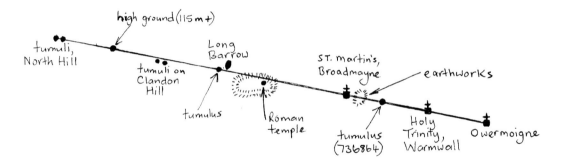

A barrow just south of it (shown on 1:25 000 maps) IS on the ley. The two tumuli on Clandon Hill, likewise, are not on the ley but close to it. However, I can confirm Devereux's claim that Maiden Castle IS visible from the tumuli on North Hill.

"ALL THE COUNTRY IS LAY'D FOR ME."

Shakespeare, Act 2, Henry VI.

MOUNT PLEASANT HENGE AND LEYS

LOCATION: This site lies on a prominent hilltop, on the eastern outskirts of Dorchester. The site is on private arable land, and permission should be sought before entry. A good view of the site can be obtained from the barrow to the SE of the henge. OS 1:50 000 sheet 194 and 1:25 000 'Purbeck & South Dorset' sheet. Grid reference: 710898.

Fig.96: The location of Mount Pleasant Henge and other features in the adjacent landscape mentioned in the text.

Below the fields of crops were found the remains of what was possibly Dorset's premiere prehistoric spiritual centre. A great henge once stood here, comparable in size with almost any henge in Britain in its heyday.

Fig.96 shows the landscape around Mount Pleasant. The data is chiefly drawn from the excavations of Geoffrey Wainwright and his team in 1970-71. His brilliant excavations of Mount Pleasant, Durrington Walls and Marden henges showed that our knowledge of them had been far too simplified.

The henge was a massive structure. The enclosure covered 12 acres (4.8-ha) surrounded by high banks. Within these banks were ditches up to 20yds wide. Various alterations to the henge were made over some 400 years. The basic henge was laid out around 2100 BC. At about 2000 BC a round timber structure was erected within the henge (the position is marked in Fig.96). At around 1700 BC this building was burnt down and replaced with a cove of stones, our chief interest at this site. A plan of the excavation of this phase of the inner enclosure is shown in Fig.97.

Many flakes of stone were found around the area, suggesting 'on site' shaping. The

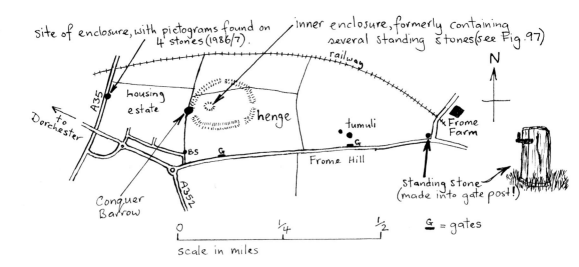

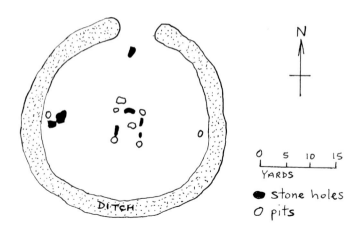

Fig.97: The inner enclosure, showing stone holes.

N

0 5 10 15
YARDS

● stone holes
O pits

DITCH

Fig.98: The leys associated with Mount Pleasant (due to the limitations of scale, the leys are not to scale). Inclusion of some features not on current maps shows the value of research using older maps. The ley to Stonehenge was plotted by Gordon Harris (unpub.).

to Stonehenge

Alvediston (church)

△ summit of Gore Hill

Berwick Down settlement & tumulus

field system, Cerne Park

● Settlement   Roman road

earthwork

N

site of Alington Avenue Neolithic Long barrow & Bronze Age enclosure (702 899)

● 2 cairns (677961) (not on OS maps)

● Dewlish (church)

site of Fordington Farm Barrows (699899)

● tumulus   ● Roman stone, Bockhampton

old maps show at stone at 681899 (now a school)

cross roads

Mount Pleasant

tumuli North Hill   tumulus (647899)   Maumbury Henge

● tumuli, Frome Hill

high point on Conygar Hill   WF   ● stone (on older 6"o.s)   Sandy Barrow

Herringston Barrow

Ridgeway tumuli   tumuli   ● Whitcombe (stone, church & earthworks)

pool by A35 with folklore

village earthworks, West Shilvinghampton   tumuli on Friar Waddon Hill

tumuli (710869)   Littlemayne Stones (former stone circle)

tumuli, by Club House   tumulus (733853)   spring (744830)

prominent hill west of Langton Herring   tumuli   ridge   tumulus on crest of hill (just off ley)

WF = site of the Medieval village of Winterbourne Farringdon.   The Knoll

△ numerous tumuli on East Hill

Fig.99: A drawing of the 1994 Samhain sunset from the barrow east of Mount Pleasant (enlarged from a photograph). The sunset is precisely marked on the landscape by the two barrows in the middle distance.

bases of some stones were still present in their holes, with stumps of sarsen remaining where the stones had been broken off. Some evidence was also found to suggest that some monoliths may have been erected within the ditch itself.

It is thought that the stones were broken up to facilitate Iron Age farming in the First Century BC, long after the henge had ceased in its importance as a ritual centre.

Wainwright suggests that Mount Pleasant marked a territorial culture group around 2000 BC that included all the coastal chalklands and the Tertiary basin of south Dorset. As well as a spiritual centre, he suggests that the henge, and ones like it, was a social hier-

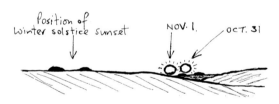

Fig.100: Observed positions of the sunset seen from Mount Pleasant over 2 days of the Samhain Festival, 1994.

archy epicentre.

A good view of the field that contains the flattened henge can be viewed from the tumuli on Frome Hill, to the east. A gate allows access (see Plate 4).

Looking down over the barren fields, it seems quite incredible that this area was the centre for ritual observances for several hundred years in the Bronze Age, nearly 3000 years ago. The importance of the henge is perhaps borne out by the fact that numerous leys emanate from the site like spokes of a wheel. Fig.98 shows the ones known to the author to date.

What can still be observed today from Mount Pleasant? The answer is: quite a lot,

including the use of the same two barrows for Winter Solstice AND Samhain/Imbolc sunsets!

From the henge (or indeed the road to the SW of it if access if not possible), the Winter Solstice is marked out beautifully by the two prominent barrows in the middle distance on Conygar Hill. However, standing on top of the barrow on Frome Hill (715896, see Fig.96), one can see the sun setting behind the Conygar Hill barrows on Samhain and Imbolc dates. The author in fact observed this at the Samhain Festival on November 1, 1994. Fig.99 is a drawing from a photograph taken by the author on that occasion. It was a beautiful sunset and one that will live in my memory forever. The sun and the landscape in harmony with Man.

Seen from Mount Pleasant itself, two sunsets are still to be seen marked out on the landscape. The two barrows on Conygar Hill, as already mentioned, mark out the Winter Solstice. But the Samhain/Imbolc sunset is more subtly marked by the meeting of Conygar Hill, Ridgeway and Maiden Castle. Fig.100 shows the view the author had on October 31 and November 1, 1994. For about 5-6 days, twice yearly, the sun sets within this 'window' between Maiden Castle and Conygar Hill.

Paul Devereux saw a similar 'Lammas window' at Avebury. Standing on top of Silbury Hill he observed that the sun, for only a few days every year, rose from behind a nearer hill, instead of the usual distant skyline. The situation at Mount Pleasant may be a 'negative' of the Avebury situation, but subtle use of the landscape by Man is readily observed.

Viewed from the henge, Imbolc and Samhain sunrises are marked by the barrow almost SE (in fact 120 degrees) from the centre of the henge. This is the barrow where we stood to see the Samhain sunset shown in Fig.99. This barrow clearly was an integral part of the Mount Pleasant ritual and astronomical system. Today, hundreds of motorists drive within yards of it everyday, not even knowing of its existence.

John North, in his book 'Stonehenge' found alignments of former posts and lintels at the henge to the stars Vega and Aldebaren c. 2100-2420 BC.

Fig.96 shows the position and a drawing of a standing stone to the east of Frome Hill (grid reference: 718896). It stands at a road junction on a grass verge. Used as a gatepost in the past, any relationship to Mount Pleasant is uncertain.

NINE STONES CIRCLE AND LEYS

LOCATION: Four miles west of Dorchester, just past Winterbourne Abbas, next to the A35. The circle is shown and named on OS maps. English Heritage maintain this Ancient Monument and although there is a fence (with a gate) around the stones, the author has always found the site 'open'. OS 1:50 000 sheet 194 and 1:25 000 'Purbeck & South Dorset' sheet. Grid reference: 611904. (NB: the road here is busy and 'fast'. Parking is best at a small pull-in at Grange Farm Dairy to the east, on the opposite side of the road.)

This fine circle nestles atmospherically under the shade of a huge beech tree but suffers, unfortunately, from its close proximity to the A35.

The circle, which dates from the period 2200-1400BC, was much visited by early antiquarians. John Aubrey visited it in the 17th Century, his sketches being included in his 'Monutmenta Britannica (1665-93)'. His figures of the Nine Stones are shown in Fig.101.

The active antiquarian and self-confessed Druid, William Stukeley, visited the circle in 1723 and the sketch shown in Fig.102 was included in his 'Itinerarium Curiosum'. As was often the case, he exaggerated the size of the stones compared to human figures. We shall return to his sketch later, regards to the tumuli shown on the distant skyline.

More recently, Alexander Thom visited the circle as part of his massive survey of Britain's stone circles. Paul Devereux also describes earth energy phenomena and a ley associated with the stone. (The folklore and phenomena related to the circle is described in Chapter 3.)

The stone circle is in fact an ellipse, elongated along the SE-NE axis. At the NE end there is a space. A record in 1872 speaks of a tenth stone hereabouts, even though the early sketches (Figs. 101 and 102) show fewer.

The internal diameter of the circle is 23.5ft W-E and 27.5ft N-S. A plan of the stones is shown in Fig.103. Alexander Thom demonstrated that the circle is laid out using the Megalithic Yard (MY) which we looked at on page 11. He gives a length of 11my for the major axis and 5.5my for the minor one.

Fig.101: John Aubrey's 17th Century drawings of the Nine Stones.

Fig.102: Stukeley's 1723 drawing of the Nine Stones. Note the alignment of barrows on the skyline with the tallest stone (see text).

Fig.102: Stukeley's 1723 drawing of the Nine Stones. Note the alignment of barrows on the skyline with the tallest stone (see text).

Fig.103: (below) The Nine Stones with alignments: 42°: high winter moonrise; 51°: summer solstice sunrise, astronomical direction. 53°: summer solstice sunrise; 63°: Beltaine/Lamas sunrise; 94°: Equinox sunrises; 300°: summer solstice sunset. (the directions above vary from the theoretical due to the close proximity of the skylines.)

The perimeter is 32.28my and varies from exact 'my' dimension by an error of just 0.22! The following quote by Thom is noteworthy:

"......1000 years before classical Greek mathematics, people in Britain were building astronomical structures using Pythagorean theorum."

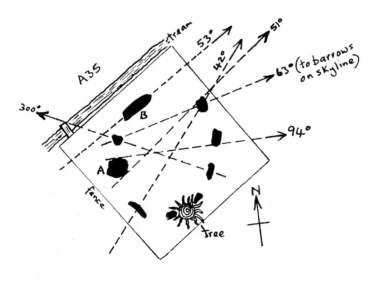

The tallest stone is stone 'A' on Fig.103. Plate 79 shows the stone from the north. It is 7ft high and weighs around 8 tons. Its pillar-like shape reminds us of many of the Avebury stones, the Broadstone and the Harp Stone. Such stones are thought to represent the male principle and phallic symbolism is so suggested.

Stone 'B' is a much squarer shape, possibly representing the Earth Goddess. It is about 6ft in height. Plate 80 shows the stone just to the left of centre. All the stones are typical hard sarsens.

So why was the circle placed where it was? Certainly, if the circle was meant for purely astronomical purposes a much better site may have been found on an adjacent hilltop. As at Rempstone and the Harp Stone, the locality is in a shallow valley on a slope with limited distant skyline views.

Clearly, a PLACE OF POWER (to use Devereux's term) is suggested, the locality on the LIVING LANDSCAPE being of prime importance to the circle's users. In China, feng-shui practitioners who laid out buildings and tombs according to the energies present, thought that at secluded and sheltered places the 'power of the dragon pulse' was at its height. They thought that in open country the power dissipates.

Even today, dowsers have proven consistently that subtle energies cross the landscape. A connection between these forces and stone sites is well proven.

Some ritual placing of the stones themselves is present: Summer Solstice sunsets go down between the two largest stones in the circle ('A' and 'B' in Fig.103). This sunset, seen from the centre of the circle, is marked by the small stone in between the two large ones, framed perfectly by the latter.

We have already seen how two barrows on the skyline to the NE mark a key sunrise (page 32 and Fig.16). Barrows visible on the skyline in Fig.102 formerly marked the Equinox sunsets. This view is now obscured by intervening trees.

Now let us turn our attention outwards to the landscape around the Nine Stones. Fig.104 shows leys associated with the Nine Stones.

The ley going from Askerswell to Flower's Barrow is one plotted by Paul Devereux, with amendments by the author. The two stones on the ley to Stonehenge, at 583873, and at Muckleford, were found by the author before any knowledge of the Gordon Harris ley was forthcoming. Independent confirmation indeed.

Despite the proximity to the busy A35, the Nine Stones are very worthy of a visit. Nestling under the branches of the huge beech, surrounded by stones erected thou-

sands of years ago, one may feel close indeed to something we lost. A 'something' that we are only now reclaiming.

"WITHIN THE PERFECT SYMMETRY OF A CIRCLE IS HELD THE ESSENTIAL NATURE OF THE UNIVERSE. STRIVE TO LEARN FROM IT ......TO REFLECT THAT ORDER."

XXI Stanza of Merlin, 12th C.

Plate 79: Stone 'A' at Nine Stones, from the north. Stone 'B' is next to the photographer.

Plate 80: The Nine Stones from the south. A gap is seen at the far side.

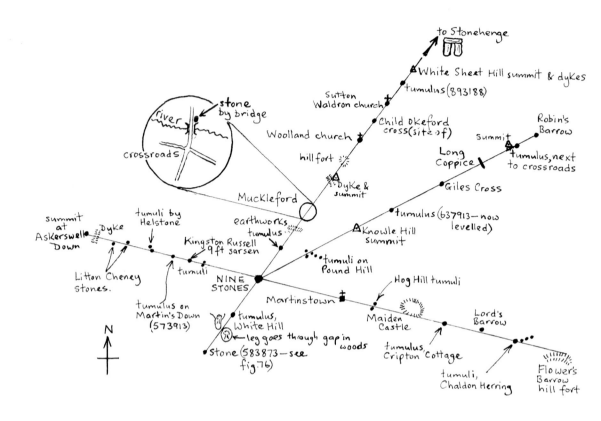

to Stonehenge

White Sheet Hill summit & dykes
tumulus (893188)

Sutton
Waldron church

stone
by bridge

river

Woolland church

Child Okeford
cross (site of)

Robin's
Barrow

Summit

Long
Coppice

tumulus, next
to crossroads

crossroads

hill fort

Giles Cross

Muckleford

Dyke &
summit

tumulus (637913—now
levelled)

summit
at
Askerswell
Down

Dyke

tumuli by
Helstone

earthworks

tumulus

Knowle Hill
summit

Kingston Russell
9ft sarsen

tumuli on
Pound Hill

Litton Cheney
Stones.

tumuli

NINE
STONES

Hog Hill tumuli

Martinstown

tumulus on
Martin's Down
(573913)

tumulus,
White Hill

Maiden
Castle

Lord's
Barrow

N

leg goes through gap in
woods

tumulus,
Cripton Cottage

Stone (583873 — see
fig.76)

tumuli,
Chaldon Herring

Flower's
Barrow
hill fort

THE PORTESHAM AREA

LOCATION: Several stones, both natural and some erected by Man, are scattered in and around Portesham and they have been grouped under one heading. Fig.105 shows the chief sites of interest. OS 1:50 000 sheet 194 and 1:25 000 'Purbeck & South Dorset' sheet.

The problem in the Portesham area is to interpret the large number of naturally weathering-out sarsens that lie around the fields, and even still litter the village centre itself. Which ones were used by Prehistoric Man?

How many are in their present localities due to field clearances? How can we tell which were once standing as a result of human endeavours?

To hopefully answer at least some of these questions, we will now go into the field using old records and folklore to give us clues. Fig.105 shows the stone site localities, designated A-H. We will look at them in this order.

For the sites to the north of Portesham village, park up at the lay-by almost opposite the track to Hampton Barn(this is the place we use for visits to the Hellstone and the Hampton Hill stone circle).

The path east is followed and, ignoring signs to the Hellstone, the second large field along will be found to be home to 3 large sarsens (site 'A', grid reference: 606869). Plate 81 shows the stones. The stones are all 6ft+ in length, one being almost 6ft square.

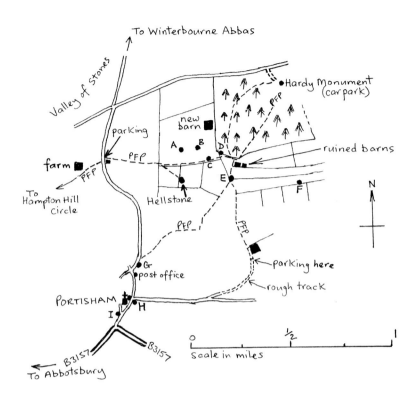

To Winterbourne Abbas

Valley of Stores

parking

new barn

A • • B

D

farm ■

PFP

PFP

To Hampton Hill Circle

Hellstone

PFP

• Hardy Monument (car park)

PFP

ruined barns

C

E •

• F

N

PFP

PFP

G

• post office

parking here

rough track

PORTISHAM

I •

• H

B3157

B3157

0   ½   1

Scale in miles

To Abbotsbury

One stone (the nearest in the plate) is smoother and semi-earthfast. The other two clearly just rest on the surface and still have loose stones and earth attached to them. Numerous small stones lie scattered around. This suggests they were quite recently either dug up or moved from elsewhere.

Hutchins, in 1774, speaks of numerous stones around here. Field trips by archaeologists in 1906 and 1908 reported four stones near to this spot. They also speak of large stones incorporated into nearby walls. The latter report also suggests that a hole was made for them and that they were 'decently interred'. The report of a 'ceremony' of sorts does suggest that the stones were either once standing or, at the very least, held with some respect by locals.

The next part of this tale takes us a little further east in the same field. Hutchins reported four stones associated with the following rhyme:

"Jeffrey and Jone,
And their little dog Denty and Edy alone."

Charles Warne reported, in 1866, that the stones had been taken up by the local farmer and built into adjoining walls. The site appears to have been destroyed around 1855. On the 1888 OS map the site is shown as 'Standing Stones (site of)'. The position is site 'B' on Fig.105 (grid reference: 607870).

The question is, do the stories of the 'ceremonial burial' and 'built into adjoining walls'

Plate 81: Sarsen stones near the Hellstone, see text.

relate to the same set of four stones? Certainly they lie in the same field which would support the burial tale. But numerous large stone blocks can be seen in nearby walls also, particularly in the foot the N-S wall at the east end of the field.

Plate 82: Stone 'C' near Portesham.

This leads us nicely to site 'C'. This stone stands against an E-W running wall, just to the east of the two previous sites (grid reference: 608868 - just west of a prominent tree that stands by the same wall).

Here, a standing stone has been utilised in

Plate 83: (below) Stone 'F' near Portesham. One yard of tape is shown.

the wall construction (see Plate 82). It is 5ft tall and has a maximum width of about 3.5ft. It is of typical hard, flinty sarsen. The top is noticeably tapered. Is this one of the 'Jeffrey and Jone' stones?

Leaving the field containing A-C, via the east gate, there is a stone lying just past the gate to one's left (stone 'D', grid reference: 608869). About 3ft across, it is noticeably hollowed out in the centre. Its age and purpose is unknown. Site 'E' was reported to the author by Sandra Harding, formerly of Portesham School.

At grid reference: 609867 (approx.), she tells us of 'one tall thick stone and two shorter ones'. They were located next to the west path of the two that go down to the old barns. The author has not as yet been able to confirm their survival.

Stone 'F' lies at grid reference: 615866, next to an E-W running dry stone wall. The stone was still standing in the 1970's, the Royal Commission on Historical Monuments describing it as 'slab-like, 3ft high'.

In October 1993, the author located what he believes to be the stone. Plate 83 shows the stone lying, as it now does, against a dry stone wall much in need of repair. The present aspect is a very sorry state of affairs. It has been dumped unceremoniously on a crumbling wall. The stone formerly lay to the north of its present position directly on, I believe, a ley. This ley is shown in Fig.82. Stone 'E' may also be associated with the same ley.

Several sarsens can be seen lying, and in some cases STANDING, within Portesham village itself. At point 'G' (Fig.105) several large stones can be seen on the east side of the lane, north of the Post Office. Several stones are set into walls. Guy Underwood found that such stones are still foci for energy lines!

Site 'H' is a group of several stones, east and north-east of the church. Two huge ones are set into the churchyard wall. Some stones are built into the walls of cottages. Plate 84 shows one such case at the corner of the road to Waddon. it is reminiscent of some of Alfred Watkin's photos of markstones. Guy Underwood found these stones had C-shaped energy patterns when dowsed.

Site 'I' is at the centre of the village, next

the a BT callbox. Two prone sarsens, up to 3ft long, show the typical flinty sarsen composition.

Whilst most of the sarsens scattered throughout the village are without question natural, some have clearly been used by locals for many generations. Early Man came to areas such as this, where sarsens were lying around in blocks at the surface, and carried off huge stones to erect sacred megalithic sites.

PUNCKNOWLE AND SWYRE

LOCATION: The neighbouring villages of Puncknowle and Swyre are about 4 miles west of Abbotsbury, on the B3157. OS 1:50 000 sheet 194 and 1:25 000 'Purbeck & South Dorset' sheet (see below for individual site grid references).

ur first stop is the churchyard of the parish church of St. Mary, Puncknowle. To the NE of the chancel stands the village cross. It formerly stood elsewhere in the village, exactly where it is not know. Plate 85 shows the cross.

The cross is dated early 15th Century and the material is Ham Hill stone. This cross appears somehow to have escaped the Puritans of the 17th Century. Perhaps, like the altar at Corton, it was hidden by the villagers.

The shaft is 8ft 6ins high and is octagonal. The socket stone below is 18" deep with moulded edges. The base may have been added, or at least altered, sometime later. At the top of the cross, the head is now absent.

To the south of the cross, at the SE corner of the churchyard, are spread around some flat, low stones. These are in fact Roman in age and were found on The Knoll in the 1960's. Note the hollows in some of them, thought to be for offerings to the gods and the dead.

At the crossroads at Swyre (grid reference: 527882, shown on 1:25 000 maps) formerly stood an old stone cross. Alfred Pope, in 1906, spoke of the demise of the stones,

which he considered to be a wayside cross, the type erected for travellers and pilgrims. Some low stones on a grass verge are all that remain of the cross today. The modern cross stands nearby.

To the north of the crossroad stands the church at Swyre (grid reference: 528882).

Plate 84: Stone at the junction of the road to Waddon, at the village of Portesham.

The author has found evidence that a large stone once lay to the east of the church. In November 1851, John Baverstock Knight painted a water colour of the church, which is reproduced in Fig.106. The stone can be seen to the left-hand side, with a figure leaning against it.

A search by the author and his wife Gemma in July 1994 failed to locate any stones in the churchyard and the fields to the east of the church. Such a large (pagan?) stone within church grounds may have caused offence!

Excavations in the late 1950's by Ernest Greenfield revealed two tumuli in the

Plate 85: The Puncknowle
Cross.

Fig.105(b): Leys associated
with stone sites in the
Puncknowle and Swyre
area (not to scale).

mation surrounded by 3 stone slabs. These
were in turn covered by a cairn of stones, possibly overlaid with a ring of stones.

We can now look at how the above sites in
the Puncknowle and Swyre area fit into the
landscape and link to other ancient localities.

Two leys passing though the site of the old
stone cross at Swyre would suggest that, once
again, the cross replaced a much older markstone (see Fig.105b). The Knoll is a prominent hill, visible for many miles around and
early Man clearly used this factor to good
effect. Further leys (additional to those shown
in Fig.105b, but not involving stones) radiate
from The Knoll, indicating its ritual importance to our ancestors. Alfred Watkins, in
'The Old Straight Track', plots a long ley running from Beacon Knap through Cerne Abbas
to Stonehenge.

RIDGEWAY SAXON STONES

LOCATION: Numerous stones line an
old Saxon boundary in the vicinity of
the Hardy Monument, NE of
Portesham. OS 1:50 000 sheet 194
and 1:25 000 'Purbeck & South
Dorset' sheet (see text for individual
site grid references).

Puncknowle parish that had stones incorporated within their structure. The first
('Puncknowle 1', grid reference: 533878) lies
on the west side of The Knoll. He found the
outer lining of the barrow to be a loose cairn
of stones, reverted by inward-sloping slabs.

The other barrow ('Puncknowle 6', grid
reference: 541871) lies on Limekiln Hill,
north of the B3157. Greenfield found a cre-

In the 1970's, Sandra Harding, then the
Head of Portesham School, lead a school
project to interpret the Saxon Charter of
1024, marking the boundary of Orc. The
results below are based on that project (pers.
comm. to the author). Fig. 107 shows the rel-

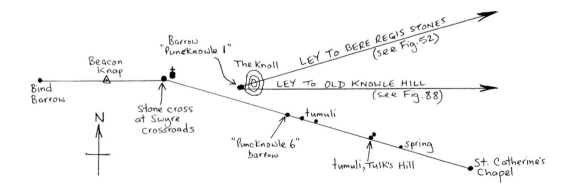

evant area with the stone sites so far encountered.

The stone slabs can be up to 4ft high but are only a few inches thick, local thin-splitting limestones being employed by the Saxons to mark out the boundaries of the land. Most appear to stand in their original positions but some (such as those used at the Hardy Monument to stop cars rolling down slopes!) have been moved. The two stones either side of the car park entrance may be in their original positions, however, as they line up with the stones further to the east (Fig.107). Numerous stones appear through the undergrowth as one walks down the lane from the car park entrance. A winter visit is best to see many of them. Along the Ridgeway Path (signposted as the Dorset Coast Path) many stone slabs can be seen.Plate 86 shows the large stones just before the gate marked in Fig.107.

The Saxon boundary turns south at Corton Down and some of the slabs have been used in the construction of stiles. Sandra Harding speaks of further stone slabs as the boundary goes west from Coryates to Portesham, some incorporated into bridges and others as gate posts.

Guy Underwood considered slab stone markers to be associated with 'Holy ways".

STINSFORD ROMAN STONE

LOCATION: Immediately west of the roundabout at Stinsford, where the B3150 meets the A35. The stone stands on the grassy bank on the south side of the B3150. OS 1:50 000 sheet 194 and 1:25 000 'Purbeck & South Dorset' sheet. Grid reference: 708912.

Fig.106: 1851 painting by John Baverstock Knight of Swyre Church. Note the large stone next to the figures.

This fine standing stone, thought to be a Roman milestone, is made of local fossiliferous limestone. At present about 3ft of stone protrudes above the grass (see Plate 87) but when it was moved in 1956

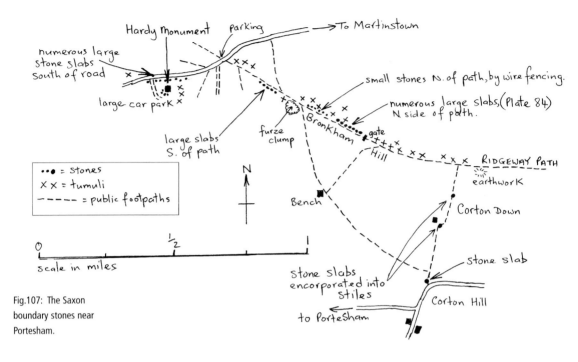

Fig.107: The Saxon
boundary stones near
Portesham.

Plate 86: Saxon boundary
stones, Bronkham Hill. The
ancient Ridgeway track
passes the stones on the
left, passing tumuli on the
skyline

(for a second time) it was measured at
5ft 10ins long (see Plate 88). A prominent
groove can be seen about 1.5ft below the top
of the stone. This groove may have been a
later addition to the stone, perhaps to attach
chains. Records on 1906 show that the stone
was known locally as the 'bull-baiting stone'.

The fact that the stone was used by the Romans to mark out their road is unquestionable. But a debate exists as to whether the Romans simply utilised and improved an ALREADY EXISTING system of STRAIGHT tracks that criss-crossed the landscape. Are we talking here of leys?

Fig.49 shows the route of the Roman road from Badbury Rings to the Stinsford stone. One can clearly see that the route is marked out by many PRE-ROMAN markers, as well as crosses and churches which, as we have seen on previous occasions, may well have evolved from pre-Roman pagan sites.

The reader is referred back to page 26 where the tale was told of an apparition of a Roman soldier along the course of the Roman road at Stinsford.

Also, whilst in the area, a visit to Stinsford Church is worthwhile. Inside is a Pre-Conquest carving of a standing angel.

VALLEY OF STONES AND CROW HILL

LOCATION: Valley of Stones and Crow Hill are both marked on OS maps. They lie to the NNE of Portesham within the parish of Littlebredy. OS 1:50 000 sheet 194 and 1:25 000 'Purbeck & South Dorset' sheet.

Fig.108 shows the area to be looked at, with particular sites in the text highlighted.

The stones to the west of Crow Hill can be reached via two gates directly opposite Basket Hill Cottage (grid reference: 595883). Permission to visit this land should be sought from Bridehead House, Littlebredy (grid reference: 589888).

The gate opposite the cottage is entered. You then head towards a second gate in front of you, near the brown tiled sheds. Standing at the second gate, one can already see stones littering the field.

The vestiges of an earthen enclosure are soon encountered, with 2 sarsen stones lying on the east side of the much-denuded bank. The older OS maps show further stones inside the banks, but these have now gone.

Although the sarsens in this valley are lying around at the surface due to natural erosion, were any of the utilised AT THIS LOCALITY by early Man? The man-made enclosure is an archaeological fact and if the stones around and IN it were not a part of its structure, why were they not cleared out of the way?

Sarsens from this valley, and the Valley of Stones, may have been used to build the ancient monuments we see scattered all around the surrounding landscape. Why dig huge stones out of the ground when a plentiful supply is lying all around?

We have seen elsewhere that sacred sites are often in valleys, or near the foot of gentle slopes. I believe that the stones seen next to this enclosure, and those which were once inside it, may have been an integral part of it.

If we continue south along the valley floor, we soon come to numerous stones of all manner of shape and size. At the far end of

Plate 87: (far left) Stinsford stone.

Plate 88: (left) The full extent of the Stinsford stone is revealed in this 1956 view, seen during relocation.

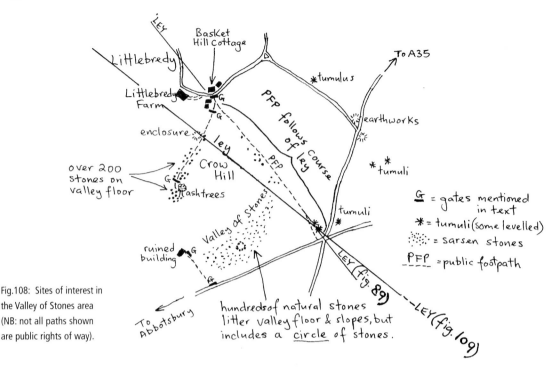

Fig.108: Sites of interest in the Valley of Stones area (NB: not all paths shown are public rights of way).

the field lies the greatest concentration. Just inside the next field, under a large ash tree, are the biggest ones seen here. Some of the stones here are over 6ft across, one being measured at +8ft. More stones nestle, encrusted with moss and lichen, under ash trees. Plate 89 sets the scene. The area is a place of quiet contemplation,.

Plate 89: Sarsen stones at Crow Hill, Littlebredy.

The reader is referred back to Fig.88. A ley running from The Knoll to Old Knowle Hill passes to within a FEW YARDS of the enclosure at Crow Hill. Once again we ask ourselves, is it just coincidence?

Another ley plotted by the author is shown in Fig.109. The ley is very 'tight', with markers close together on the landscape.

Of interest are the former standing stones at the eastern extremity of the ley. These are described on page 143 and Fig.105 (site 'B'). On several occasions the author has encountered seemingly isolated stones (and old reports of ones now departed) that were found at a later date to lie on leys and thus CONNECTED with other sites.

Also in the area, the woods around grid reference 584888, west of Littlebredy church, are called 'Stone Hills Plantation', another possible inference of former stones.

We will now turn our attention to the nearby Valley of Stones. As the reader may recall, the hundreds of sarsen stones that litter the valley were reputed to have been thrown there by the Devil. The stones have in fact weathered out naturally and have been lying around as such since Prehistoric times.

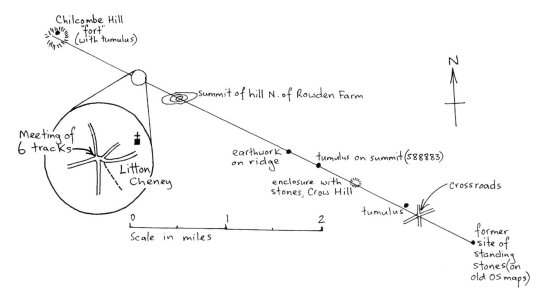

Chilcombe Hill "fort" (with tumulus)

Summit of hill N. of Rowden Farm

N

Meeting of 6 tracks

Litton Cheney

earthwork on ridge

tumulus on summit (588883)

enclosure with stones, Crow Hill

crossroads

tumulus

0   1   2

Scale in miles

former site of standing stones (on old OS maps)

It seems only logical to assume that this plentiful supply of large stones would have been used by Neolithic and Bronze Age Man for megalithic construction.

But were any of the stones erected for ritual purposes IN THE VALLEY ITSELF? Trips early this Century by archaeologists noted some stones appeared to be arranged into circles, which some of them took to be 'enclosures' (a nice term: they didn't know if they were houses, animal paddocks or stone circles per se. 'Enclosure' helps archaeologists out now and then!).

The Historical Monuments Survey of 1952 noted two circles 'NE of Black Down Barn'. They in fact produced a clear photograph of a circle of stones, shown in Plate 90. Plate 91 shows a 1909 photo of the same circle.

The author has visited the site on several occasions and clear views such as these can only be obtained during winter/early spring, due to the tall grasses and nettles that carpet the valley at other times.

As a guide, the circle lies just west of the first telegraph pole that actually stands within the gentler slopes of the valley, as opposed to the ones that line the steeper east slopes. The circle is 71ft x 60ft and all the stones lie

prone. The circle was clearly designed by the removal of stones that would formerly have littered the inside.

What the author found curious was that two of the largest sarsen stones of the valley occur very close to the circle, in fact on OPPOSITE sides of it. Fig.110 shows their position. Stone 'A' (arrowed in plates 90 and 91) lies half prone approximately 40yds NE of the circle. It is 10ft long and about 2.5ft thick. It leans out of the ground at about 40 degrees.

Fig.109: Ley associated with the Crow Hill enclosure and stones.

Plate 90: 1952 photo of a 'sarsen enclosure', Valley of Stones (stone 'A' - see text)

Fig.110: Stones 'A' and 'B' described in the text, near the circle of stones, Valley of Stones (non-relevant sarsens are now shown).

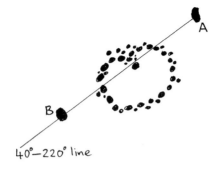

B

40°–220° line

Plate 91: A 1909 view of the same circle of stones, from the east slopes of the valley.

Guy Underwood called these sloping stones 'Rostra'. He found the tips of them to mark energy nodes.

On the other side of the circle, on a heading of about 220 degrees from the circle and at around the same distance, is stone 'B'. This huge stone is 10ft x 6.5ft and around 3ft thick. This stone is full of hollows and pot-holes, which are common enough features of sarsen stones, it must be said. However, one hole on the top surface (shown in Plate 92) may be a different matter. This cavity is 5" deep and conical, tapering up to a 5" diameter opening.

The purpose of the cavity is unknown. It may have been a post-hole. Another possibil-ity is that it may have ritualistic origins, such as certain Roman stones, which have hollows for offerings to the gods. The stone is typical of Underwood's 'basin stones'. He found energy nodes associated with them.

Plate 92: Cone-shaped cavity in stone 'B', Valley of Stones.

WHITCOMBE

LOCATION: Whitcombe lies 1.5 miles SE of Dorchester, on the A352. OS 1:50 000 sheet 194 and 1:25 000 'Purbeck & South Dorset' sheet. Grid reference (of the church): 717883.

Three stones of interest can be seen in and around the 12th Century church. As one crosses the field from the road, a stone can be seen leaning into the churchyard wall, to the right of the gate. The stone is arrowed in Plate 93 and a close up of it is shown in Plate 94. Alfred Watkins saw in his native Herefordshire many old stones occurring in churchyard walls.

limestone and leans into the wall at about 45 degrees. The wall has clearly been built AROUND THE STONE, indicating its antiquity.

Moving now into the churchyard, a 14-15th Century cross shaft and base can be seen SW of the porch (see Plate 95). The rectangular shaft is 2ft 8" in height and 12" square at its base. It fits very badly into a plain square base, which appears to be older. Both shaft and base are of Portland-Ridgeway limestone.

The interior of this small church is very atmospheric and has an ancient feel to it.

Plate 93: Whitcombe Church. The arrow marks the stone seen in close-up in Plate 94.

Plate 95: (left) The old churchyard cross at Whitcombe.

Plate 94: Stone leaning into the churchyard wall, Whitcombe Church.

Watkins took this as a sure indication that many Christian sites had 'grown' from ancient ley markers and other pagan sites. At nearby West Stafford, another small stone can similarly be seen against the churchyard wall (grid reference: 726896; see Fig.82 for association with ley).

The Whitcombe stone is 17" wide and 35" protrudes out of the earth. It is a block of

Plate 96: The Saxon stones inside Whitcombe church (inset shows interlacing).

Directly in front as one enters the chancel are two fragments of Saxon 10th Century crosses. They were discovered built into the east wall of the chancel during repairs in 1912. The interlaced carving still stands out well in relief. Plate 96 shows the fragments. More fragments of possible Saxon age lie loose at the west end of the chancel.

The stone by the churchyard wall and numerous earthworks found around the church may indicate a much older, pre-Christian, sacred site. To the SW of the church a line of barrows stand out on the sky-line between 190 and 230 degrees. These, and others, mark out Winter Solstice, Samhain and Imbolc sunsets as seen from Whitcombe (the barrows at around the 240 degree heading are now obscured by trees).

Fig.91 shows how the church lies on a ley associated with both the great henge at Mount Pleasant and the Littlemayne stones. This is a sure sign of a pre-Christian site.

Plate 97: The remaining stones of the Winterbourne Steepleton Cromlech.

WINTERBOURNE STEEPLETON CROMLECH AND CROSS

LOCATION: Winterbourne Steepleton lies about 3 miles west of Dorchester, and the junction of the A35 and B3159. OS 1:50 000 sheet 194 and 1:25 000 'Purbeck & South Dorset' sheet. Grid references: Church 629898; Cromlech 614897. (Permission to see the cromlech stones should be sought from Combe Farm. The stones lie to the rear of it.)

Stones probably representing a chambered barrow can be located on the slopes above Combe Farm. The stones are marked 'Burial Chamber (remains of)' on the 1:25 000 map. Older maps show it as 'rems of Cromlech'. Charles Warne, in 1872, described the stones as lying 'in a confused heap covered by nettles'.

Plate 97 shows the present state of the site, which seems to have improved since Warne's lifetime. The largest stone is 8ft x 5ft. To the east it is another, 4ft x 2ft. Three smaller stones are also in attendance. The stones are thought to lie at the east end of a levelled E-W orientated mound. The mound is now reduced to a slight rise, less than 2ft high.

Plate 98: Cross base outside the church at Winterbourne Steepleton.

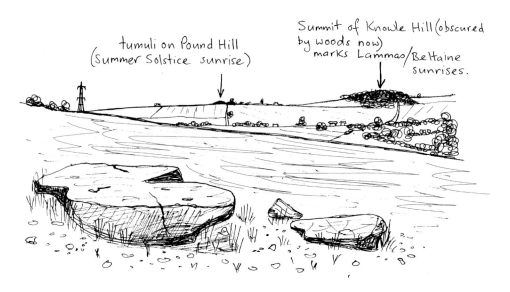

tumuli on Pound Hill
(Summer Solstice sunrise)

Summit of Knowle Hill (obscured
by woods now)
marks Lammas/Beltaine
sunrises.

Fig.111: Key sunrises marked on the landscape as seen from the Winterbourne Steepleton Cromlech (drawn from a photograph by the author).

Geomantic aspects of this site have already been touched upon. On page 33 we saw how the same barrows are seen to mark sunrises of DIFFERENT pagan festivals depending on whether they are viewed from the Nine Stones or this site. Fig.16 shows the barrows from the Nine Stones. Fig.111 is a view towards the same barrows from the cromlech stones.

From tumuli just west of the cromlech Lammas and Beltaine sunrises are marked by Knowle Hill on the skyline. I believe that the Winter Solstice sun rising over the summit of the hill to the SE of the cromlech also influenced its siting.

In Winterbourne Steepleton village we find the church of St. Michael. In the churchyard, next to the porch door, lies the base of a medieval cross. It lies loose and solitary. Plate 98 shows it next to the porch wall.

Inside the church is the famous 'Flying Angel'. This is a Saxon stone relief some 25" x 15" in size. It was formerly on an external wall but is now fixed to the wall of the inner chancel. Fig.13 shows a sketch of the stone. Similar ones have been found at Bradford-on-Avon.

The chancel is also graced by a 12th Century font.

Fig.13 also shows the church to lie on a ley that runs south from Holwell. Fig.52 shows that another ley passes the church on its way from Woodbury Hill to the Knoll. Both leys point to a site of some antiquity, prior to the building of the present church. Site evolution rearing its persistent head once more.

"CRAWL TO YOUR EARTH
MOTHER SHE WILL SAVE YOU
FROM THE VOID."

Rigveda, XVIII, 10.

Chapter Eight

The WEST AREA

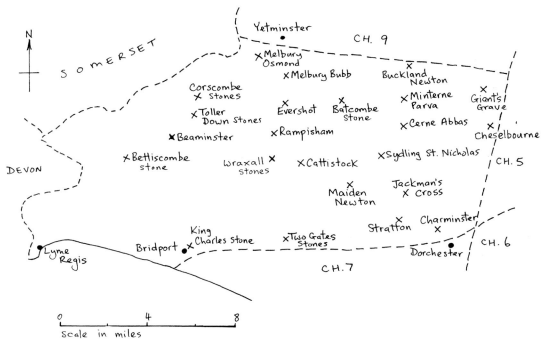

Fig.112: Location map for sites in the West area. NB: additional sites may be found under these main site headings

he countryside included in this area is shown in Fig.112, which also shows the localities to be visited. The region is covered with rolling hills and picturesque villages and many of the sites of interest lie in unspoilt areas. The western boundary of the area is defined by the borders with Devon and Somerset. The southern limit approximates with the A35 between Bridport and Dorchester. The northern and eastern borders meet at the village of Ansty Cross.

BEAMINSTER AND BROADWINDSOR

LOCATION: The Robinson Memorial in the centre of the town marks the site of an old cross. OS 1:50 000 sheet 193. Grid reference: 480013.

his old stone cross is reported to have been 'wantonly destroyed' around 1750. It is suggested here that the cross was in fact a replacement of an older stone that formerly marked out the course of a ley. Fig.113 shows the proposed ley and its route will be seen to pass three more stone sites; at Rampisham (2 stone crosses) and Minterne Parva (an obviously Christianised stone) and the stone at Sliding Hill.

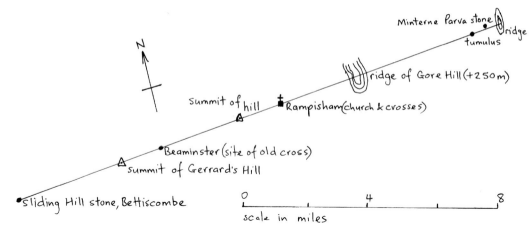

Fig.113: Ley associated with the former Beaminster cross and other stone sites.

Fig.114: Ley associated with Sliding Hill (after Hitching, with amendments by the author).

At Broadwindsor, a 2ft stone lies on the church side of the crossroads in the village centre. This is further evidence of a ley previously plotted by Gordon Harris which runs from Lamberts Castle right up to Stonehenge, via other ancient sites.

BETTISCOMBE STONES

LOCATION: On the slopes of Sliding Hill, NE of Bettiscombe Church, within the grounds of Bettiscombe Manor (permission to see the stone should be sought).
OS 1:50 000 sheet 193.

n the hill, the Ordnance Survey mapped a megalith in 1887. It was reported to be 4ft high and up to 7" thick. The stone has since disappeared.

However, near the northern foot of the hill (directions from the Manor) there lies a sarsen some 9ft x 7ft. Jeremy Harte noted in 1986 that the title of 'standing stone' seems to have been transferred to the sarsen. In fact, Sliding Hill may have acquired its name from the local folklore that the stone goes down the hill on Midsummer Eve, to return the next day.

Francis Hitching cites a very compact ley involving Sliding Hill (which is shown in Fig.114) in his book 'Earth Magic'.

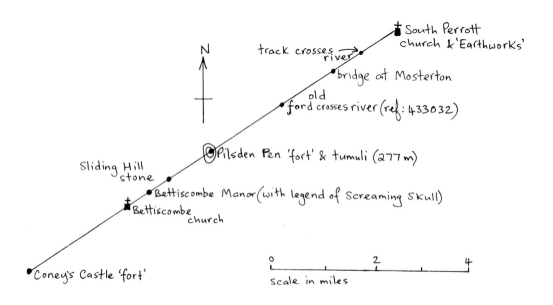

BUCKLAND NEWTON WARRIOR

LOCATION: Buckland Newton is situated on the B3143, 3 miles NE of Cerne Abbas. The stone is in the Church of the Holy Rood. OS 1:50 000 sheet 194. Grid reference: 687053.

The stone 'Warrior' is a Saxon pre-Conquest carved stone. It is set into the wall over the south doorway. It is 7-8th Century. The matrix is mica schist and it measures 13" x 10". It shows a warrior with bow and spear, thought to be of a northern European style.

It was discovered in the vicarage gardens in 1910. Plate 99 shows the stone.

CATTISTOCK

LOCATION: Cattistock is situated 2 miles N of Maiden Newton, north of the A356. OS 1:50 000 sheet 194. Grid reference (of church): 592995.

Inside the parish church of St. Peter and St. Paul there are hints of pre-Christian traditions, plus signs of early Christianity which was a fusion of the old ways and new. The church may be 19th Century but the site is Saxon.

The church is full of dragon symbolism. This includes paintings, fine wooden carved decorations and stained glass windows. All this in a church not even dedicated to St. Michael or St. George!

Before the coming of Christianity, the Dragon was seen to represent beneficence.

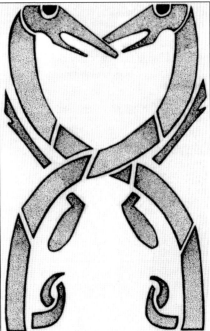

Fig.115: Two Celtic dragons.

Plate 99. (Left) The Buckland Newton Warrior.

Famous Celtic researcher, Bob Stewart, considers that dragons symbolised earth energies to the Celts. King Arthur 'Pendragon' used dragon heraldry. It was only later on that Christian hierarchy used the symbol against paganism in its efforts to eradicate the Old Ways.

In the Far East, the dragon still represents beneficial qualities and earth energies. Appropriately the title 'Dragon Project' was chosen by the team that set up monitoring of the energies of the Rollright Stones.

The church at Wynford Eagle also displays dragon carvings (see Plate 111).

With all this in mind, it may be of little surprise to find that the church at Cattistock stands on two leys. The first is shown in Fig.12. Its course was discovered by John Michell, but the Minterne Parva and Brockhampton stones are additions by the author. The second ley is shown in Fig.36 and the stone sites at Giant's Grave and Milton Abbas lie along its path.

Plate 100: The stone cross in the Abbey churchyard, Cerne Abbas.

"CUM SAXUM SAXORUM IN DUERSUM MONTUM OPARUM DA, IN AETIBULUM, IN QUINATUM - DRACONIS!"

Druidic Evocation of The Dragon.

Also of interest in the church is a Pre-Conquest, early 11th Century cross, set into a recess in the north wall to the left of the main altar.

It shows a central marigold with ornamentation on each side. One arm remains, showing a foliage design. It was discovered in 1857.

CERNE ABBAS CROSS

LOCATION: The cross stands in the abbey churchyard, which is through a gate near the Abbey entrance. OS 1:50 000 sheet 194.
Grid reference: 666014.

The cross, shown in Plate 100, is soon reached to the right-hand side of the main path through the churchyard. It is probably 'a 15th Century preaching cross' according to Alfred Pope (1906), probably not in its original position. The 2.5ft high shaft is around 14" in diameter, and is set into a base and plinth measuring 2.5ft in height. The material is red sandstone.

Several leys intersect Cerne Abbas village but we cannot tell which the cross may have been originally associated with.

The Cerne Abbas Giant is obviously the main attraction around these parts and a good view of it can be had from a viewing car park on the A352 (grid reference: 662018).

Gerard of Trent (ms 1622) found evidence of pagan stones at Cerne Abbas. When St. Augustine came to the village he 'came break-

Plate 101: The old stone cross at Charminster.

ing down the altars of the Saxon God Heile, whom they honoured as the conferer of their health'. St. Augustine's Well is a place of quiet contemplation, an ancient sacred locality.

In "The Ley Hunter's Companion", Devereux & Thompson find the well to lie on a ley stretching from Holwell to Cerne Abbas. The author has been able to extend this ley further south, as shown in fig. 13.

CHARMINSTER CROSS

LOCATION: Charminster is situated 1 mile north of Dorchester on the A352. The cross lies at the parish church of St. Mary. OS 1:50 000 sheet 194 and 1:25 000 'Purbeck and South Dorset' sheet.
Grid reference: 679927.

he shaft of a Medieval stone cross lies loose in the churchyard next to the wall of the south aisle. It is a tapered shaft, 3.5ft long, with a maximum diameter of 1ft.

In the 18th Century, John Hutchins noted a barrow to the SW of Charminster. It was on the Bradford Peveril to Dorchester road. He described it as being 'surrounded at the base by rude stones'.

Its exact locality remains unknown and it is now probably gone.

CHESELBOURNE CROSS AND BARROW

LOCATION: Cheselbourne is situated approximately midway between Dorchester and Blandford Forum, north of the A354. OS 1:50 000 sheet.
Grid references: Church 763996; Barrow 739995.

he parish church of St. Martin is our first stop. North-east of the north porch stands the cross shown in Plate 102. A photograph by Alfred Pope, taken prior to 1906, shows the cross in a much worse condition, with stones missing and the whole structure covered in ivy. Today, the cross is in a good state of repair, having been subsequently restored. Some modern stones have been added.

almost completely with an impenetrable mass of bramble, furze and small trees. I was unable to locate the stone.

The stone may indeed still be there, but extensive site clearance may be necessary to find out.

Two other barrows lie in the field, but no stones were found on these.

"A ROUND BARROW IS ALWAYS LOCATED ON ONE OR MORE BLIND SPRINGS. THIS MARKS ITS MYSTIC CENTRE."

Guy Underwood

CORSCOMBE STONES

LOCATION: Corscombe is situated near the Devon border, 8 miles NW of Maiden Newton. OS 1:50 000 sheet 194. Grid reference: 514048.

Fig.116 shows the locality of the stones. Access is afforded via public paths. Leaving the A356, a track is taken east before the village is reached. Two chalets are soon seen on the right and the stones can be seen in the valley beyond. A public footpath goes right through the site.

Plate 102: The old stone cross at Cheselbourne

The cross is dated as 15th Century, its shaft set diagonally into a rectangular pedestal and plinth. The shaft is 4ft high and tapers between 13" at the bottom and 10" wide at the top. The plinth and steps together reach nearly 6ft in height and the whole 10ft structure is visible some distance away. The material is Ham Hill Stone.

Fig.116: Location of the Corscombe stones.

About 1.25 miles west of Cheslbourne church is a barrow of interest. On the 1:50 000 sheet there is a clutch of 4 barrows between Kingcombe and Hog Leaze. A bridlepath passes close by the barrows to the east of them. The barrow of note is the northern-most. This is the 'Cheselbourne 7' barrow and Leslie Grinsell reported (in his 1959 'Dorset Barrows') a 4.5ft high 'stone column'. The barrow is 6ft high and formerly had a diameter of 65ft, although the latter now seems to have diminished. The author visited the site in 1994 but was met with a barrow covered

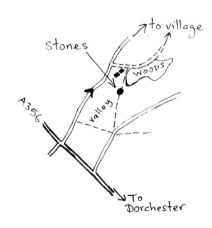

5 large stones and numerous smaller ones are strewn along approximately 50yds of the floor of a small, steep-sided valley.

In 1925 Vere Oliver thought the site to be a chambered long barrow, similar to The Grey Mare and Her Colts. The Royal Commission listed the site as 'three standing stones'.

To the author's amazement, the site is not a listed Ancient Monument, a status which it certainly seems to warrant.

Fig.117 is the author's site plan carried out in the autumn of 1994.

Stones A-C certainly do stand similar to the megaliths at the 'Colts' barrow, with the hint of a crescental forecourt. The smaller stones (F) nearby may suggest that the barrow was orientated SE-NW, the most popular direction of barrow orientation, as shown in Fig.2.

Stone A is locally called 'The Devil's Chair', although 'Granny's Armchair' has also been cited. Plate 103 shows the stone on the right side of the view and the ledge allowing seating is clearly seen. Stones that enable seating crop up throughout Britain and may have been for meditation and rituals. The stone is 4.5ft tall. A stone seat at Bradford-upon-Avon is of a similar design.

Next to it stands stone B, the tallest. It reaches nearly 6.5ft and is noticeably pointed at the top. At the Nine Stones and elsewhere we have seen how taller columnal stones are positioned between more squarish, lozenge-shaped stones. This method of stone selection is most noticeably at Avebury.

Stone C lies on its longest axis and is notable for a deep round hole, low down on the north side. This may be obscured by nettles during the summer.

The stones at point F are all smaller and can likewise vanish under a tangle of nettles during summer months.

Some 50yds south along the footpath are stones D and E. They nestle beneath an elder. The largest is 8.5ft long and 2ft thick. The other is 6ft in length. They are both prone and lichen-covered.

Here we have another stone site lying at the floor of a valley. Dowsing by the author located at least four bands of energy, running parallel to each other, passing through the

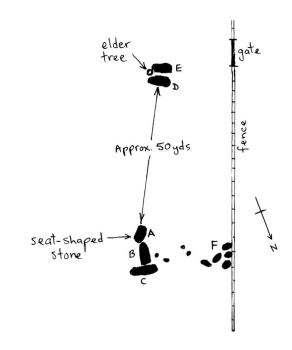

Fig.117: Site plan of the Corscombe site.

site. They run parallel with the fence and pass through the vicinity of the stones cited.

A ley has been found that passes close to stones D and E and this is shown in Fig.118.

"......THERE SEEM TO BE CERTAIN FAVOURED PLACES ON THE EARTH WHERE ITS MAGNETIC AND EVEN MORE SUBTLE FORCES ARE MOST POWERFUL AND MOST EASILY FELT BY PERSONS SUSCEPTIBLE TO SUCH THINGS."

J.D. Evans-Wentz (1911)

CROSS AND HAND STONE - BATCOMBE

LOCATION: Batcombe is situated 3 miles NW of Cerne Abbas. The stone stands on a minor road joining Holywell and Minterne Magna, about 0.75 mile east of Batcombe church. OS 1:50 000 sheet 194. Grid reference: 632038.

The folklore tales associated with this stone (all nine of them!) were described in Chapter Three. The stone stands on the north side of the road, some 250yds west of woods. The shape of the stone is unique to Dorset and some debate has taken place in the past regarding its origin. Plate 104 shows the stone from the road. The stone is featured in Hardy's 'Tess of the D'urbervilles' as well as in his poem 'The Lost Pyx'. Alfred Pope and others considered it Pre-Conquest, whilst some consider it Roman. It is similar in shape to stones at Clackmannan (near Stirling) and Langholm Mercat (Dunfrieshire), and Derek Bryce, in his 'Symbolism of the Celtic Cross', points out what he considers to be pagan phallic symbolism. Janet and Colin Bord, in 'Earth Rites' describe several more examples. They even include a photograph of stones, similar to the Cross and Hand Stone, standing in Ethiopia!

The shaft stands 3.5ft high and the top is 11" across. The hand, said to have been carved on one side, has now eroded away.

A ley is suggested here for the first time to prove antiquity of the stone. Perhaps such an obvious phallic stone survived the Church's purges due to the priest who witnessed the 'pillar of fire' at the spot (page 25). Was the priest observing earth energy phenomena on a ley?

Fig.118 shows the route of the ley. Details of the Milton Abbas cross can be found on page 55, whilst the Corscombe and Minterne Parva stones are dealt with in detail in this Chapter.

Plate 103: Stones A-C at Corscombe

"SOME SAY THE SPOT IT BANNED; THAT THE PILLAR CROSS-AND-HAND ATTESTS TO A DEED OF HELL; BUT OF ELSE THAN OF BALE IS THE MYSTIC TALE THAT ANCIENT VALE-FOLK TELL ......"

from 'The Lost Pyx', Thomas Hardy

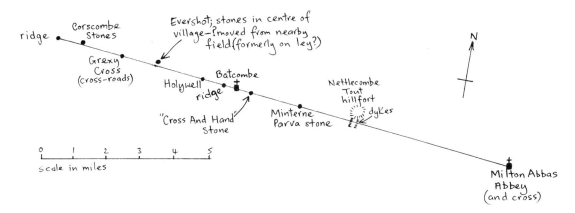

ridge • Corscombe Stones

Grexy Cross (cross-roads)

Evershot; stones in centre of village—?moved from nearby field(formerly on ley?)

Holywell ridge

Batcombe

"Cross And Hand" Stone

Minterne Parva stone

Nettlecombe Tout hillfort

dykes

N

0 1 2 3 4 5
scale in miles

Milton Abbas Abbey (and cross)

On a trip to the area in 1994, the author 'stumbled' upon the stones shown in Plate 105. They stand at the north end of the village, on a green opposite Swiss Cottage. Three stones have been incorporated into a bench. The largest is 5ft high and all three are composed of fossiliferous Jurassic limestone, so are not sarsens. I believe these are the 3 dumb sisters of the tradition. They echo stone naming elsewhere in Britain. There are the Nine Maidens of Devon, the Merry Maidens of Cornwall, and 'Seven Sisters' occurs quite commonly.

Fig.118: Ley associated with the 'Cross and Hand' stone (as well as four other stone/cross sites).

Plate (left) 104: The Cross and Hand standing stone.

Plate 105: The Evershot stones.

EVERSHOT STONES

LOCATION: Evershot is situated some 5 miles NNW of Maiden Newton. It is one mile west of the A37 at Holywell. OS 1:50 000 sheet 194. Grid reference (of stones): 576046.

Back in 1895, the Dorset Field Club visited Evershot. A field was referred to called 'Dumb Maid's Plot' where '3 dumb sisters danced to while away the time ,......on the green there'.

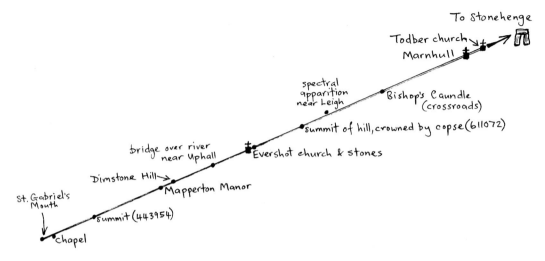

To Stonehenge
Todber church
Marnhull
spectral apparition near Leigh
Bishop's Caundle (crossroads)
summit of hill, crowned by copse (611072)
bridge over river near Uphall
Evershot church & stones
Dimstone Hill
Mapperton Manor
St. Gabriel's Mouth
summit (443954)
chapel

Fig.119: Ley associated with the stones at Evershot (after Gordon Harris, with amendments by the author)

A ley has already been shown (Fig.118) that passes near to the stones. But work by Gordon Harris results in the ley shown in Fig.119. It will be seen that the ley passes right past the village green and the stones.

It seems to me an injustice that once-proud standing stones have now been reduced to the role of supporting a bench seat. But, at least, they are still standing near their original site, and the erection of the bench may have, ironically, secured their survival!

GIANT'S GRAVE AND NORDON HILL

LOCATION: These two localities lie about 3 miles west of Milton Abbas. The nearest village is Melcombe Bingham. Both sites are named on OS maps. OS 1:50 000 sheet 194. Grid references: Nordon Hill c.750030; Giant's Grave 757017.

These two sites are described together for two reasons. Firstly, they share the same folklore tale about a stone throwing contest between two giants (details on page 18). Secondly, it has been shown that the two localities are connected by a ley, details of which are shown in Fig.14. Is the folklore a distant memory of some ancient ley and/or earth energies?

Giant's Grave lies on the western slopes of Henning Hill, below the line of trees. The sarsen lying on it is in fact visible from the road below, if one knows where to look. C.W. Bingham, reporting on the site in 1866, cites 'two large stones' on a mound here. The traces of a mound can still be seen running north from a solitary stone, which has lost its companion since Bingham's day.

The remaining sarsen measures 7ft long, 4ft wide and 3ft thick and is typical flinty sarsen stone. It is very weathered and roughly triangular. The stone's longest axis aligns with Nordon Hill on the skyline. This may fortuitous (?). Fig.36 shows the stone also lies on another ley, bearing east-west. Dowser Roger Sleet has map-dowsed an energy line that goes straight through the Giant's Grave, heading E-W.

The stone is said to move when the cocks crow at nearby Cheselbourne. This could be another folklore memory of energy anomalies known to occur at sunrise at stone sites. These have been recorded (such as during the Dragon Project at the Rollrights in Oxfordshire) with scientific instrumentation.

About a mile north of Giant's Grave is the summit of Nordon Hill. It is known that at one time 3 sarsens lay on top of the hill, which now seem to have disappeared. The hill has a prehistoric past for sure: tumuli can be seen here and there and the Romans once had a camp. The Ancient British camp at

Plate 106: The sarsen at Giant's Grave.

Nettlecombe Tout lies about one mile west along the same ridge. Next to the camp is the Dorset Gap, from which 8 ancient hollow ways radiate.

KING CHARLES STONE

LOCATION: 1 mile east of the centre of Bridport, at the junction of the A35 and Lee Lane. Shown as 'Mon' on OS maps. OS 1:50 000 sheet 193 and 1:25 000 'Purbeck and South Dorset' sheet. Grid reference: 479933.

The stone stands under the shade of a large oak tree on the west side of the lane. It stands about 4.5ft tall and is 3.5ft wide at the base. The stone is a massive block of the local Bothenhampton Stone from the nearby Wanderwell Quarry. It rests on a plinth of Portland Limestone, which is full of fossils.,

This memorial stone is not an 'ancient' one as such, but has been included in this guide to dispel any doubts the reader may have had should he have chanced upon it. It is also a fine example how beautiful stone can be left in a rough and semi-natural state and not squared and cut to excess.

The stone was erected in 1901, and was unveiled at a ceremony to mark the 250th anniversary of the escape down Lee Lane on April 23 1651 of Charles II from his Roundhead pursuers, years prior to his coronation. It was designed by G. Milverton, a former pupil of Bridport School of Art.

On the stone the inscription reads:

KING CHARLES II
ESCAPED CAPTURE THROUGH THIS
LANE
SEP. XXIII MDCLI
WHEN MIDST YOUR FIERCEST FOES
ON EVERY SIDE
FOR YOUR ESCAPE GOD DID A LANE
PROVIDE.
THOMAS FULLERS WORTHIES.
ERECTED SEP. XXIII MDCCCI.

Photographs taken at the time show the stone high on a bank, not at road level as it is at present. Miss J.E. Burrell (Bridport Museum's Officer) informed the author that

MAIDEN NEWTON AREA

LOCATION: Maiden Newton is situated about 7 miles NW of Dorchester on the A356. There are several sites of interest in the area and individual localities are given in the text. OS 1:50 000 sheet 194.

The first stop is the junction in the village, where the A356 passes through. Here stands the 15th Century village cross. It stands in the middle of the road mounted on a square modern base.

The cross is now only a shadow of its former glory. An account of 1780 tells us that it

Plate 107: The King Charles Stone at Bridport

Plate (right) 108: The Maiden Newton Cross, seen in April 1994.

the stone was probably moved in the 1970's, due to road widening.

Also in Bridport is a possible ancient stone, 2ft across leaning against a wall at the corner of Gundry Lane and South Street.

Whilst in the area, visit the church of St. Wite at Whitechurch Canonicorum. On the north side of the chancel is a rare Saxon shrine dated the 9th Century. It is a place of pilgrimage for catholics and is unique in England.

The village of Powerstock is 3 miles NE of the King Charles stone. A large cross formerly stood here. John Hutchins, the antiquarian, reported its destruction which was some time prior to 1863.

Plate 109: The Maiden Newton Cross, seen after restoration, August 1994.

Fig.120: Ley associated with the Maiden Newton cross (after Gordon Harris, with amendments).

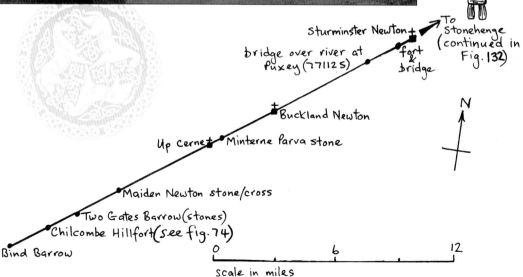

Sturminster Newton┼ To Stonehenge (continued in Fig. 132)

bridge over river at Puxey (771125)

fort & bridge

┼ Buckland Newton

Up Cerne┼ ● Minterne Parva stone

N

● Maiden Newton stone/cross

● Two Gates Barrow (stones)

● Chilcombe Hillfort (see fig.74)

Bind Barrow

0   6   12

scale in miles

was restored and set onto a modern base, of similar stone (see Plate 109).

The socket stone is about 15" deep and over 4ft of shaft rise from it. On the west face of the shaft can be seen the weathered remains of figures standing on a corbelled projection, reminding us again of the cross at Stalbridge.

Independent work by Gordon Harris resulted in the ley shown in Fig.120. It will be seen that the cross lies directly on the ley. Once again, we may have here the Christianisation of a much older stone marker.

Our next port of call is the church of St. Mary in the village (grid reference: 596978). In the churchyard, south of the south transept, is a stone cross, probably dating from the 15th Century. The material is Ham Hill Stone, and the cross is covered in lichen. The 3ft long tapered shaft projects upwards from a 3ft wide octagonal base, which is 1ft 8" deep.

The cross was probably a wayside cross originally, and was placed in its present position in the 19th Century. A spring visit to the churchyard rewards the visitor with an array of daffodils.

Plate 110: (above) The stone cross in the churchyard at Maiden Newton.

Plate 111: Dragon symbology on the Wynford Eagle tympanum.

could be 'bettered only by the famed Stalbridge cross'. In the 18th Century it was moved due to Turnpike road construction and lost its original base. During this century the cross was gradually being encroached upon by tarmac and road signs alike (see Plate 108). During the summer of 1994 the cross

Next we go to the village of Wynford Eagle, which lies about 1.5 miles SW of Maiden Newton.

At the church of St. Lawrence, a fine late-11th Century tympanum can be seen. On it is carved 2 fighting dragons. Opposing dragons crop up in certain Celtic legends. We saw more dragon symbology at Cattistock.

Prior to 1864 a Roman pavement was discovered immediately SW of Wynford Manor. More was uncovered in 1935. Designs on it included foliage and dolphins.

About 1.5 miles west of Maiden Newton is the small village of Toller Fratrum. At the church of St. Basil are 2 early stone relics of interest.

Firstly, set into the east wall of the chancel is a stone mural. It is of Saxon, Pre-Conquest age and dates from c.1100. It is 17" x 7" and is thought to show Mary Magdalene anointing the feet of Jesus The Christ.

Secondly, there is a fine 12th Century font.

MELBURY BUBB CROSS AND FONT

LOCATION: Melbury Bubb lies about 5 miles north of Maiden Newton, just east of the A37 Dorchester to Yeovil road. The church of St. Mary is in the centre of the village. OS 1:50 000 sheet 194. Grid reference: 596065.

Plate 112: The old stone cross at Melbury Bubb

n the churchyard, SE of the porch, is the old stone village cross (Plate 112). It is 15th Century and made of Ham Hill Stone. Only 13" of shaft now remains, this being 12" square at its base. It is set into a 15" deep. The remains today are in a poor state. The modern cross, erected in 1898 and standing south of the church, is said to be a '.......true reproduction of the old cross.'

Inside the church we find one of the oldest and one of the most interesting of Dorset's old stone fonts. It is shown in Plate 113. It is Saxon, c.1000 in date, and has carved on it many animal figures, all upside-down! It is thought that it may be a hollowed out old column, perhaps even Roman. The carvings are of hounds chasing deer, a stag, a horse, a wolf and even what looks to be a dolphin; a whole assemblage of animals perhaps representing pagan mythology.

It may have been that the transition of an older pagan stone into a font, and the upside-down display of the carvings, was meant to

Plate 113: The Saxon font at Melbury Bubb.

show suppression of the old pagan ways by the Church.

Looking for a pre-Christian origin to the site of the church and cross, it may be relevant, in our ley studies, that the churches of Yetminster, Melbury Bubb and Frome St. Quinton lie very nearly on a straight line.

MELBURY OSMOND CROSS

LOCATION: Melbury Osmond lies just 1.5 miles NW of Melbury Bubb (see previous locality), just off the A37 Yeovil to Dorchester road. The church stands in the centre of the village. OS 1:50 000 sheet 194. Grid reference: 574078.

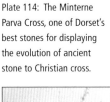 t the SW corner of the churchyard, next to the gate and a tall old lamp, lie the remains of the old village cross. It is thought to be 14-15th Century and is made of Ham Hill Stone. Only the octagonal base now remains, measuring 38" diameter and 15" deep (most of the latter is now beneath the ground).

Parts of the cross were used, apparently, to restore the Norman Font in 1887. These parts were incorporated into the base of the font and can be seen in the church.

Plate 114: The Minterne Parva Cross, one of Dorset's best stones for displaying the evolution of ancient stone to Christian cross.

MINTERNE PARVA STONE

LOCATION: Minterne Parva is a small village, just off the A37, 1 mile north of Cerne Abbas. OS 1:50 000 sheet 194. Grid reference: 664034.

eaving the A37, one crosses the river and stops at the first cottage. The stone can be seen high up on a bank, next to a round building. The stone is largely obscured during summer/autumn.

The stone is similar in appearance to the older half if the Tarrant Crawford Cross (see Plate 11). This fact, plus the discovery that the Minterne Parva Cross stands on several leys, lends itself to the suggestion that once again we are dealing with the modification of an ancient, pre-Christian stone.

The shaft is 2ft 4" stump, tapering upwards from a 15" wide base. It is mortised into an octagonal base, 3ft across, which is much worn away. Below is a stone plinth, 3ft square and over 1ft deep.

Alfred Pope, in 1906, thought the cross to be 14th Century and considered that its position on the high bank was not its original locality. The stone stands at an ancient crossroads marked by the public footpath to the west and the old gate to the east. The cross may have been moved when the present tarmac road was evolving from a dirt track.

In 1994 the author noted a cup-shaped depression on the base stone. This may have been for either offerings of a religious nature, or else for the giving of alms for the poor. In Pope's day, carvings were still to be seen on the stone.

"ALMOST ALL WAYSIDE AND CHURCHYARD CROSSES EVOLVED FROM (LEY) MARK STONES."

Alfred Watkins, 'The Old Straight Track'

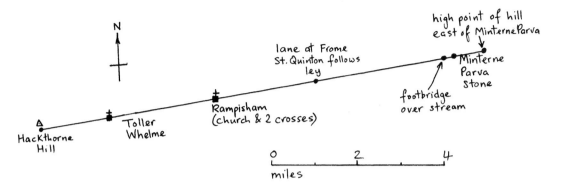

high point of hill
east of MinterneParva

N

lane at Frome
St. Quinton follows
ley

Minterne
Parva
Stone

footbridge
over stream

Rampisham
(church & 2 crosses)

Toller
Whelme

Hackthorne
Hill

0   2   4

miles

Where this stone really 'comes into its own' is when one applies ley line studies. At least 4 leys pass within yards of the stone, as if to confirm its ancient status.

Gordon Harris plotted a ley that stretches from Bind Barrow, on the coast, right up to Stonehenge (see Fig.120). The stone is on the ley. John Michell has mapped a ley from Old Sarum, near Salisbury, down to Powerstock. This is shown in Fig.12. The Minterne Parva stone is situated on it (although not shown on Michell's original map). A ley suggested by the author in Fig.118 also has the stone on its course. Another ley is shown above in Fig.121. This all leads us nicely to our next locality, Rampisham, which lies on the ley.

to help cure the rector's insomnia! The cross is thought to be 15th Century.

The square shaft is 4ft high and tapers from 15" to 12". On the west face is a carved figure, now much denuded. It is thought to be St. Michael standing on a dragon. The base is octagonal with remains of piers or broaches on 4 faces. The shaft is grouted into the base with lead.

Fig.121: One of the leys associated with the Minterne Parva Stone/Cross (see text for others).

Plate 115: The wayside cross at Rampisham.

RAMPISHAM CROSSES

LOCATION: Rampisham is situated 4 miles NW of Maiden Newton, 1 mile north of the A356 Crewkerne to Dorchester road. OS 1:50 000 sheet 194. Grid references: church 562021; wayside cross 565025.

Two old stone crosses stand in the village of Rampisham. The first is near Broomfield Farm. It stands on the east side of the lane, opposite the old rectory (grid reference: 565025). Plate 115 shows the cross.

The cross used to stand on the green, opposite the Tiger's Head, but was moved to the present site near the Old Rectory in 1800

Plate 116: The churchyard cross at Rampisham, with tomb built into its base.

Plate 117: The stone cross at Stratton churchyard.

has the date 1516 on its base, whilst the adjoining tomb is dated 1606. Here and there dole holes can be seen. The socket stone is richly carved with religious scenes.

It is reported that another stone cross also once stood in the churchyard. Also of interest is the tale of a Roman pavement found at Rampisham. It was discovered on common land in 1799. However, soon afterwards, the pavement was broken up by 'ignorant neighbours', who thought that treasure was buried beneath.

STRATTON AREA

LOCATION: Stratton is situated on the A37, 3 miles NW of Dorchester. Several sites of interest lie within a 2 mile radius of the village. Grid references are given in the text as each site is described. OS 1:50 000 sheet 194 and 1:25 000 'Purbeck and South Dorset' sheet.

Back at the church of St. Michael and All Angels, an early 16th Century cross can be seen next to the church. Plate 116 shows how an altar tomb has been built into its base. About a foot of shaft still projects from the square base. This base is set onto a pedestal, which has projections and is inscribed. Below this two steps form a foundation. The cross

Our first destination is the churchyard of the village church in Stratton (grid reference: 651938). Between the churchyard gate and the porch stands the old stone cross (Plate 117), 3ft of shaft stands out of an octagonal socket stone. Below this, the base stone is 7ft square and the whole structure has been restored somewhat, with signs of grouting and newer stones. The cross is thought to be late 14th Century.

Next stop is the bridge over the River Frome at Muckleford, 0.5 mile west of Stratton (grid reference: 643936). A stone lies just north of the bridge, on the east side of the road (see Plate 118). The stone was located by the author in October 1994, when 'walking' the ley shown in Fig.13 (plotted originally be Paul Devereux) to see in any further markers still remained in between those seen by Devereux. Bridges over rivers frequently occur along the course of leys. The author was happy to add the bridge itself to the markers, but only an actual VISIT TO THE SITE revealed the stone. The importance of the stone, bridge and the nearby crossroads is borne out in Fig.104. It can be seen that the

locality is associated with a ley running right up to Stonehenge.

The stone itself measure about 5ft x 3ft, the long axis being N-S. It is prone and lies up to 1ft above the road surface. It appears to be earthfast.

The next locality is 1.5 miles north of Stratton, on Grimstone Down. Alfred Pope reported in 1906 the base of Jackman's Cross lying to the north of the intersection of tracks (grid reference: 650960). The cross is still marked on 1:25 000 OS maps. On a visit to the area in the autumn of 1994 the author failed to locate the stone.

Pope saw a socket stone of Portland limestone 2ft square by 1ft deep, with a mortise 11" x 8", which formerly took the shaft. He noted a cup-shaped cavity on the stone, which may have been used for the reception of alms. There is a tradition that a sheep-stealer called Jackman was hanged at the cross in the 18th Century.

The author has found that this ancient stone site lies on a ley going from Holwell to Winterbourne Steepleton (see fig. 13.)

One mile NE of Jackman's Cross is the Holy Trinity Church at Godmanstone (grid reference: 666974). Inside the church, look for the column to the right of the altar. At the base, next to two steps, is a rectangular block of stone, on which the column stands. Faint inscriptions can still be made out on this block. These were revealed in 1964 during work on the church. They are Roman Latin inscriptions and it appears as if the Norman builders of the church used the stone as the base of the column. The script is dedicated to 'Jupiter Optimus Maximum'. It is thought to have originally been a Roman altar stone and may have come from a villa site a mile to the south.

About 0.5 mile SSW of Stratton is a plateau centred around grid reference 645928, NW of Penn Hill. Three barrows formerly stood here and one of these contained a massive stone slab 'that took 6 horses to remove'. It may be worth noting that a straight line can be plotted on the map that starts at the stone by Muckleford Bridge (Plate 118), proceeds through the barrows on the plateau, passes the tumuli at the summit of

Penn Hill before heading SE to terminate at the Roman Temple at Maiden Castle. A possible ley is suggested.

Plate 118: The markstone at the bridge at Muckleford (notebook rests on stone).

SYDLING ST. NICHOLAS

LOCATION: This village is situated midway between Maiden Newton and Cerne Abbas, 1 mile east of the A37. A stone cross and an older stone are both situated in the centre of the village. OS 1:50 000 sheet 194. Grid reference: 632994.

At the village crossroads stands a stone cross, on the west side of the road, by the bus shelter. Plate 119 shows the cross and it appears identical in appearance to when Alfred Pope photographed it in 1906. It is a wayside cross of about the 15th Century and probably stands at an ancient crossroads. The track following the N-S course of Sydling Water meets the E-W route from Maiden Newton to Cerne Abbas at the crossroads.

The shaft is 4.5ft high and is formed of two octagonal blocks mortised together. It is slightly tapered and is 1ft 3" square at the base. The

Plate 119: The cross at
Sydling St. Nicholas

Fig.122: Ley associated
with the cross and stone at
Sydling St. Nicholas.

The cross used to stand under the shade of the 'Cross Tree', a huge elm which had a hollowed centre 'capable of containing several men', according to Pope.

It was blown down in 1880. The village stocks once stood close by. The village school stood opposite the cross between 1836-1966. The pupils used to play around and on the cross, causing much erosion in the process.

On the opposite side of the road, on the corner, lies a stone (see Plate 120). The stone was found by the author in December 1993. Such a stone, lying as it does close to the cross, suggests site evolution in the marking of an ancient track (and ley also?).

The stone appears to be limestone and is potholed and weathered. It is 3ft long and 2ft deep.

To confirm the antiquity of the stone, and to further the case for site evolution, a search was made for a ley that passed through the crossroads. In due course one was realised and this is shown in Fig.122. It is a very instructive ley, with a variety of differing types of ley marker such as stones, churches, crossroads, tumuli, prehistoric settlements and a mighty hillfort Maiden Castle. Also of interest

join of the shaft and base is run with lead. The base stone is an equal-side octagon, measuring 1.5ft on each face, and is 2ft deep.

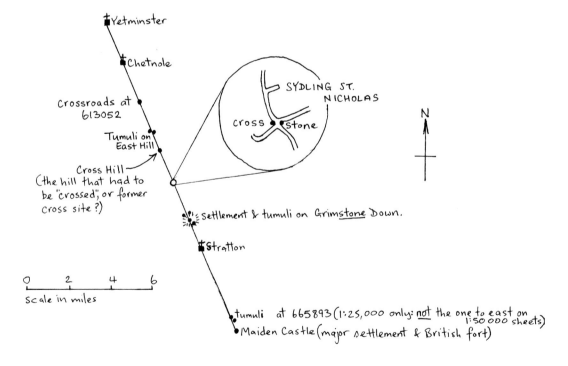

Yetminster

Chetnole

Crossroads at
613052

Tumuli on
East Hill

Cross Hill
(the hill that had to
be "crossed", or former
cross site?)

SYDLING ST.
NICHOLAS

Cross   Stone

N

Settlement & tumuli on Grimstone Down.

Stratton

0   2   4   6
scale in miles

tumuli   at 665893 (1:25,000 only: not the one to east on
                                                    1:50 000 sheets)
Maiden Castle (major settlement & British fort)

are two place names on the ley, Grimstone Down and Cross Hill, which may be memories of further stone localities.

Half-a-mile north of the village is a cross-roads (grid reference: 631003). The ruins of a stone cross was still in evidence there at the end of the 18th Century. In 1812 a fragment of the shaft was still visible and on it the much eroded figure of a saint. Pope, in 1906, declared the cross 'totally disappeared'. The cross was called 'Mat's Cross' by locals. This differs from Rodney Legg, who recently described the locality as 'Marr's Cross (see 'Dorset', No. 3, March/April 1995). The OS favours the latter name on their maps.

In October 1994 the author visited the locality and a search made through the grass banks etc. The only stones found were on the south-west corner of the crossroads, next to a drain. Two stones are seen at road level, up to 2.5ft long. Are these fragments of the 'lost' cross, exposed since Pope's day?

lie in low-fenced enclosures, either side of the slip road of the A356, south of Urless Farm. OS 1:50 000 sheet 194. Grid reference: 517034.

Plate 120: The markstone at Sydling St. Nicholas. It stands opposite the village cross.

TOLLER DOWN STONES

LOCATION: On the A356 road, 3.5 miles NE of Beaminster. The stones

hese two large stones are known locally as the 'Hoar Stones'. They are named on 1:25 000 sheets as 'Hore Stones'. This title is found elsewhere, as at Verwood, and means 'boundary stone'.

Fig.123: Ley associated with the stones at Toller Down (after Jackman, with amendments by the author).

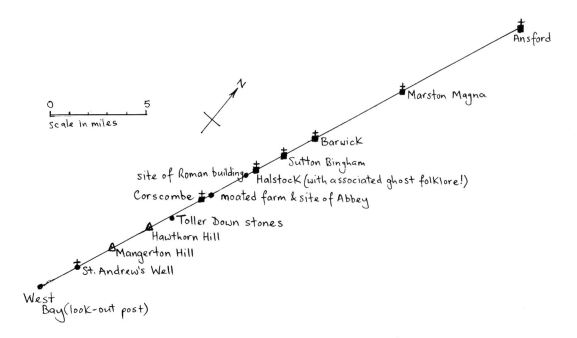

Plate 121: One of the Toller Down stones, showing the present overgrown condition of the site.

a huge correspondence in response. The ley is 30 miles long. The Toller Down stones lie about 150yds east of the ley but they are close enough to it to be thought relevant by Jackman. The author is inclined to agree. We do not, after all, know if the stones were moved and other stones may have once stood nearby, on the ley.

> "THE PRIMARY PURPOSE OF
> THESE STONES WAS NOT TO
> ACT AS BOUNDARY - BUT AS
> WAY-MARKS; IT IS OBVIOUS
> THAT PREHISTORIC WAYS
> MUST HAVE BEEN IN USE
> BEFORE OWNERSHIP OF
> LAND EXISTED."
>
> *Alfred Watkins, 'The Old Straight Track'*

Folklore says the Devil hurled the stones in an attempt to block the road. The stones presently lie at road level on either side of the sliproad. Fencing at least preserves the stones but both are very overgrown and little can be made out unless visited in winter/early spring. Brambles and nettles are awaiting anyone wishing a closer inspection!

The northern stone is 7.75ft x 7ft and 3ft thick. It is rich in quartz. The other measures a grand 11.25ft x 8.5ft and is over 3ft in thickness. Old 6" OS maps show 4 stones in the vicinity. Dowsing by the author in June 1994 picked up a band of energy running between the two stones. The band continued north across the A356 and headed down the valley towards Corscombe.

Fig.123 shows a ley found by Brian Jackson. He described the ley in an article in the Sunday Times early in 1974. It attracted

TWO GATES STONES

LOCATION: Two Gates and the burial chamber nearby are marked on OS maps, less than a mile SE of Eggardon Hill. The site is 1.5 miles north of the A35. OS 1:50 000 sheet 194 and 1:25 000 'Purbeck and South Dorset' sheet.
Grid reference: 554938.

At the junction of the lane to West Compton, there is a gate on the east side of the lane. The stones lie in the field beyond, 150yds from the gate. The stones are obscured by crops in the growing season. They lie roughly in between two telegraph poles.

Two stones are to be found today, thought to represent the remains of a chambered barrow. Older records of the stones speak of them 'standing 4ft high'. They are now both prone. An 1872 drawing by Charles Warne (reproduced in Fig.124) shows the stones in a more erect posture than the present view (Plate 122).

The stones lie close together and are of similar length, about 6.5ft. The field is culti-

Fig.124: An 1872 view of the Two Gates Stones.

vated and all traces of barrow mound material have long since vanished.

Another tomb if reported to have been formerly visible to the SE, south of the E-W lane. This lane follows a Roman road, running from Dorchester up past Eggardon Hill. Work by Gordon Harris (unpub.) resulted in the ley shown in Fig.120. The ley goes from Bind Barrow, on the coast, right up to Stonehenge. It will be seen that the Two Gates Stones lie very close to the ley.

Another ley (shown in Fig.128) was plotted by John Michell (shown in 'Dorset Countryside', 1vii, 1976) which goes from Old Sarum near Salisbury down to Cerne Abbas. The author has now extended this line further SW, to include the church at West Compton and terminating at the Two Gates Stones.

In 1945, at nearby Eggardon Hill Farm to the north of the Two Gates Stones, a mound was reported at grid reference 552945, north of the public path. 'Large limestone blocks' were noted on it. No traces appear to have survived.

Also nearby, the Bell Stone is named on OS maps, at the NW tip of the hillfort.

WRAXALL CROMLECH
LOCATION: Wraxall is situated NW of both Maiden Newton and Cattistock.

Stones are reported to the west of the village, on the A356 road, south of the Kingcombe Crossroads. OS 1:50 000 sheet 194. Grid reference: 557006.

 certain J. Davidson reported, in 1833, stones from a possible chambered long barrow at 'Crock Lane'. Leslie Grinsell (in 'Dorset Barrows', 1952) included Davidson's note and the grid reference given above.

Davidson noted that the uprights were removed prior to 1833, but that the stone he took to be the capstone was 'recently........still there'. This stone was 5ft long and 3ft wide. The most interesting feature was a 'hollow place in the middle ......1ft in diameter ......locals called "The Crack".'

Davidson goes on, 'the stone was held in superstitious veneration by the neighbouring peasantry'. We cannot tell from the description if the 'Crack' was a depression in the stone or a hole straight through. But we obviously have another ancient healing stone which served the local community with benevolent properties.

A search by Wraxall resident, Derek Sowton, in 1995, at the author's request, failed to locate any of the stones. They may now be 'lost'.

Chapter Nine

NORTH AREA

Fig.125: Location map for stone sites in this chapter. NB: additional neighbouring sites may be found under these main location headings.

So we come to the last area in our survey of Dorset's ancient stone sites. The area is shown in Fig.125. The area is rich with stone crosses which often stand midst quiet villages off the beaten track. Site evolution is again suggested, with many of these monuments standing on leys. Tales of older megaliths are encountered at Brockhampton Green, Ibberton and Child Okeford, whilst surviving ones can still be found at and near Egbert's Stone in the far north of the county.

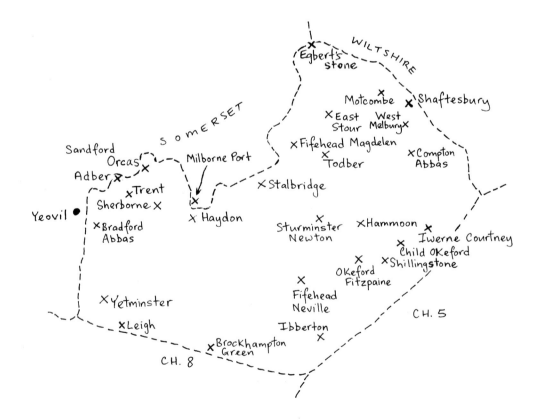

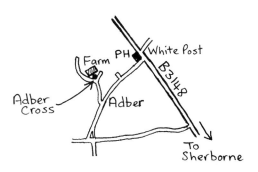

BRADFORD ABBAS CROSSES

LOCATION: Bradford Abbas is situated 3 miles SW of Sherborne on the Somerset/Dorset border. A cross stands in the churchyard of the parish church of St. Mary. OS 1:50 000 sheet 194. Grid reference: 587143.

Fig.126: Location of the old stone cross at Adber.

Plate 123: (left) The Adber Cross.

Plate 124: Bradford Abbas stone cross.

ADBER CROSS

LOCATION: Adber is situated on the Dorset/Somerset border, 3 miles NW of Sherborne just off the B3148. Fig.126 shows the position of the cross. OS 1:50 000 sheet 183. Grid reference: 598203.

This 15th Century stone cross was moved to its present site in 1963, as the accompanying plaque testifies (Plate 123). It formerly stood near the site of St. Mary's Chapel and older OS maps still show the cross's former location.

The shaft is 2.5ft tall and 9" wide at the base, narrower than the average shaft diameter for Dorset stone crosses of this age. The shaft is fitted into an 18" base stone.

orth west of the tower stands a very fine 15th Century stone cross (Plate 124). The shaft is 7.5ft tall and about 15" square at the base. Carvings on the shaft can still be made out. The figures are thought to be that of the Virgin Mary and John The Baptist. The cross head is now absent.

The socket stone below also has carved figures and ornaments. Sculptured panels are evident on the four sides and on the west side a figure of an angel was once more clearly discernible. The stone is about 4ft square.

Below the socket stone is an octagonal base and step, together being about 3.5ft in height. The base step measures about 4ft on each face of the octagon. The whole structure of the cross is composed of stone from Hamdon Hill, near Yeovil, just over the border into Somerset.

Alfred Pope noted, in 1906, that the style is similar to the crosses at Rampisham and Stalbridge. The cross was still being used for Rogation services in his day. The chief damage to the cross seems to have been inflicted by Cromwell's Roundheads c.1642-9.

The cross stirred W.H. Hamilton Rogers into the following poetic mood.......

"the churchyard cross, a hoary presbyter among the tombs, still existent and preaching for all the eternal lesson - the present only is yours; the morrow may find you at rest beneath my shadow."

(1888)

Standing amidst the tombstones and tall yews one feels somewhat humble and conscious of something more than our transitory selves.

Another fine cross formerly stood in the centre of the village. In 1815 John Hutchins reported that an arched stone building called The Cross once stood, being of a similar design to the conduit at Sherborne, but of smaller dimensions. It was apparently taken down 'by the overseer, to the great regret of many of his neighbours, without any advantage to the parish'.

There appears to be no traces left of this structure.

Plate 125: The stone at Brockhampton Green

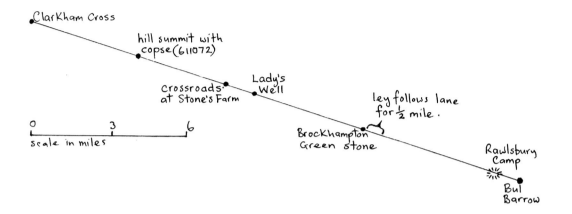

BROCKHAMPTON GREEN

LOCATION: Brockhampton Green is a small hamlet, about 5 miles NE of Cerne Abbas. It lies about 1 mile east of the B3143. A stone lies east of the crossroads. OS 1:50 000 sheet 194. Grid reference: 718062.

On page 18 we saw how folklore tells of a stone at Brockhampton Green, so large that 'it would take 12 strong men to move it'. One of the tales tells of it being thrown by a giant. It was said to be round, but with a 'flat top'. No record exists of its demise, but it was subsequently broken up.

The author searched the area in 1994 for any fragments of the stone. One stone was found, but may have not been part of the huge monolith. The stone lies to the east of the crossroads, just west of a small bridge. It lies opposite a cottage, on the south side of the road. Plate 125 shows the stoneThe stone is 5ft long and a depth of 2ft is visible. It appears to be earthfast. Fig.12 shows a long ley going from Powerstock up to Old Sarum near Salisbury. It will be seen that this small, seemingly insignificant, stone lies WITHIN YARDS of the ley. Another ley is suggested by the author in Fig.127. The ley includes the famous Bul Barrow and the sacred Lady Well at Hermitage.

CHILD OKEFORD STONE

LOCATION: Child Okeford is situated 5 miles NW of Blandford and 1 mile north of Shillingstone. A stone formerly stood on the village green. OS 1:50 000 sheet 194. Grid reference: 835127.

In 'The Old Stone Crosses of Dorset' (1906), Alfred Pope informs us of a stone on the open space in the village. This is where 5 roads and tracks meet directly opposite the pub. The modern cross now stands on or near the spot.

Pope saw "a huge block of green sandstone ......34" square, and is 16" deep". He saw no signs that the stone had ever been part of a cross, with no mortise or broaching. His conclusion was that it probably never formed part of a cross. He did note a basin-like depression on the top of the stone, which he thought to be a dole-hole for the giving of alms. A tradition exists that in the 19th Century a woman was whipped on the stone for stealing hurdles!

The importance of Child Okeford on the landscape is highlighted in Fig.128. Two leys cross at the village, the E-W one passing right through the site of the former stone on the village green. John Michell plotted the ley coming down from Old Sarum. The author has

Fig.128: Three leys
associated with Child
Okeford church and stone

Child Okeford church &
site of former stone

To
Old
Sarum

Ashmore

bridge over
river at
Angiers Farm

New Cross
Gate
(crossroads)

Park
Vale

Iwerne
Courtney
Cross

Chettle
Long
Barrow

Cursus

N

Okeford
Fitzpaine

Belchalwell

Stourpaine

Mappowder

site of cross

stone at Shorts Lane,
Blandford

Cerne Abbas (Abbey site)

Blandford
St. Mary

West Compton (saxon site)

Charlton Marshall

Two Gates Stone (barrow
site)

Spetisbury
Rings

Plate 126: The old stone
cross at Compton Abbas.

extended the ley to include West Compton and
the Two Gates Stones. The reader is referred
back to Fig.104. This shows a ley, plotted by
Gordon Harris, that extends from the south of
Nine Stones to Stonehenge. Child Okeford can
be seen to lie on the ley.

COMPTON ABBAS

LOCATION: Compton Abbas is
situated 3 miles south of Shaftesbury,
just off the A350. A stone cross
stands in the churchyard of the
ruined church of St. Mary at East
Compton (not to be confused with
the more recent church, next to the
main road). OS 1:50 000 sheet 183.
Grid reference: 876188.

he cross stands in the old churchyard,
south of the remains of the tower.
Plate 126 shows the cross with the
tower behind. Only 18" of shaft now remains,
being 12" square at its base. It is set onto a
socket stone that is 19" wide and 19" deep.
Below is a step, nearly 6ft square and 14"
deep. The base of the cross is 7.5ft square and

nearly 2ft deep with a prominent weather drip. The whole structure is of Ham Hill Stone and is thought to be 15th Century.

Back at the main road stands the new church of St. Mary. On the other side of the road is a bus shelter and next to this can be seen a stone on a grassy bank (grid reference: 868184). It was found by the author in December 1993. Some 18" of stone projects above the earth and some shaping appears evident. The stone is not marked on OS maps as either a boundary stone or a milestone.

The stone may have marked out a pilgrim's way going north to Shaftesbury. The old cross at West Melbury (1.5 miles to the north) appears to mark the same route.

Fontmell Magna lies about a mile south of Compton Abbas.

Alfred Pope, writing in 1906, tells us of a cross that formerly stood in the centre of the village near the stocks and the maypole. Some of the older villagers he spoke to remembered the cross. They spoke of a 'broken pillar' standing on 4 steps which were about 9ft square at the base.

At around 1860-70 the cross had become so dilapidated that the parish authorities ordered it to be demolished. It was said to be 'doing no credit to so respectable a village'.

EAST STOUR CROSS

LOCATION: East Stour is situated 4 miles west of Shaftesbury and 3 miles south of Gillingham. OS 1:50 000 sheet 183.

In 1939 a fragment of a 10th Century Saxon cross was found at East Stour. This is shown in Plate 127. The stone is 2ft 4" high and is very richly decorated with Saxon/Celtic vine scrolling and interlacing.

The stone is now in the collection of the British Museum, in London.

Plate 127: The Saxon cross fragment from East Stour.

EGBERT'S STONE

LOCATION: At the village of Bourton, 3 miles NW of Gillingham. See Fig.129 for locality. OS 1:50 000 sheet 183. Grid reference: 774312. (On private Golf Course. The owner is usually obliging and gave the author some useful information.)

Fig.129: Location map for the Egbert's Stone area.

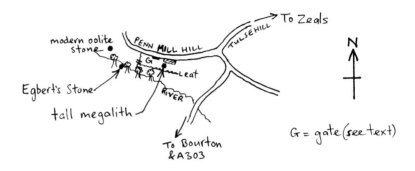

mounted on a small plinth, next to the river that runs through the Golf Course. It stands amidst trees and to the south of the 4th/13th tee. Leaving a modern gate (see Fig.129), one heads SW crossing a small bridge where a stream and leat meet, and straight on down to the river. The stone will soon be seen on the far side (wading is possible).

The stone stands about 3ft high on a brick plinth and is moss covered. It is composed of

Plate 128: Egbert's Stone, Bourton.

gbert's Stone marks the meeting of the counties of Dorset, Somerset and Wiltshire. The stone can be seen,

greensand, a local sandstone. According to the Golf Course owner, John Freeman (pers. comm.), the stone was set on the plinth for its own safety after being found thrown in the river.

According to a recent article by Rodney Legg ('Dorset', No. 3, 1995), the stone is no longer in its original spot (which it is) but has been transported up the hill, near Penn Mill Lane. He produces a photograph of the stone and here the mystery is solved. This megalith can be found immediately SE of the gate, next to some buildings adjacent to an old metal gate (see Fig.130).

John Freeman assures me that this stone was recovered from the leat, close by to the south, in the mid 1980's. He remembers its erection and the fact that a 20p coin was buried beneath it! Legg appears to have mistaken this stone for Egbert's Stone, possibly because of the similar circumstances of both stones being recovered from a watery grave.

This taller megalith, reaching about 5ft tall, is also composed of Greensand and does

tioned in the 17th Century.

Fig.130: (left) Megalith at Bourton (see text).

> "WHEN, AS WAS CUSTOMARY,
> TWO OR MORE MONOLITHS
> WERE USED AS BOUNDARY
> MARKS, THE BOUNDARY RAN
> ALONG THE GEODETIC
> (ENERGY) LINE CONNECTING
> THE TWO."
>
> *Guy Underwood (dowser).*

FIFEHEAD MAGDALEN CROSS

LOCATION: Fifehead Magdalen is a small village situated about 5 miles west of Shaftesbury. The cross stands in the churchyard of St. Mary Magdalene. OS 1:50 000 sheet 183. Grid reference: 783216.

indeed appear to be an ancient stone. Possibly it also helped mark out the borders of Saxon land. At present, it stands just south of the Dorset/Wiltshire border.

Egbert's Stone is called 'Ecgbryhtes Stan' in the Saxon Chronicle. It is named after Egbert, who ascended in 802 as ruler of the West Saxon Kingdom. King Alfred mustered his army at the stone on the eve of the decisive victory over the Danes in 878 AD at the Battle of Edington. The stone, and the taller one nearby, may of course have a much older history. The Saxons may have simply utilised existing PREHISTORIC megaliths.

John Freeman told me that he once found someone kneeling at the foot of the taller megalith. This person told him the stone was 'very special' and that 'we are very lucky to have it'.

Do not be confused by two other stones that stand on the Golf Course close by. These are of fresh-looking oolitic limestone and were erected by the owner quite recently 'because' he told me 'I like raising stones'.

Less than 2 miles east of Egbert's Stone is a place where 3 parishes meet (grid reference: 795309). The boundaries of Gillingham, Milton and Mere (Wiltshire) meet NE of Silton Hill, north of Redmoor Farm. Tradition has it that a bush called 'Dead Man's Bush' marks the boundaries and that a stone lay close by. We have seen before how 'dead man' may indeed refer to a stone. The stone is men-

o the SE of the chancel a tall cross can be seen. The shaft and the steps are modern and it is the socket stone in the middle that is of interest. Pope saw the stone lying loose in 1906. It was discovered not long prior to this face down in the soil here. It has since been reused to support the village cross shaft, the second time in its history it has served this purpose.

The stone is thought to be 15th Century and is cut from a single block of Ham Hill Stone. It is octagonal, 21" deep and 32" across at the base.

The two modern steps below are unusual. They are cut into patterns that cannot be better described than star-shaped!

FIFEHEAD NEVILLE

LOCATION: This village is situated 2 miles south of Sturminster Newton. Several interesting sites occur around the village. OS 1:50 000 sheet 194. Grid reference (of church): 768110.

ur first stop is the parish church of All Saints. After entering the south doorway, turn about-face. Above the door can be seen a large block of brown fossiliferous stone. It is thought to be the vestiges of a former cross shaft. Traces of decoration can be made out. The wall is dated c.1500, so presumably the stone is at least as old as this.

To the east of the church the River Divelish passes under a very pretty bridge at a picturesque ford. In the field to the NE (grid reference: 773113) a Roman Villa has been excavated. It was dated at 200-300 AD. But our interest in this area lies in a report dated September 1903, describing a visit by members of the Dorset Field Club. NW of the villa, a field is called Holywell Meadow. Here members found a clear stream of WARM water. The flow was seen to be received into a stone basin which had grooving for a sluice and a hatch for alternating the supply.

The writer thought the stone to be Roman in age, adjacent as it is to the Roman Villa. The fact that the Romans liked warm baths is only too well known, as the extensive buildings at Bath testify. I believe the Romans would have also attached religious significance to the place, seeing the waters as being issued from the underworld of the Earth Goddess.

200yds east of the bridge is a junction (grid reference: 775112). Separate incidents involving the sighting of a spectral ghost and a phantom rider have occurred here. Bearing in mind the siting of the villa, and the warm water story, were the apparitions emanations of earth energy phenomena at a "PLACE OF POWER"?

HAMMOON CROSS

LOCATION: Hammoon is situated 2 miles east of Sturminster Newton, 1.5 miles north of the A357. The cross stands at the village crossroads. OS 1:50 000 sheet 194. Grid reference: 817146.

n 1906, Alfred Pope saw the socket stone of an ancient cross lying face down at the rear of the church. He also saw a cross shaft nearby at a spring. He noted that a cross stood in the centre of the village until 1869-70, when the village was largely rebuilt. An inscription tells us that the cross was moved back to its original site in 1913. It also confirms that the fragments were once near the church.

The shaft is 3ft high, with the remains of one arm still evident. It stands on a socket stone that measures 30" square by 15" deep. The whole cross is of Ham Hill stone. Pope considered the cross to be 14th Century.

Plate 129: The Hammoon Cross

HAYDON CROSS

LOCATION: Haydon is situated 2 miles east of Sherborne. The cross stands in the churchyard of St. Catherine's. OS 1:50 000 sheet 183. Grid reference: 671157.

his locality is very atmospheric, an old churchyard with many dilapidated old stones lying around. A trip to the site on a dull cloudy day is very moving indeed. Although Haydon was in Dorset in 1906, as it is now. Alfred Pope seems to have missed it, even though it is a prominent, well preserved cross. Was the cross moved here from elsewhere, such as from over the nearby border with Somerset? Research into leys, however, suggests that the cross may have stood somewhere close by (perhaps the nearby crossroads) since it was built. Details are given below.

Some 4.5ft of shaft still protrudes from the socket stone. The shaft tapers from 1ft diameter at the bottom to 9" at the top. The socket stone is octagonal at the top, on a square base. It measures 34" diameter and is 18" deep. The base is 5ft 3" across and is visible to a depth of 23". Some modern stones appear to have been incorporated into it, probably when it was restored.

The cross has been dated as simply 'Medieval'.

A ley plotted by Gordon Harris is shown in Fig.131. It will be seen that Haydon lies on the ley. In fact the ley cuts RIGHT THROUGH THE CHURCHYARD, within yards of the cross!

Plate 130: The Haydon Cross

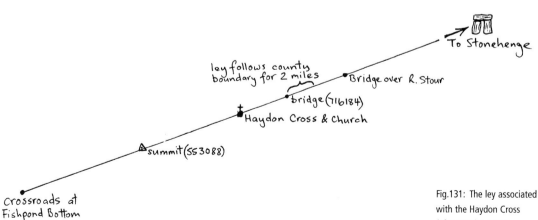

ley follows county boundary for 2 miles

To Stonehenge

Bridge over R. Stour

bridge (716184)

Haydon Cross & Church

summit (553088)

Crossroads at Fishpond Bottom

Fig.131: The ley associated with the Haydon Cross (after Gordon Harris, unpub. Amendments by the author).

> "STAND YE IN THE WAYS, AND
> SEE, AND ASK FOR THE OLD
> PATHS, WHERE IS THE GOOD
> WAY, AND WALK THEREIN,
> AND YE SHALL FIND REST
> FOR YOUR SOULS."
>
> *The Bible, Jeremiah 6:16*

A tale has been told, on page 26, of local villagers who went to dig up a local stone. As they attempted this, smoke emanated from below. A hollowness was also encountered underfoot. Robert Courage gave me the approximate locality of the event. It was 0.5 mile SE of the church, next to a N-S hedge (grid reference: c.797065).

Plate 131: The remains of the old stone cross at Iwerne Courtney.

Plate 132: (Top right) Cross at crossroads at Leigh.

Plate 133: (Bottom right) The remains, much dilapidated, of the cross in the churchyard at Leigh.

IBBERTON

LOCATION: Ibberton is a small village situated about 5 miles west of Blandford Forum. It is 3 miles south of the A357 at Shillingstone. OS 1:50 000 sheet 194. Grid reference (of church): 789075.

Local tradition has it that halfway up the steep hill above Ibberton there was formerly a stone. It was said to have come down to drink at the village well, but only made it halfway up afterwards. On a visit to the village in 1994, I spoke to a life-long village resident, Robert Courage. He remembered the stone when he was younger. He described it as 'a square stone ......chalky'. He went on to tell me that a farmer moved it and pointed out the former locality. It was next to the second gate on the left going up the steep road up to the top of the hill, above the village (grid reference: 792075).

The ridge above has many prehistoric remains, such as tumuli, cross dykes and a settlement. The road across the top of Ibberton Hill and Bell Hill follows an ancient track.

IWERNE COURTNEY CROSS

LOCATION: Iwerne Courtney (also known as Shroton) is located 4 miles NW of Blandford Forum just off the A350 road to Shaftesbury. The cross lies at the village crossroads next to a brick wall. OS 1:50 000 sheet 194. Grid reference: 859129.

Alfred Pope noted the cross in 1906, in the same locality. Today only the socket stone remains, very worn and moss-covered (Plate 131). The maximum height is about 2ft and the diameter 2.5ft. The mortise hole in the centre is 14" wide. The shaft is now absent, but Pope spoke to some of the older inhabitants of the village who remembered a stump of the shaft still fixed in the mortise. It appears to have been removed around the 1860's.

Fig.128 showed a ley running from Salkeld Bridge to the Dorset Cursus. The cross lies WITHIN YARDS of the ley. The cross may, once again, have been the modification or replacement of a more ancient stone.

LEIGH CROSSES

LOCATION: Leigh is set 2 miles SE of Yetminster. Two crosses stand in the village. The first is at the crossroads (grid reference: 621086). The other is in the churchyard of St. Andrew's Church (grid reference: 617087). OS 1:50 000 sheet 194.

The crossroads cross is a fine example of 14th-15th Century work and has some interesting features. The whole structure has been remounted onto a modern base with a step. Onto this the socket stone is set. It is 33" square, 23" deep and has much worn convex broaching. It is a solid block of Ham Hill stone. Onto this can be seen at 2-3" stump of a shaft, some 15" square. It is fixed to the socket with lead.

Above this can be seen a join. Alfred Pope noted the fact that the major part of the shaft was attached onto an older part beneath. What is unusual is that he considered the upper part to be 13th Century, OLDER than the stump and socket stone below. The local vicar of the time, Rev. T.L. Jenkins, studied the stone. He noted that three sides of the stone have ornamentation, whilst the fourth does note. This blank side shows signs that it may have been attached to some building on this face. 'It may likely,' he says, 'have been part of a pinnacle surmounting a buttress or flanking a tower' (1905 quote).

The tapering shaft is 5ft high and composed of a coarse gritstone. The sculptures are now practically eroded away but at one time were more clearly seen. Carvings depicting St. Christopher carrying Jesus The Christ and St. Michael slaying a dragon were depicted.

The cross head is comparatively modern, having been placed in position when the cross was re-erected around 1847.

Our second locality is the village churchyard. To the SE of the church of St. Andrew stands the dilapidated remains of a stone cross, under the branches of a tall Yew. A socket stone, 33" square and 18" deep, still retains the stump of the shaft. The shaft was broken off almost level with the base stone

and is 11" diameter. The whole structure is built of Ham Hill stone.

The remains are thought to be a 14-15th Century preaching cross.

Also at Leigh, comes a tale of spectral apparition. A ghostly black dog has been reported in the lane at grid reference 628084, 0.5 mile east of the church. The phenomena took place very close to the ley plotted in Fig.119. Was this another manifestation of either earth energies or else 'site memory'?

MILBORNE PORT CROSS

LOCATION: Milborne Port lies just across the Somerset/Dorset border, 2.5 miles east of Sherborne on the A30. The cross stands on a green at the junction of the A30 and Bathwell Lane. OS 1:50 000 sheet 183. Grid reference: 675185.

Purists may argue that a Somerset stone may not belong in this present work. The cross, however, lies just 0.5 mile from the Dorset border. In addition to this, anyone using this guide to visit north Dorset sites is surely at some time to follow the A30, next to which the cross lies. It seemed a pity, then, not to include it.

The cross lies on a green under the shade of trees on the north side of the road. An inscription tells us that it was moved from the centre of the village in 1959. It would appear to be the base stone of a 14-15th Century stone cross. It is 39" diameter and reaches 18" at maximum. It is worn smooth. On it can be seen a basin, which is off-centre. It may have been an alms hole.

The present site, and the former site to the east, both lie very close to a ley running SE up to Stonehenge, perhaps indicating the Christianisation of a more ancient stone. Other sites on the ley include the church at Pendomer, the bridge and Tithe Barn at Bradford Abbas and the centre of Sherborne.

MOTCOMBE

LOCATION: Motcombe is situated 2 miles north of Shaftesbury. OS 1:50 000 sheet 183. Grid reference (of church): 849253.

In the churchyard of the parish church of St. Mary, stands a stone cross. It stands close to the south porch. Alfred Pope considered the cross to be late-14th Century, on account of plain structure. He also considered it to be a preaching cross. Two solid steps form the base of the cross, the lower one being

Plate 134: The stone at Milborn Port (Somerset).

8ft square, whilst the upper one is some 5ft square. These steps are 14" and 9" deep respectively.

Above this is a socket stone, 2ft square and 16" deep. The upper bed is chamfered. Into this the base of the shaft stands, set with lead. Only just over 2ft of shaft survives and it appears to have been of a tapered octagonal design, of unknown height. The whole structure of the cross is of Ham Hill stone.

The church at Motcombe lies on another ley plotted by Gordon Harris, which proceeds SE from Motcombe up to Stonehenge. Other ley markers include Penn Cross (grid reference 347944), the hill summit at Newtown (grid reference 911291) and the church at Chilmark (Wiltshire).

In 1954 Mrs Harfield reported (in Proc. Dorset Nat. Hist. & Arch. Soc.) 4 or 5 stones upended in a hedge by the Shaftesbury to Mere road, west of Thames Farm (grid reference 862244). They were thought to be the vestiges of a chambered long barrow. There are no reports of them since.

OKEFORD FITZPAINE CROSS

LOCATION: Okeford Fitzpaine is located 5 miles west of Blandford Forum. It is signposted from the A357 at Shillingstone. The cross stands at the village crossroads. OS 1:50 000 sheet 194. Grid reference: 806109.

Opposite the village stores the stone cross now stands where the village green once existed, NW of the church.

The cross comprises two steps capped by a socket stone. The basement step is rectangular, measuring 8ft x 9ft. It is composed of local Tisbury Sandstone and is 14" deep. The second step is also rectangular, measuring 6ft x 5.5ft. The step is 9" deep and is built of Ham Hill stone.

The socket stone is made from a solid block of Ham Hill stone and is also rectangular, measuring 3.5ft x 3ft. It is 1ft 9" in depth and the upper bed is cut octagonally. Pope, in 1906, saw the base of the shaft of the cross

still sitting in its mortise, sawn off level with the upper surface of the socket stone. On a visit to the cross in October 1993, the author found the mortise to be empty, all traces of the shaft having gone. The size of the mortise seems to bear out Pope's dimensions of the shaft as being 16" x 15" diameter.

Plate 135: The Motcombe Cross.

Plate 136: The cross at Okeford Fitzpaine.

The cross is thought to be 14-15th Century. Interestingly, the Abbots of Glastonbury provided for the services at the cross up until the time of Henry VIII. The nearby church is on a ley, first suggested by John Michell, which is shown in Fig.128. A plaque near the cross, dated 1953, explains some historical information.

2.5ft of square to octagonal shaft remains, which has a diameter of 12" at its base. The socket stone below is 20" in height and is fashioned into an octagonal upper surface.

Whilst in the churchyard, note the stone of ancient appearance under the Yew next to the path, west of the cross. It is 4ft long and noticeably flat-bottomed.

Plate 137: The Sandford Orcas cross.

SANDFORD ORCAS CROSS

LOCATION: Sandford Orcas is located on the Dorset/Somerset border, 2.5 miles north of Sherborne. The cross stands in the churchyard of St. Nicholas. OS 1:50 000 sheet 183. Grid reference: 623211.

The cross is located south of the church. After ascending the steps up to the churchyard, the path to the right is taken, ignoring the one to the porch. The cross will be seen to the left (north) of the path. The cross once stood nearer the church but in 1871 was moved 20ft east during restoration.

The shaft and socket stone are 15th Century, set upon two modern steps. Some

In the porch of Trent church (see page 200) is an old map of the Trent and Sandford Orcas area. On it there is a stone marked in the field immediately north of the churchyard at Sandford Orcas, on the slopes leading down to the river. In March 1995 a search was made by the author, but to no avail. It is uncertain if there is any connection to the stone under the Yew in the churchyard.

SHAFTESBURY

LOCATION: This ancient town lies midway between Yeovil and Salisbury. The town appears to have had at one time as many as 6 crosses. These are dealt with individually below. OS 1:50 000 sheet 183.

n the Middle Ages, Shaftesbury had a thriving Abbey and the town was the focus for pilgrims from far and near. This is reflected in the large number of crosses that once stood in the town. John Hutchins wrote of 5 crosses that still stood in his time (1773) and another that had 'recently been removed'. Alas, only two survive to this day and we will look at these first.

Our first stop is the churchyard of the Holy Trinity (grid reference: 862229). A fine cross stands SW of the tower (Plate 138). The cross head is modern but the shaft, socket stone and steps are c.15th Century.

The shaft is octagonal, about 7ft long and composed of a single piece of hard limestone. Below this is a 2ft square moulded socket stone. This rests on 2 steps and a base. This base may be the top of another step. Fig.4 shows an old (pre-1773) view of the cross. The 'extra' step is clearly seen. The cross was restored around the mid-19th Century.

The other remaining cross stands in the grounds of the Abbey, now a museum. The site has restricted opening times so check first (grid reference: 862228). The monastery is said to have been founded by either King Alfred the Great or his brother, King Ethelbald, in AD 880.

The cross was moved to its present locality in 1931. Alfred Pope records (in 1906) the cross standing at the site of St. John's Church. It has been reset on a stepped base in the ruins of the abbey chancel.

The cross head, shaft, base stone and steps stand proudly at around 10ft tall. The structure is built of Ham Hill stone. The most interesting features of the cross, however, are carved alabaster panels. They show angels, a vesica piscis and other worn features.

John Hutchins (1773) noted 4 more crosses still standing in his day, plus another that had only recently been removed:

The first was Gold Hill Cross, which stood near St. Peter's Church. It was removed to build the Guildhall in 1827. An old engraving of the cross is reproduced in Fig.5 Another, St. Mary's Cross, stood on St. Mary's Green at Bimport. It was a preaching cross and was removed about the year 1798. The Fish Cross is shown in a map dated 1615, to

the west of the aforementioned Guildhall near St. Peter's Church. It was taken down around 1783.

The last cross was known as the Butter Cross. It is also shown on the 1615 map and stood in the Butter Market. Hutchins says that it was taken down in 1727.

The large number of former crosses in the town, plus the Abbey, certainly shows Shaftesbury to have been once a place of great spiritual importance. The sanctity of the area probably goes back pre-Christian times. Records exist that show that prior to the establishment of the monastery a large standing stone stood on the site! It may be relevant that Gordon Harris has plotted a ley that comes up from Bridport, passes through the heart of

Plate 138: The cross in the churchyard of the Holy Trinity.

Shaftesbury, before proceeding on its way up to Stonehenge. Indeed, a stone can be seen against a garden wall in a lane off St. James Street. A ley relic?

3 Miles SW of Shaftesbury sits the Popple Stone, at Doncliffe Hall Farm (permission to be sought to enter land). It is a 3½ft+ rounded stone with a flat top, which enables seating. Popple derives from the Dutch word 'popelen' meaning 'to throb'; ancient memories of earth energies? The stone lies exactly on a ley running from Thorncombe Beacon, via several sites, up to Stonehenge: Coincidence? Folklore says it was thrown by the devil from Bul Barrow

SHERBORNE

This ancient town once possessed 3 stone crosses, all of which appear to have been 'high crosses', of a similar design to the one still standing at Stalbridge. One stood in Newland and one at the top and at the bottom of Cheap Street. One was still standing as late as 1774, for it was described by John Hutchins in that year. Alfred Pope surmises that the other two were demolished during the puritan purges of 1643.

In Sherborne Museum is the pedestal stone of a 15th Century stone cross. it is octagonal with carvings and inscriptions. It was found built into a house at Bishop's Down, 4 miles SE of Sherborne.

Plate 140: The old stone cross in the churchyard at Shillingstone.

SHILLINGSTONE

LOCATION: Shillingstone is situated on the A357, midway between Blandford Forum and Sturminster Newton. There are 3 sites in the village plus notes on a former one (location details below). OS 1:50 000 sheet 194. Grid reference (of church): 825114.

The village cross stands prominently next to the main A357 road, at its junction with the lane leading to the church (grid reference: 824113). The cross comprises of two phases. The steps and socket stones are thought to be 15th Century. The cross was restored in 1903 and the modern shaft and cross head were built onto the ancient stones below.

The base of the cross is 9ft square with a weather drip. The second step is plain. The socket stone above is a solid block of Ham Hill stone. It is square at the base but has an octagonal top surface. It was noted at the time of restoration that the old shaft was still embedded in its mortise, sewn off level with the top of the socket stone. The new shaft was set up at a different angle to the old one, so as not to obscure what remained of the latter.

Next stop in the village is the church of the Holy Rood. In the churchyard, to the SE of the chancel, are the remains of a 15th Century cross. It lies to the right of the path leading to the church.

It comprises a step and base stone, both of Ham Hill stone. The basement step is 7ft square and 18" deep, with a bold weather drip. The stone above (which is possibly a second step) is in fact formed of three blocks of stone, nearly 5ft square and 11" deep in total. There are no socket stone or shaft remaining.

Tradition has it that formerly bread and alms were distributed to the poor once a year.

We next proceed into the church itself to look at one of the most unusual stones that we will encounter on our tour of Dorset stones.

Fixed onto the wall of the chancel, near the bell ropes, is an ancient stone slab with an accompanying descriptive plaque.

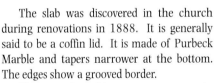

would seem to imply a Romano-British age and it is curious that the 'Inventory of Historical Monuments.......of Dorset' gives its age as late as the 14th Century.

The stone slab is the only one of its kind in Dorset and is well worth a visit, whether one's standpoint is pagan or Christian.

Returning to the churchyard, note the towering Hambleton Hill and Hod Hill to the NE and E. Barrows can be seen on the skyline. Neolithic and Iron Age settlements once occupied the summits and the Romans built a fort on Hod Hill.

John Hutchins noted, in the mid-19th Century, another stone cross still in evidence at the southern extremity of the village. It stood on the north side of the A357. No other details are known and all traces of it seem to have vanished.

Plate 139: The old stone cross at Shillingstone.

Plate 141: Inscribed slab in Shillingstone church.

The slab was discovered in the church during renovations in 1888. It is generally said to be a coffin lid. It is made of Purbeck Marble and tapers narrower at the bottom. The edges show a grooved border.

The incised markings are very pagan in design. The sun symbol has been taken to represent Jupiter, whilst the crescent moon is thought to represent Diana, or some similar deity. The symbols were later taken to represent Christ and Mary, hence the stone's survival.

A lengthy descriptive plaque is fixed to the wall next to the slab. It states that the stone 'dates from the twilight of the pagan-Christian era' and goes on 'thought to be the tomb slab of a Saxon lord'. The markings

STALBRIDGE CROSS

LOCATION: Stalbridge is situated 6 miles east of Sherborne and 4 miles NW of Sturminster Newton on the A357. The cross stands beside the main road. OS 1:50 000 sheet 183. Grid reference: 734180.

The cross is the best of its kind in all Dorset. It is of the High Cross variety and survived the 1643 Puritan fury, when so many crosses were destroyed or damaged.

The shaft is about 12ft tall and is cut from a single block of Ham Hill stone. On one side (visible in Plate 142) is carved a standing figure (thought to be Jesus The Christ) standing over a lamb. The shaft is 18" square at the base but tapers slightly upwards.

The octagonal abacus, stone shrine and spire above the shaft are a faithful replica of the original work, the latter of which fell down in 1950.

Plate 142: Stalbridge Cross.

Below the shaft, the socket stone is cut from one block of Ham Hill stone. It is 38" square by 28" deep and all four sides are sculptured. Scenes representing the Resurrection were formerly seen, but are too worn today.

The three steps below total about 2.5ft in height. They are octagonal and the basement step measures just under 4ft on each face.

The whole structure reaches up nearly 30ft tall and is well worth a visit. The date of erection was once thought to be as early as the 14th Century but the 15th seems a more feasible alternative. At one time a Latin inscription was to be seen on the cross containing a prophecy.

It foretold that if ever the words were erased then the Island of Rhodes would fall to an invader. In Henry VIII's time it was erased and the island was duly conquered by Solomon the Magnificent!

STURMINSTER NEWTON CROSS

LOCATION: The remains of a stone cross can be seen on the east side of the main street, opposite the White Hart Inn, 200yds NW of the church. OS 1:50 000 sheet 194. Grid reference: 786141.

The fine remains of the steps, surmounted by another stone, are worth a visit. It is thought to be 15th Century, although Alfred Pope considered it to be 13th, probably on account of its relative simplicity.

Most of the structure is a calvary of 4 steps. The basement step has a diameter of 11.5ft. The steps above gradually become smaller, and the top one measure 4.5ft diameter. These steps are chiefly of Melbury Greensand with a few pieces of Ham Hill stone intermixed. This mixture of stones came about when the cross was restored c.1800. The steps are very worn at several places.

Fig.120 shows how the church at Sturminster Newton lies on the path of a ley from Bind Barrow to Stonehenge (plotted by

Plate 143: The old market cross at Sturminster Newton.

Gordon Harris, pers. comm.). The bridge over the River Stour is likewise on the ley. The main road through the town may have evolved from the ley, thus making the cross a possible contender as an 'evolved' ley marker.

At nearby Hinton St. Mary, a fine Roman mosaic dating from the 4th Century was found. It showed a mixture of pagan and Christian symbology. It can be seen in the British Museum. Barry Cuff informs the author of a 3ft high stone south of the village by the main road at grid reference: 787155.

TODBER SAXON CROSS

LOCATION: The village of Todber is situated 4 miles SW of Shaftesbury. It lies on the B3092 midway between Sturminster Newton and Gillingham. OS 1:50 000 sheet 183. Grid reference (of church): 799201. (The church is often closed; details of where to obtain the keys are shown.)

ragments of a 9th/early 11th Century Saxon cross shaft can be seen in the church (Plate 144). Two pieces of stone can be seen incorporated in a reconstruction, showing where they may have been posi-

tioned on the original cross shaft. These fragments were formerly incorporated into another cross in 1889 which stood in the churchyard. Pope shows this cross in his 'Old Stone Crosses of Dorset' (1906). The fragments were discovered around 1879. The stones were brought into the church in 1983 to protect them from further weathering.

Plate 144: Saxon sculptured stones in Todber Church. (The smooth lighter parts are modern.)

On the lower fragment one sees a cross repeated with vineal coils and vine leaves. The upper fragment has spirals and vines in the design. One can compare this design with the similar Saxon fragments seen in Whitcombe Church, seen in Plate 96.

The church is of early English character, Pope notes, with a low tower and chancel and nave only. The church may have succeeded a chapel of earlier date and this may account for the early sculptured fragments. The site may indeed have a much more ancient heritage. Fig.119 shows a ley running from St. Gabriel's Mouth on the coast up to Stonehenge. The church at Todber stands directly on the ley.

Beside the cross are some photographs and information on the fragments.

Plate 145: The stone cross at Trent. The arrow marks the join of the 15th Century and modern parts of the shaft.

TRENT CROSS

LOCATION: Trent is a small village situated 3 miles NW of Sherborne, and 2 miles NE of Yeovil. OS 1:50 000 sheet 183. Grid reference (of church): 589185.

n old stone cross stands in the churchyard of the parish church of St. Andrew directly in front as one enters the churchyard. The cross was excluded from Alfred Pope's 1906 survey because at that time Trent was in Somerset. The cross head, most of the shaft and the steps are modern. It is the lowest part of the shaft and the socket stone that is of interest in our ancient survey. These parts are dated 15th Century.

At the top of the steps the socket stone sits. It is round and 18" deep. Into this is mounted the shaft, 1ft in diameter. Close inspection will show that only about 2.5ft of original shaft is present. A join can be seen, with the newer part above moulded to a similar shape and design. Leaf ornamentation is present, more worn on the original shaft section.

WEST MELBURY CROSS

LOCATION: West Melbury can be located 1.5 miles south of Shaftesbury. An ancient socket stone can be found at Cornhill Cottage, Cornhill, west of A350 Shaftesbury to Blandford road. OS 1:50 000 sheet 183. Grid reference: 866204. Permission to view should be sought at the cottage.

ust inside the front gate, to the right, is the socket stone of a 15th Century cross. It is 2ft x 2.5ft in size. A 1ft diameter mortise is visible which would have at one time housed the shaft.

The remains represent a wayside cross which would have stood at the crossroads nearby. The north-south road that passes by here was at one time a pilgrim way from

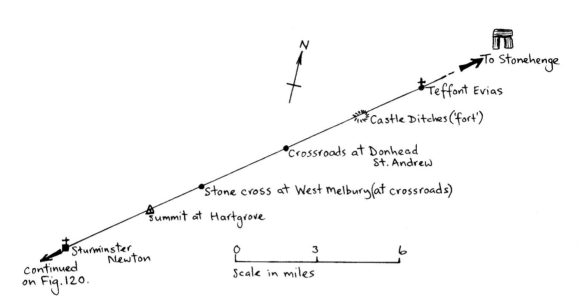

continued on Fig.120.

south Dorset to the monastery at Shaftesbury. But I think that this lonely overgrown stone may have a more ancient heritage than the cross it was possibly modified into. Fig.120 shows a ley running from Bind Barrow to Sturminster Newton, plotted by Gordon Harris (pers. comm.). Fig.132 above shows its continuation going NE towards Stonehenge.

It is relevant that the ley passes RIGHT THROUGH the crossroads at Cornhill, the site of the cross. Can there be any doubt that the crossroads also marked an ancient ley with a stone as a sentinel?

It is independent correlation such as this, by keen amateurs, that is helping to bring archaeology (often kicking and screaming at times!) into the Aquarian Age.

"......BY NUN'S WOOD YEWS, AND HUNGARY HILL, AND THE CORPSE WAY STONES ALL STANDING STILL."

John Masefield, 'Reynard the Fox'.

YETMINSTER STONE AND CROSS

LOCATION: Yetminster is situated 4.5 miles SW of Sherborne. The village lies 2 miles east of the A37 Dorchester to Yeovil road. A cross fragment and a wayside stone are to

Fig.132: Ley running from Sturminster Newton towards Stonehenge (after Gordon Harris, with amendments by the author).

Plate 146: Stone at Tark's Hill, Yetminster.

be visited. OS 1:50 000 sheet 194. Grid references: Church 594206; Stone 593102.

Plate 147: Saxon cross shaft in St. Andrew's Church, Yetminster.

Just south of the village centre is Tarks Hill (marked by a signpost with the grid reference on the top). On the bend there is a junction with another lane heading off in the direction of Melbury Osmond. On the north side of the road, next to the signpost, stands a stone (Plate 146). It stands 46" out of the ground and is 12" x 9.5" wide. It is earthfast and leans slightly south. The top appears to have been rounded. It is composed of a fossiliferous sandstone.

OS maps do not show any milestone or boundary stone at the locality, and indeed the stone is nowhere near any boundary. The author would welcome any information on the stone.

Our next stop is inside the parish church of St. Andrew. On a window ledge, to one's left as the church is entered, is an ancient cross fragment (Plate 147). It is part of a 10th Century Saxon cross shaft and until recently stood in the churchyard. It is 2.5ft tall and 9" across. There is an accompanying notice.

The shaft shows busts under arches, and other work, carved on it. The shaft is of a round type typical of those found in Mercia (North-Central England). It is thought to be Wessex's only example so far known.

A glance at Fig.122 reveals that Yetminster church lies at the northern end of a ley running up from Maiden Castle.

"BRICK AND STONE WILL DECAY, AND TIME DESTROY THE LABORS OF THE ABLEST ARCHITECT; BUT THE WORKS OF THE LEARNED WILL ENDURE SO LONG AS REASON AND GOOD SENSE SHALL HAVE ANY BEING IN THE WORLD."

Inigo Jones ('Stone-Heng', 1725)

FURTHER INFORMATION

The following contacts may help the reader to get in touch with those people of 'like minds' in the Earth Mysteries field.

THE LEY HUNTER:

The foremost Earth Mysteries magazine in the world. Published 2-4 times a year. Danny Sullivan recently took over the Editorship from the innovative Paul Devereux. Write to: The Ley Hunter, PO Box 258, Cheltenham, GL53 0HR.

WESSEX DOWSERS:

Holds monthly meetings in Wareham. Members have many years experience in dowsing, including work on stone sites. Beginners welcome and instruction given. Write to: Paul Craddock, 6 Library Road, Parkstone, Poole, BH12 2BE.

EARTH MYSTERIES WORKSHOPS:

The author holds workshops and field trips to sacred sites around Dorset. If you would like details write to: EM Workshops, c/o 14 Maxwell road, Winton, Bournemouth, BH9 1DJ.

WESSEX RESEARCH GROUP:

Holds monthly meetings and workshops on subjects such as UFO's, earth mysteries and sacred sites.
Write to: Pat Law, 6 Burnham Drive, Queens Park, Bournemouth BH8 9EX.

The following museums have notable archaeological exhibits:

DORSET COUNTY MUSEUM, DORCHESTER
(TEL: 01305 262735)
RED HOUSE MUSEUM, CHRISTCHURCH
(TEL: 01202 482860)
SHERBORNE MUSEUM, SHERBORNE
(TEL: 01935 812252)
BRIDPORT MUSEUM, BRIDPORT
(TEL: 01308 422116)
ABBEY MUSEUM, SHAFTESBURY
(TEL: 01747 852910)

BIBLIOGRAPHY

Aubrey, John. **Monumenta Britannica**, 1665-93.
    Ed Dorset Publishing Co. 1980
Bord, Janet and Colin. **Mysterious Britain**, Garnstone, 1972.
    The Secret Country, Paul Elek, 1976.
    Earth Rites, Granada, 1982.
    Ancient Mysteries of Britain, Grafton, 1986.
Bryce, Derek. **Symbolism of the Celtic Cross**, Llanerch, 1994.
Burl, Aubrey. **Prehistoric Stone Circles**, Shire 1979.
    Prehistoric Astronomy and Ritual, Shire, 1983.
    Megalithic Brittany, Thames and Hudson, 1985.
    Prehistoric Henges, Shire, 1991.
Devereux, Paul. **Places of Power**, Blandford, 1990.
    Earth Memory, Quantum, 1991.
    Symbolic Landscapes, Gothic Image, 1992.
Devereux, Paul and Main, Laurence. **Earth lights**,
    Thornsons, 1982.
    The Old Straight Tracks of Wessex, Thornsons, 1992.
Devereux, Paul and Thomson, Ian. **The Ley Hunters Companion**,
    Thames and Hudson, 1979.
Field, N. **Dorset and the Second Legion**, Dorset Books, 1992.
Field, N. and Bugler, J. **The Ancient Monuments of Dorset**,
    Dorset Natural History and Archaeological Society, 1972.
Forbes, J.F. **The Unchronicled Past**, Simpkin Marshall, 1938.
Gerard of Trent. **Survey of Dorsetshire**, copy of 1622 ms,
    pub. 1732.
Graves, Tom. **Needles of Stone Revisited**, Gothic Image, 1986.
Grinsell, Leslie V. **Dorset Barrows**,
    Dorset Natural History and Archaeological Society, 1959.
    Barrows of England and Wales, Shire, 1979.
    Folklore of Prehistoric Sites in Britain,
    David and Charles, 1976.
    Dorset Barrows Supplement,
    Dorset Natural History and Archaeological Society, 1982.
Hadingham, Evan. **Circles and Standing Stones**, Heinmann, 1975.
Hamilton-Rogers. **Memorials of the West**, 1888.
Harte, Jeremy. **Cuckoo Pounds and Singing Barrows**,
    Dorset Natural History and Archaeological Society, 1986.
Hawkins, Gerald. **Beyond Stonehenge**, Hutchinson, 1973.
Heselton, Philip. **The Elements of Earth Mysteries**, Element, 1991.
Hitching, Francis. **Earth Magic**, Cassell, 1976.
Hutchins, John. **The History and Antiquities of the County of
    Dorset**, 1774, 3rd ed. 1861-70 by W. Shipp.
Johnson, Walter. **The Later History of the Megaliths**,
    Hark Back ed., 1991.
Lancaster Brown, **Peter. Megaliths, Myths and Men**,
    Blandford, 1976.
Legg, Rodney. **Mysterious Dorset**, Milborne Port, 1987.
Lonegran, Sig. **Spiritual Dowsing**, Gothic Image, 1986.
Mills, A.D. **The Place Names of Dorset**,
    English Place Names Society, 1977.

Michell, John. **The Old Straight Track in Dorset Countryside**,
    Vol.1, 1976.
    The New View Over Atlantis,
    Thames and Hudson, 1983.
Osborn, George. **Exploring Ancient Dorset**,
    Dorset Publishing co., 1985.
    Dorset Curiosities, Dovecote, 1986.
Palmer, Kingsley. **Oral Folk-Tales of Wessex**,
    David and Charles, 1973.
Pennick, Nigel and Devereux, Paul. **The Lines on the Landscape**,
    Hale, 1989.
North, John. **Stonehenge**, Harper Collins 1996.
Pope, Alfred. **Old Stone Crosses of Dorset**, Chiswick, 1906.
Reeks, Pam and Coulthard, Hill. **A Brief History of Verwood**, 1984.
Royal Commission on Historical Monuments.
    Inventory of Historical Monuments of Dorset, HM
    Stat. Office, 1959-75.
Stukeley, William. **Itinerarium Curiosum**, 2nd ed., 1776.
Sydenham, John. **Baal Durotrigensis**, W. Pickering, 1841.
Thom, Alexander. **Megalithic Sites in Britain**,
    Oxford University Press, 1967.
Thomas, Nicholas. **Guide to Prehistoric England**, Batsford, 1976.
Udal, John S. **Dorsetshire Folk-Lore**, Hertford, 1922.
Underwood, Guy. **The Pattern of the Past**, Abacus, ed. 1972.
Wainwright, Geoffrey. The Henge Monuments, T
    hames and Hudson, 1989.
Waring, E. **Ghosts and Legends of the Dorset Countryside**,
    Compton, 1987.
Warne, Charles. **Ancient Dorset**, 1872.
Warren, F.C. **Dorset Legends and Traditions in The Dorset Year
    Book for 1951/2.**
Watkins, Alfred. **The Old Straight Track**, Metheum, 1925,
    reprinted by Garnstone, 1970, and by Abacus, 1974.
White, Sydney J. **The Stone Circles of Dorset in The Dorset Year
    Book for 1951/2.**
Whittle, Jane. **Twenty Wessex Walks Exploring Prehistoric Paths**,
    Hobnob, 1988.
Wilson, Roger. **A Guide to Roman Remains in Britain**,
    Constable, 1975.
Wood, John Edwin. **Sun, Moon and Standing Stones**,
    Merrivale, 1978.

Useful articles on Dorset stone sites also occur periodically in the following magazines:

**Proceedings of the Dorset Natural History
and Archaeological Society**

Dorset Countryside	**The Ley Hunter**
Dorset Life	**Dorset Year Book**
Dorset: The Colour Magazine	

INDEX